ALSO FROM
VISIBLE INK PRESS

Handy Bug Answer Book

Handy Dinosaur Answer Book

Handy Earth Answer Book

Handy Geography Answer Book

Handy History Answer Book

Handy Physics Answer Book

Handy Science Answer Book

Handy Space Answer Book

Handy Sports Answer Book

Handy Weather Answer Book

THE
HANDY
GARDEN
ANSWER
BOOK

THE HANDY GARDEN ANSWER BOOK™

Karen Troshynski-Thomas

Detroit • London

The Handy Garden
Answer Book™

Published by Visible Ink Press™
a division of Gale Research

Address until September 15, 1998:
835 Penobscot Building
645 Griswold St.
Detroit, MI 48226-4094

Address after September 15, 1998:
27500 Drake Rd.
Farmington Hills, MI 48331-3535

Visible Ink Press is a trademark of Gale Research

Most Visible Ink Press™ books are available at special quantity discounts when purchased in bulk by corporations, organizations, or groups. Customized printings, special imprints, messages, and excerpts can be produced to meet your needs. For more information, contact Special Markets Manager, Visible Ink Press, 835 Penobscot Bldg., Detroit, MI 48226 until September 15, 1998 or 27500 Drake Rd., Farmington Hills, MI 48331-3535 after September 15, 1998. Or call 1-800-776-6265.

Art Directors: Michelle DiMercurio and Cindy Baldwin

Typesetting: Graphix Group

ISBN 1-57859-067-1
Printed in the United States of America
All rights reserved
10 9 8 7 6 5 4 3 2 1

ABOUT THE AUTHOR

Karen Troshynski-Thomas's overlapping careers as gardener, writer/editor, and mother of 6-month-old Jack Henry have been nurtured into Taproot Writers Collective, a home-based business in Berkley, Michigan. Karen's gardening experience began with tomato plants grown at her college apartment. (They were pitched from a terrace during a neighbor's party.) Undaunted, she is currently working toward her Master Gardening certificate through the Michigan State University Extension Service in Oakland County, Michigan.

ABOUT THE PHOTOGRAPHER

Robert J. Huffman has been a photographer of natural subjects for nearly 20 years. His images have appeared in books, magazines, advertisements, and electronic media. He lives in Old Rosedale Gardens, an historic section of Livonia, Michigan and the backdrop of many of the photos used in this book.

Contents

PLANT AND SOIL SCIENCE ...3

Plant Science . . . Plant Parts . . . Plant Functions . . . Plant Hardiness . . . Soil Science . . . Fertilizers

SEEDING, PROPAGATION, AND PLANTING ...27

Seed Selection . . . Starting Plants from Seeds . . . Caring for Seedlings . . . Other Methods of Propagation . . . Selecting Plants . . . Preparing the Soil and Planting

CARE AND FEEDING ...47

Watering . . . Fertilizing . . . Composting . . .
Weeding . . . Mulch . . . Garden Tools . . . Other
Maintenance

PROBLEMS ...75

Four-Legged Pests . . . Insects . . . Disease . . .
Disease and Pest Control . . . Environmental/
Cultural Problems . . . Problem Prevention

GARDEN DESIGN ...99

Garden Making . . . Plant Shapes, Textures, and
Colors . . . Garden Designs . . . Garden
Hardscaping

GARDENS, GARDENERS, AND GARDENING ...119

Famous Gardeners . . Famous Gardens . . .
Careers in Gardening

TREES AND SHRUBS ...223

Woody Ornamental Types . . . Planting . . . Fertilizing and Care . . . Training and Pruning . . . Roses

LAWNS AND GROUNDCOVERS ...251

Establishing a Lawn . . . Lawn Care . . . Lawn Trivia . . . Groundcovers

HERBS ...271

Herb Planting and Care . . . Herbs for Particular Uses

Introduction

Welcome to the world of gardening. If you're a new gardener or an old hand, I hope you'll find something to learn here (or at least something to amuse you). I know I learned a great deal in putting this book together.

I have been gardening for over ten years (a drop in the bucket for many "dirt gardeners"). Like many gardeners, I started with annuals and a few vegetables, graduated to too many perennials, and have branched out, so to speak, into trees and shrubs. My interest in gardening grew after signing up for a Master Gardener certification course through the Oakland County Cooperative Extension Service in Michigan. I don't profess to be a Master Gardener yet as I am still finishing up my volunteer work. If you'd like more information on the Master Gardener program, contact your county's Extension Service.

Although the glossy new publications springing up everywhere would have you believe gardening is the latest and greatest hobby, it has actually been America's favorite pastime for quite a while. These same publications profess that there is a right and wrong way to garden. While botany is a science, gardening is more of an art. Every gardener has her or his own particular ways of doing things. I've tried to provide you with the more common methods of tackling gardening tasks, but there are certainly others.

I do admit to a basic bias toward gardening organically. The act of gardening is always an invasive one, as it imposes one's will on plants and soil. However, with native plant and animal species rapidly disappearing, I feel it is important for modern gardeners to tread as lightly as possible on the earth. So you won't find information on ad-hoc tomato-dusting and rose-spraying in this book. What you will find is information on good gardening practices that put nutrients back into the soil, maximize watering efficiency, and promote healthy plants which will be better equipped to fend off insects and disease.

As I write this, the morning sun is shining on our vegetable garden and perennial border. Despite an early, warm spring, we got a late start this year. It looks like everything has caught up rapidly in our raised beds, including the weeds. My son is singing his happy, good-morning tune that signals he's ready to go out into the garden. So am I. And with this book, I hope you will be too.

Karen Troshynski-Thomas

Acknowledgments

Writing a book, even on something you enjoy, is difficult at best. A newborn son makes things even a little more complicated. This effort would not have been possible without the support of my husband and partner in gardening, Tim Thomas. From his patented "baby belly bounce" to soothe Jack's fuss, to keeping the household going on top of his own career, to fine-tuning my questions and answers and adding a few of his own, Tim kept it all together. Thanks for everything darling.

Thank you Jack Henry Thomas—your love of the outdoors and inquisitive nature have shed new light on your Mom's used-to-be favorite pastime.

Thanks also to both our families who provided much-appreciated support throughout these busy months: our parents Jim, Rena, Kathie, and Brian for regular babysitting while "Mom" worked or when we really needed to get out for a night; Bob and Tina for Jack-watching and drop-in visits; Don, Angelica, and John for encouragement and a really great reference source; Grandma M. for her lovely notes and support.

Thanks, too, to my mom, Kathie and my father-in-law, Jim for their gardening inspiration. Mom's beautiful flower beds reveal her painterly eye for color and form while Jim's mostly-organic vegetable garden is an amazing sight. I am also inspired by the beautiful and unique backyard gardens of my neighbors in Berkley.

I can't overemphasize the value of the terrific information to be found through your local Extension Service. I really enjoyed the Master Gardener course offered through the Oakland County Cooperative Extension Service. The lecturers and text were wonderful, as was the energetic Martha Ferguson, coordinator of the program. Thanks, too, to the Master Gardeners Society of Oakland County for providing an arena for local gardeners to learn more about gardening and to share their expertise with one another and others.

The folks at Visible Ink and Gale Research were most crucial in getting this book to you. Thank you firstly to Terri Schell for suggesting a Garden Handy book and me to do it! Thanks Julia Furtaw who championed the idea, Devra Sladics for ushering the project through, Bob Huffman for the beautiful photos, and Cindy Baldwin (a fellow MG candidate) and Michelle DiMercurio for the striking page and cover design.

And finally, thanks to you, the reader, for selecting this gardening book in the midst of dozens of them. I hope these questions and answers will help you in your own backyard endeavors and provide you with enough confidence to keep you experimenting. Happy gardening!

Photo Credits

Parts of a flower illustration courtesy of Fred Fretz.

USDA Plant Hardiness Zone Map courtesy of the United States Department of Agriculture.

All others courtesy of Robert J. Huffman/Field Mark Publications.

PLANT SCIENCE

How are **plants classified**?

Plants are classified by different categories of similarity. The method of classification gives two names to each plant (binomial nomenclature). Plants that share similar flowering and fruiting habits belong to the same *family*. This information can be helpful to the home gardener since plants in the same family can be susceptible to similar diseases. For example, roses and pear trees belong to the *Rosacea* family. On a plant tag, you will often see three names, with the first two in Latin and the last in English. The first name and the next level of classification for a plant is its *genus*. These plants share similar flowers, roots, stems, buds, and leaves. The genus is always capitalized and underlined or in italics. The second name—a plant's species—refers to a primary descriptive characteristic of a plant such as its coloring. The species is italicized but not capitalized. The third name is called a plant's *cultivar* or *variety*. The cultivar can refer to a wide variety of characteristics the plant may have from hardiness to flower color. Whatever the characteristic, it is retained in the plant after it is reproduced.

What are the advantages and disadvantages of **hybrid seed**?

Hybrid seed is the result of cross-fertilization of certain plant species or varieties in order to produce plants which grow more vigorously, produce more fruits of a uniform quality, and have greater disease resistance. They tend to be more expensive than open-pollinated seed.

What is a **cultivar**?

A cultivar is a group of plants that have the same characteristics (such as color, height, and flavor) which they retain even when reproduced.

What do **grass, cattails, corn, iris, and bamboo** have in common?

All of these plants are monocots or belonging to the monocotyledons group of flowering plants. The leaves of a monocot have veins which run parallel. Because of this, monocots are generally small-stemmed since their leaves will not support anything larger. As seedlings, monocots grow just one seed leaf.

PLANT PARTS

What is the difference between **plants and animals**?

The basic difference is in their cells. Plant cells have a rigid cell wall that provides support to the plant. Animal cells do not have these since they receive internal support from their skeleton.

What do beans, marigolds, and maple trees have in common?

All of these plants are dicots (part of the dicotyledons group of flowering plants). As seedlings, dicots generate two seed leaves. Later, their leaf venation forms branches rather than running parallel, enabling the leaves themselves to be larger and to provide more support for a large-stemmed plant. Some herbicides selectively impact either monocots or dicots which is why a broadleaf herbicide can kill dandelions but not grass.

How does a plant receive **food and water**?

Vascular tissues known as the xylem and the phloem move food (the result of photosynthesis) and water throughout a plant. Xylem tubes carry water and some minerals upward mainly from the root system to the rest of the plant. The phloem tubes take food released through photosynthesis to other parts of a plant.

What are the main functions of **plant roots**?

Roots provide a secure mooring for the plant by branching out. Roots also ensure the plant receives water and nutrients by absorbing these from the soil. Roots also provide storage for the plant—housing carbohydrates to be used later.

What is a **taproot**?

A taproot is a deep-growing large root that has fine small roots branching off it. Carrots and parsnips are taproots. Plants with taproots are difficult to transplant or uproot since the root system runs deep. The beloved dandelion is a prime example of this.

What are some **alternative root systems** grown by plants?

English ivy grows aerial roots at various places on its stem. These adhere to surfaces and penetrate cracks in order to provide firm support to the plant. Periwinkle grows roots from nodes on its stem. New plants can be produced by cutting sections of the stem that have these roots. Some rainforest trees such as banyans grow additional roots above the ground in order to provide extra support when the tree is mature.

What are the functions of a **plant's leaves**?

The flat surface of most leaves helps them to efficiently absorb sunlight in order for it to be used in photosynthesis. Leaves also may protect another part of the plant or be used to reproduce it.

What do **a rhizome, a bulb, a corm, a tuber, a stolon, and a runner** all have in common?

All are specialized types of stems which can be used to propagate a plant, but each reproduce differently. The rhizome, the tuber, the bulb, and the corm are below ground stems. A rhizome grows horizontally and can be divided into pieces in order to generate new rhizomes. Tubers have eyes (think of a potato) or nodes where shoots develop; they remain stationary and multiply. Bulbs multiply by generating bulblets from the "mother

The dandelion's (*Taraxacum officinale*) long taproot tends to snap when pulled, which is why it is one of the most persistent lawn weeds.

bulb." Corms are similar to bulbs and generate cormels. However, unlike bulbs, the main mother cormel doesn't survive this. Stolons and runners are aboveground stems which can be divided into sections with nodes. These new cuttings can then be rooted to produce new plants.

What can you tell about a plant from the **growth rings** of its stem?

By examining the stem's growth rings, you can learn about what happened to the plant in a particular year. Each ring signifies one growing year in a plant's life. The width of the ring is related to the amount of

Leaves of Boston Ivy (*Parthenocissus tricuspidata*). Despite its common name, this ivy is imported from Asia. Also called Japanese ivy. Woodbines like Boston Ivy are cousins of grapes and climb in two ways: by twining tendrils and by modified roots equipped with adhesive pads that cling to walls and other surfaces.

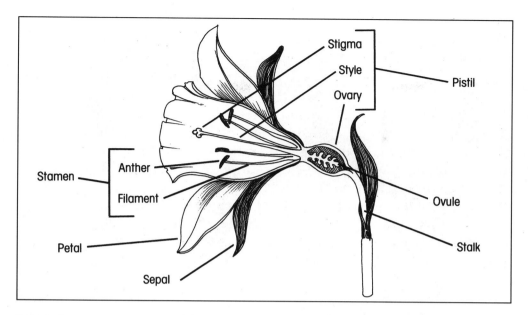

Parts of a flower.

growth the plant experienced that year—the wider the ring, the better the growing season. Irregularities in a growth ring might signify damage or injury to the plant.

How does a plant's different **leaf shape and thickness** help it to withstand a particular environment?

Plants that grow in shady areas tend to have larger leaves so that they have a bigger surface area for absorbing light. The needles of conifers help them to withstand particularly windy conditions. A plant that receives a great deal of sunlight will have smaller leaves with thicker cuticles (a waxy layer that covers a plant's epidermis) in order to retain moisture in the plant. The leaves of cactus have transformed themselves to thorns with photosynthesis occurring in the plant's stem.

What are the major **parts of a flower**?

The major parts of a flower include the pistil, the stamen, the ovary, the sepal, and the petal. See the illustration shown above.

Why does the Christmas cactus need to be placed in a dark, cool area for a period of time to force its bloom?

Plants have different requirements for light and temperature. Light duration or the photoperiod is the amount of time a plant is exposed to light or dark. All plants are either short-day, long-day or day-neutral. The Christmas cactus is a short-day plant which means it forms buds only when the day length is less than 12 hours. Long-day plants form buds only when days are longer than 12 hours. Day-neutral plants are not impacted by the day length. The Christmas cactus also has a "chilling requirement" meaning it requires low temperatures in order to bloom.

PLANT FUNCTIONS

What is the difference between **photosynthesis and respiration**?

Photosynthesis is the process by which plants produce their own food. By absorbing carbon dioxide from the air, light from the sun, and water from the soil, a plant converts these to sugar, storing energy for later and releasing oxygen in the process. In respiration, a plant uses the food produced by photosynthesis in order to grow. The process releases carbon dioxide and water and does not require sunlight to occur. Both photosynthesis and respiration are required for plant growth.

What is the concept of **apical dominance** and how does it impact pruning?

A terminal or apical bud (a bud on the growing tip of a stem) causes a hormone, auxin, to be produced in a plant. Auxin prevents the growth of buds below the terminal bud. When the terminal bud is pruned away, the hormone is no longer present and the lateral buds will begin to

Why do you need to have a "boy" holly bush and a "girl" holly bush in order to have berries?

Most hollies are dioecious. In order to self-pollinate, a plant needs both male (stamen) and female (pistil) flower structures. Holly plants have either all staminate flowers or all pistillate flowers. In order to produce berries, a pistillate holly needs to have a staminate holly nearby for pollination. The holly bush which produces berries is the female/pistillate holly.

grow. This concept is significant in pruning trees and shrubs. Hedges and shrubs that have not been pruned in some time begin to look tall and thin because the presence of terminal buds on the limbs and auxin in the plant prevents growth below the terminal bud. If you remove the terminal bud from a limb, the lateral buds below it will begin to grow, causing the shrub or hedge to become fuller and solid-looking.

What is a **self-fruitful plant**?

A self-fruitful or self-pollinated plant is one whose flowers are able to pollinate themselves since they have both stamens and pistils. Most plants are self-fruitful. Some plants have flowers that are incomplete (have either stamens or pistils) with the male and female flowers being found on either the same plant (monoecious) or different plants (dioecious—see below).

Why do flowers have **fragrance**?

Flower scents aid in plant reproduction. The fragrance entices bees, flies and other insects to investigate the plant. In landing on the flower, their bodies brush against the anther, collecting pollen. The insects move from flower to flower, unknowingly picking up and dropping pollen as they go.

11

PLANT HARDINESS

How can I find out what my **hardiness zone** is?

You can determine your hardiness zone by referring to the USDA hardiness zone map which breaks down the U.S. into 11 zones, based on a range of the area's average annual low temperatures. Most states contain more than one hardiness zone, so be sure to pinpoint your location on the map. Plants are then categorized by zone, based on their ability to withstand that region's annual low temperature.

I purchased a plant whose tag said it would **survive in zones** 3–5 but when I checked an encyclopedia, the same plant was listed as surviving in zones 2–5. What gives?

It is quite possible that the nursery and the encyclopedia were referencing two different hardiness zone maps. There are actually 3 different hardiness zone maps: the USDA map as noted in the previous question, the Arnold Arboretum map, and the Rutgers University map. The USDA map lists 11 zones, the Arnold Arboretum map lists 9 zones, and the Rutgers map breaks the country into 23 different zones. While the Rutgers map could be argued to be the most accurate as it takes into consideration other weather factors such as wind, sunshine, and humidity, the USDA map is the one most commonly used by nurseries and seedsmen.

I'm interested in growing some plants that are borderline hardy for my region. What can I do to improve their **chances of survival**?

While USDA hardiness zones are important indicators of a plant's ability to survive in your landscape, every area has its own microclimate—even sections of your backyard! Large bodies of water, protection from the wind, an adequate amount of moisture, and a porous soil can all help to increase a plant's hardiness. You can "baby" your plants by seeking out warmer portions of your yard to plant them in. Identify these microclimates by watching for early growth and bloom of plants as compared to other areas of your yard. You can also mulch these plants well, ensuring

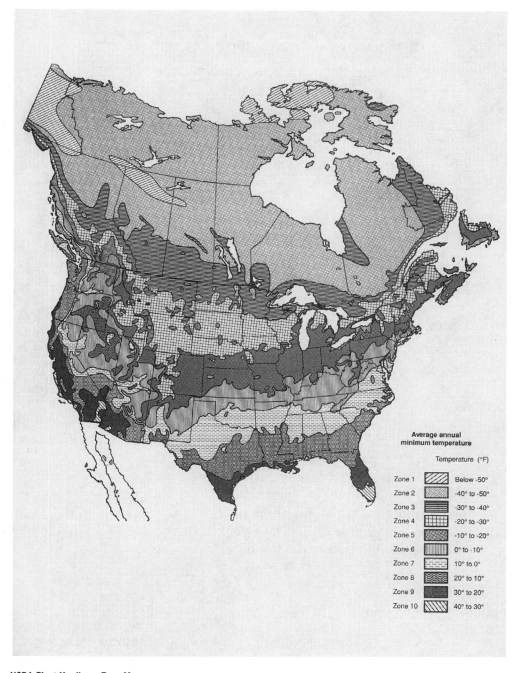

Average annual
minimum temperature

Temperature (°F)

Zone 1	Below -50°
Zone 2	-40° to -50°
Zone 3	-30° to -40°
Zone 4	-20° to -30°
Zone 5	-10° to -20°
Zone 6	0° to -10°
Zone 7	10° to 0°
Zone 8	20° to 10°
Zone 9	30° to 20°
Zone 10	40° to 30°

USDA Plant Hardiness Zone Map

What is the correlation between elevation and the length of the growing season?

For each thousand feet of elevation, the growing season is shortened by a week or so at both the beginning and end of the season. This leaves mountainous areas of Colorado in hardiness zone 3, while its high plains are in zone 5.

protection from wind and preserving moisture in the winter. While you may choose to invoke more drastic measures such as burlap shelters for "iffy" plants, remember it is always best to select the proper plant for your site. Providing a plant with the soil, light, and warmth it requires is the best way to ensure its survival.

I live in a **cold region**. How should I site my garden to improve plant hardiness?

In the north, a garden that slopes to the south will receive more direct sunlight. By planting your garden on a southern slope, the resulting microclimate will be warmer earlier in the spring, and stay warmer in the fall. By planting on a southeastern slope, you can also shelter your plants from wind which mainly comes from the northwest. In the south, however, you will want to plant your garden on a northern slope to decrease the influence of the sun during the summer months.

How does a **coastal climate** impact a plant's hardiness?

In inland states, most precipitation occurs in the summer and seasons are usually distinct. Warm weather in the spring encourages new growth in plants followed by a hot summer in which the growth is able to mature and survive the cold winter. In coastal areas, precipitation occurs throughout the year and the weather is moderated by the large

I live in zone 2.
Why can't I grow a plant that is hardy to zone 3?

You can if you find a warmer, sheltered spot in your yard. If your plant is exposed to temperatures that are below its normal level of tolerance, it may not die immediately. However, repeated exposure to these conditions will damage and stress the plant, killing it or weakening it to the point that other threats such as pests and disease finish it off.

body of water. Temperatures can fluctuate which means new plant growth is unable to mature before being hit with freezing temperatures.

SOIL SCIENCE

What is in **dirt**?

I'm assuming you are referring to soil! The first thing to remember as a prospective gardener is that dirt is something you scour from your bathtub but soil is what you plant in! Soil is made up of minerals and the remains of previously living organisms as well as pores that are filled with water and air.

What is the ideal **soil composition** for plants?

A soil made up of 45% minerals, 25% water, 25% air and 5% organic matter would be ideal for plants. In the real world, however, soil is constantly changing and would not remain at this ratio for long. In addition, every plant requires a slightly different soil, so this ideal is just a composite of those different needs.

15

What does soil do for plants?

Soil provides a medium for plants to grow in. It provides support to keep the plant stationary. It also provides the water, air, and nutrients a plant needs carry out its processes. Finally, although plants can still be affected, soil serves to absorb the impact of contaminants.

What is **soil pH**?

Soil pH measures the acidity or alkalinity of a soil and assigns it a number on a scale from 1.0 to 14.0 with 7.0 being neutral. An acid or "sour" soil has a pH below 7.0, with 1.0 being the most acidic soil. An alkaline or "sweet" soil has a pH range above 7.0, with 14.0 being the sweetest soil. The pH of most soils is between 4.5 and 8.0, while most plants grow best at a pH between 6.0 and 7.0.

Which plant has blooms that can indicate the **pH level of the soil** they are grown in?

Hydrangea macrophylla produces flowers which may be either pink or blue, depending on the pH of the soil they are growing in. If your hydrangea has pink flowers, your soil's pH is most likely above 7.0. If your hydrangea has blue flowers, your soil's pH is probably below 6.5. If your soil is somewhat neutral, your hydrangea may show both pink and blue flowers. Keep in mind, however, that pH levels can vary from place to place in your yard.

How does **wood ash** impact the pH of the soil?

Wood ash increases the pH of the soil, making it more alkaline. It should be used with care, however, since its fine texture means ash is absorbed into the soil quickly.

Wood ashes contain 1% to 10% potash and 1.5% phosphorus—valuable nutrients for plants.

My nosy neighbor says my soil doesn't have enough tilth. What can I do to improve it?

What your neighbor is referring to is your soil structure. Soil binds together in clumps. Without clumps, water and nutrients run right through soil, passing up plant roots in the process. But if the clumps are too large or form horizontal plates, the soil retains water and prevents air from reaching plant roots. A soil that is slightly clumpy, called "friable" soil or soil that has "crumb" or feels "mellow", is the ideal. In most cases, adding organic matter such as peat or compost improves soil structure.

How does **peat moss** impact the pH of the soil?

Peat moss decreases the pH of the soil, making it more acidic. However, if your soil is very alkaline, it would require an impractical amount (that is to say, expensive) of peat moss to make an immediate difference in the soil pH.

What is **soil texture** and how does it impact plant growth?

Soil texture refers to the amount of sand, silt, and clay particles that make up the mineral portion of the soil. The most coarsely textured soil is sand. Since sand particles are large, they allow water and nutrients to move through the spaces between them rapidly while retaining oxygen. Also known as light soils, sandy soils warm up quickly and are easy for plant roots to penetrate but can dry out and lose nutrients too quickly. Clay particles are very small and as a result, stay closer together and hold water and nutrients much more tightly, leaving less air between particles. While clay or heavy soils can be slower to warm up, they tend to be more fertile. Different plants have different needs but most tend to appreciate the benefits of both clay and sandy soil. A soil that is balanced between the different types of mineral particles is called a loam and is the goal of most gardeners.

How can I avoid compacted soil?

Soil is most commonly compacted by walking on it, since this closes up the pores between soil particles. You can avoid compacting your soil in flower beds and borders by creating paths or inserting stepping stones at intervals. In your vegetable garden, you may choose to plant your vegetables closer together, leaving paths around the beds or create wide spaces between your rows for weeding, watering, and feeding in order to minimize the amount of foot traffic around your prized plants.

What is the **saturation point** of soil?

Soil reaches its saturation point when its large pores are unable to absorb any more water and do not contain any air. This occurs following a soaking rain before the water is able to drain out.

The weather turned warm early this year so I raced out with my new rototiller and spent hours **turning clods into beautiful loam**. But now it's midsummer and my soil is dry and crusty looking. What gives?

In your zest to use your new toy, you overworked the soil and broke desirable clumps into individual soil particles. When rain hit the soil, it formed a crust at the surface which prevents water and air from reaching the soil underneath. You can come clean by adding organic matter to the soil, gently working it into that top soil layer. Next year, go easy on the tilling.

What are the **major elements** plants need and how do they impact plant growth?

Nitrogen, phosphorus, potassium, magnesium, calcium, and sulfur (known as macronutrients since plants need them in large quantities) are the most important elements to plants. Nitrogen is important for

19

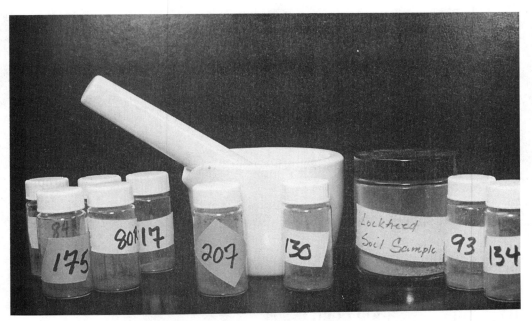

Soil samples in labeled containers. State Agricultural Research Stations will perform soil tests for home gardeners and report on nitrogen, phosphorus, potassium, trace elements and soil acidity.

good leaf and stem growth and also keeps plants green. Since it is highly water-soluble, it tends to leach from the soil quickly—not the best thing for groundwater. Plants that don't have enough nitrogen look pale and spindly. However, an overabundance of nitrogen can cause plants to grow too rapidly, making the stems and leaves soft and susceptible to problems such as disease and insects. Too much nitrogen can also cause plants to focus on growing new leaves when they should be setting fruit or growing new roots.

Phosphorus helps a plant's root system to develop and to encourage the setting of fruit and seeds. It is not as water-soluble as nitrogen and so does not leach out of the soil as easily. Plants that don't have enough phosphorus can become stunted in their growth, have fewer flowers, and have discolored leaves. Potassium keeps plants vigorous, with strong stems and a better resistance to disease and insect problems. Plants that don't have enough potassium can also become stunted in their growth and show chlorosis or yellowing of their leaves. Potassium is also highly water-soluble. Not enough magnesium in the soil can cause some chlorosis or cupping in the older leaves of a plant and reduces the number of seeds the plant produces. A shortage of calcium in the soil can cause weak stems and adversely impact budding and fruiting. An overabundance of either calcium or magnesium interferes with a plant's ability to use the other element as well. A shortage of sulfur, while rare, can cause yellowing in the entire plant.

What is done in a **soil test**?

In order to properly test your soil, you need to take 10–15 small samples of soil—about a cup's worth each—from all over the garden or bed you'd like tested. If a portion of the bed or garden has been fertilized differently than the rest of the garden or is located next to a street (where it might receive salt), leave it out of the testing. Then, mix these samples together and provide your local Cooperative Extension Service or other testing service with a half-cup sample, noting the past (if known) and planned use for the bed. You will receive back an analysis of your soil which generally includes soil pH, macronutrient quantities, and fertilizer recommendations. You can also purchase do-it-yourself soil test kits. If you can afford it (soil tests range widely in price starting at around $10/sample), at least test your soil's pH annually.

What is **humus**?

Humus is the slowly degrading organic matter that is left after the initial decompostion of organic matter takes place. It is high in nitrogen and is able to absorb water and nutrients.

FERTILIZERS

What is the impact of too much **manure** on the environment?

Nitrogen from fresh manure used as topdressing can vaporize into the air as ammonia. Excess nitrogen from the manure can also leach into and pollute groundwater, making it unsafe.

What are some characteristics of slow-release fertilizers?

Slow-release fertilizers take longer to be available to the plant but provide a more constant source of nitrogen. They tend to leach into the soil and burn plants less frequently than water-soluble fertilizers. However, they are more expensive and don't always work well in cool weather.

What are some characteristics of **water-soluble fertilizers**?

A water-soluble fertilizer is available very quickly to the plant. Unfortunately, it is also available to everything else nearby because they leach quickly as well. As a result, it can burn a plant if it is overapplied or not watered in well at the time of application. They can lower the pH of a soil and work well in cool weather. They tend to be inexpensive. For all of these reasons, they tend to be the most misused fertilizers by home gardeners, causing problems ranging from plant or turf burn to groundwater pollution.

Why are **slow-release fertilizers** better for the environment?

Since the nitrogen in slow-release fertilizers is released over a long period of time, plants use most of what is released and there is less left over to leach into the soil and groundwater.

What do those **numbers on a bag of fertilizer** stand for?

Those numbers, like 4-6-8 or 15-15-15, refer to the percentages by weight of macronutrients found in the fertilizer. The first number stands for nitrogen (N_2), the second for phosphorus (expressed as phosphate or P_2O_5), and the third for potassium (expressed as potash or K_2O). In order to determine the actual amount of each element in the fertilizer, multiply the percentage by the fertilizer's total weight in pounds. For example, in a 50 lb. bag of 15-20-15, there are 7.5 lbs. of nitrogen, 10 lbs. of phosphorus, and 7.5 lbs. of potassium. The remaining pounds are filler. By law, both organic and inorganic fertilizers must be labeled in this manner.

SEEDING, PROPAGATION, AND PLANTING

SEED SELECTION

My ten-year-old son wants to try his hand at **starting plants from seed**. Are there any that are easier to start with than others?

Choose plants with larger seeds such as beans or peas—they are easier for smaller (and larger) hands to plant. Plants that grow quickly such as lettuce, carrots, and radishes will provide almost instant gratification (important for short attention spans). Finally, if you're starting the plants indoors, be sure to stay away from plants which don't transplant easily (see below).

I've never grown plants from seed before. Are there any that are difficult to **transplant**?

Be sure to check seed packets that advise outdoor sowing before you purchase them. Plants that are best sown directly in the ground include beans, corn, cucumbers, melons, pumpkins, California poppy (*Eschscholzia californica*), cockscomb (*Celosia cristata*), balloon flower (*Platycodon grandiflorus*), moss rose (*Portulaca grandiflora*), dill, chervil, and coriander.

27

What are some plants that self-seed easily?

Beefstake plant (*Perilla frutescens* 'Atropurpurea'), larkspur, love-in-a-mist (*Nigella damascena*), Iceland poppy (*Papaver nudicaule*), opium poppy (*Papaver somniferum*), tobacco plant (*Nicotiana*), verbena, mountain spinach (*Atriplex hortensis*), Johnny jump-ups (*Viola*), columbine, hollyhocks (*Alcea*), perennial forget-me-not (*Brunnera macrophylla*), spider flower (*Cleome*), four-o'clocks (*Mirabalis jalapa*), chives, and foxglove (*Digitalis purpurea*) are just some of the plants that self-seed easily. Many are biennials which set seed in order to survive. Warm weather plants like tomatoes and marigolds (Tagetes) will even self-seed in cold areas if the conditions are right.

What is an **heirloom seed**?

An heirloom variety is one which has been around for more than 100 years, before modern seed production and food distribution systems. They were originally discovered by regional seed growers who collected them from individual gardeners. These backyard gardeners selected them due to their qualities such as disease or pest resistance, taste, and appearance—qualities which continue to make them popular today.

If I don't use up all of the **seeds in a packet**, can I plant them next year?

You can save seed from year to year if you keep your leftovers properly. Seed viability can be reduced by heat and moisture. After opening the seed packet and planting the number of seeds you need this year, keep the remaining seeds in an airtight jar such as a recycled baby food jar. Place the jar in a cool, dry place. Next year, before planting all the remaining seeds, try sprouting a few (see question below) to determine the viability rate of the remaining seeds.

What is a seed tape?

In order to assist with proper spacing of seeds, some seed companies implant their seeds onto biodegradable tapes. When planting, cut the tape into the length needed for your plot and plant it according to its proper depth in the ground. Don't forget to provide proper spacing between rows. Seed tapes are useful for small seeds such as carrots which are difficult to plant singly and enable a gardener to forgo thinning in most cases.

You can create your own tapes using paper towels cut in long sections and a "glue" mixture of cornstarch and water to adhere the seeds to the tapes.

STARTING PLANTS FROM SEED

What **supplies** do you need to start plants from seed?

In order to start plants from seed, you need a growing medium (see below), containers to grow seedlings in, a watering can and bottle, labels to mark your newly-sewn seeds, and, needless to say, the seeds themselves. You can recycle plastic flats from nurseries but be sure to sterilize them in a diluted bleach solution (roughly 10% bleach) to avoid contamination. You can also use butter tubs or the bottoms of milk cartons or purchase peat pots or new flats to start your seeds.

Seeds actually require warmth to germinate rather than light. While the heat from a grow light or sunny window can be enough for some, others require a heat source underneath the seeding container to germinate. By being placed on a refrigerator or a seed-starting heating pad (available from catalogs and some garden centers), seeds like tomatoes and peppers can successfully germinate. Keep the seeds moist by planting them in a moist mix and covering the container with plastic wrap. Once the seeds have sprouted, they need light and oxygen to grow and flourish so be sure to check your seeds daily. At the first signs of life, remove

29

Garden expos are excellent ways to introduce young people to the joys gardening. Here, a youngster learns the proper technique to plant seeds.

the wrap and place them in a location where they will receive between 8–10 hours of light per day. Water them carefully using a spray mister in order not to knock the fragile seedlings over or wash away the soil. Use a highly diluted fertilizer (I use watered-down fish emulsion) every other time you water.

What **kind of soil** should I use to start plants from seed?

You want to start with a good soil mix. It should be light enough so that the seeds can push through the soil (and also be reached by water, heat and fertilizers) but not so porous as to fall apart once the roots start growing. It's important that the mix is sterile to avoid spreading disease to your new seedlings. You can either mix your own or purchase a mix. Mix your own using equal parts peat or fine compost, soil, and vermiculite or perlite for aeration and drainage. If you buy your mix, be sure it's meant for seedlings. Avoid bags marked potting soil— these usually don't include vermiculite or perlite and are too heavy for seed starting.

I've waited until late in the winter to get my seeds started. It's already three weeks before my frost-free date. Can I still start tomato and pepper plants from seed?

Yes you can. Although seed companies usually recommend starting tomato and pepper plants 8–10 weeks prior to a region's frost-free date, it's actually better to start seeds too late rather than too early. Go ahead and start them inside. Once they're as wide as they are tall, begin to harden them off in preparation for outside planting. In the artificial environment of your house or greenhouse, it is difficult to keep plants watered and fed properly without getting leggy or undernourished. Seedlings that are a little small when set out usually catch up to their earlier-planted cousins.

I have some seeds I bought a few years ago that I never got around to planting. Are they **still good**?

To test the viability of older seeds, you should presprout them. Place ten seeds on a wet paper towel, spacing them apart so that they don't touch each other. Roll up the towel and place it in a plastic bag, loosely tied to be sure air can enter the bag. Set the bag in a warm place such as the kitchen or on top of the refrigerator. Check the seeds in a few days. By multiplying the number of sprouted seeds by ten you get a rate of germination. While anything less than 50% is considered poor, you could still plant the seeds by sowing them more thickly than recommended.

Can I successfully **start seeds in my sunny kitchen window**?

It depends. Is your window leaky? Most seeds require warmth more than sun to germinate. Seeds such as tomatoes and peppers require a warmer soil to germinate than others. You may be better off starting these plants

31

under lights close to the soil, moving the lights up as the plants grow. Better yet, start them on a warming pad made for seed starting or even on top of your refrigerator. Check them carefully every few days. Once they've sprouted, they need light to grow.

I've just bought a packet of morning glory seeds and can't wait to see them climbing up my mailbox. The directions on the packet tell me that I need to **scarify my seeds**. What does that mean?

Seeds like morning glories, sweet peas, and baptisias which have a hard outer covering need to be scarified or scratched in order to absorb water for germination. Methods of scarification include scratching the coating with a knife or rubbing them with sandpaper. If you have more than a few seeds to scarify, line a container such as a coffee can or a jar with sandpaper. Place the seeds inside the container and shake them until the coating wears down.

What is **stratification**?

Stratification is the practice of exposing seeds to cold temperatures for a certain period of time in order for them to break their dormancy and germinate. Some plants that require stratification include bleeding heart, cardinal flower, birch, spruce, and dogwood. Plants that are double-dormant require a warm, moist period followed by a cold period in order to germinate. These include arborvitae and lilac.

I'd like to start **saving seeds** for planting next year. What do I need to do?

Begin by deciding which seeds you'd like to save. To begin with, you can only save seeds from cultivars that are grown from open-pollinated seed. This means the plants will produce seeds that are somewhat similar to its parent. Plants grown from hybrid seeds will not be true to the parent and may even be inferior to it. Once you've determined that your chosen plant is an open-pollinated cultivar, select individual plants that are healthy and have particular traits you want to reproduce. For instance, you noticed a dianthus that produced a deep red flower in the sea of pink flowers that you had purchased. If you're able, keep the plants you've chosen for seed-saving far away from other blooming plants of the same species by at least 200 feet to avoid crossing the plant with others.

You need to harvest the seed pods when they have turned brown, dry and brittle but before they break apart and spill their precious cargo. Seeds from plants such as tomatoes and cucumbers can be saved by allowing the fruit to get overripe on the plant (but before it rots!). Remove the seeds from the fruit and wash them well in clean water, soaking if needed to remove any remaining fruit. Let the seeds dry for a week or so on newspaper, then place them in airtight jars and store them in a cool, dry location for next year.

CARING FOR SEEDLINGS

How do I know when to **transplant my seedlings**?

Seedlings should be generally be transplanted at two different times. If the seeds were started in flats, they should be transplanted to a larger container after they have grown their first set of true leaves (leaves that look like tiny leaves rather than small stubs). They shouldn't need to be transplanted again until they're ready to be planted out unless the weather turns cold despite the arrival of the frost-free date or if they're outgrowing their containers.

How do I **transplant my seedlings**?

Fill your new containers (peat pots, larger plastic cells or clay pots) with wet soil mix. Dampen the mix by combining water and soil mix in a separate container until the soil is thoroughly wet without being soggy. Gently dig out a seedling or group of seedlings from its original home. I use a plastic spoon for larger transplants and its other end for smaller ones. Carefully hold the seedling by one of its leaves being careful not to crush it or the stem. Create a small hole in the damp soil mix using the opposite end of the spoon and place the seedling inside. Gently move the soil back around the seedling and return it to its sunny window or grow light.

What is **damping off**?

Damping off is a soil-borne disease which attacks young seedlings causing their stems to shrivel and collapse at soil level. To prevent it, you must be sure the pots or flats you plant in are sterile. To do this yourself, you should scrub previously used containers using dish soap and water, followed by a soak in a chlorine bleach/water solution (using a 1:10 ratio) and a final rinse to remove the bleach.

What is **hardening off**?

This is the process of acclimating your newly-grown seedlings (or newly purchased plants) from the climate in your house or greenhouse to the outdoors. Temperature, wind, and sunlight can all impact your fragile seedlings or plants. With seedlings, start by bringing them outside into a sheltered, somewhat shaded spot for a few hours each day, gradually increasing their exposure to the elements over a week or two. If the weather takes a drastic turn for the worse (here in Michigan, it usually does), you might consider holding off for a few days or take extra precautions to be sure you don't freeze, burn, or wind-scorch your plants.

What is grafting?

Grafting is a form of plant propagation in which a bud, shoot, or scion of a plant is inserted in a groove or cut in the stem or stock of another plant. The plant then continues to grow. This is a common method for propagating rose bushes and fruit trees.

OTHER METHODS OF PROPAGATION

What is the difference between **sexual and asexual propagation** in plants?

Sexual propagation of plants uses seeds to reproduce plants while asexual propagation of plants uses actual parts of plants such as a leaf or stem to propagate.

When and how do I **divide a plant**?

Dividing a plant separates a plant into several smaller plants. Bulbs, suckering shrubs, ornamental grasses, and perennials that form clumps are some of the plants that you can divide. The best time to divide a plant is when it is dormant, though division can occur at any time with a healthy parent plant. Also, in order not to disturb bloom, plants that bloom in the spring and summer should be divided in the fall, and fall-blooming plants should be divided in the spring.

To divide a plant, gently loosen it from the soil using a spade. Lift it from the soil and examine the roots to see where smaller plants have formed. Separate these from the parent using a sharp spade or knife. Each new plant should have its own root system. If the center of the parent plant is extremely woody, remove it and cut the healthy ring that is left into individual pieces. Plant all new plants as soon as possible, making sure to water them deeply and provide mulch to protect the tender roots.

A greenhouse worker at Henry Ford Estate, Fair Lane in Dearborn, Michigan divides a plant.

What is **cutting**?

Cutting is the most common form of plant propagation in which a leaf or a part of a stem or a root is cut from a plant in order to create a new plant. Most plants can be successfully propagated in this manner. When a cutting is formed from a stem and placed in either water or a highly porous rooting medium, new roots form at the stem node (a section on the stem where a bud or leaf forms). Herbaceous plants root quite easily while woody plants sometimes need assistance in the form of a rooting hormone. Other plants such as the African violet are propagated through leaf cuttings. Raspberries and some perennials are propagated through root cuttings.

What is **layering**?

Propagation by layering is a method of inducing a section of a plant's stem to sprout new roots. It can be done by merely bending a branch to the ground and burying a part of its stem with soil. After the stem roots, it is cut away to form a new plant. With air layering, plants that are difficult to bend or propagate in other ways, may be reproduced. The stem of the plant is wounded, then "bandaged" with moist sphagnum moss or a similar medium. The wound will eventually root, revealing the roots through the moss, and the new plant can be removed from its parent.

SELECTING PLANTS

How can I tell the **healthy plants** from the sickly ones at the farmer's market or my local nursery?

When selecting plants, you should avoid ones with wilted or yellowed leaves. These can indicate that the plant hasn't been watered frequently enough, that it is diseased, or worse. While it might improve once it's in your garden, it's usually best to make another selection. Look for plants that are short and bushy and green, without buds. You want to have the

37

A selection of hanging plants and beds of plants at a greenhouse at Henry Ford Estate, Fair Lane in Dearborn, Michigan.

plant do most of its growing once it's in your garden, otherwise it may poop out early. Check the root ball by giving a gentle tug at the base of the stem and examining the bottom of the pot. If the plant feels loose when you tug on it, it may be damaged or have rotted roots. The roots should appear white and firm and should not be growing out of the bottom of the pot—this indicates its been growing in the pot too long. Check the leaves and stem of the plants, if they appear damaged or plagued by bugs or disease (spots, odd curling, mushiness), don't buy them! Finally, while you can buy a plant in bloom (especially if you're not confident that its color matches the tag), try to avoid it. Again, you want to have your plant do its growing in your garden.

Where is the **best place to purchase** plants?

This is really a matter of opinion but I would try to avoid any place that sets out its plants in between the hammers, the shoe polish, and the cereal. While you can always find a good deal and sometimes even a healthy plant, these places don't have knowledgeable staff to help you decide if that wonderful blooming azalea is one that will survive the cold in your state or if it is meant to brighten your dining room for a few weeks. Farmer's markets can be a good source for plants, although not all the vendors grow the plants they're selling. Try to find one who does. Smaller nurseries that do their own propagation can be an excellent source of new cultivars and those that are probably best suited to your climate. But while they're more reliable and certainly knowledgeable, they can be more expensive. I would tend to purchase my big-ticket items such as trees and shrubs from a local nursery (since these purchases are a true investment), perennials at the same nursery or a farmer's market, and an occasional whimsical purchase at the five and dime.

I've never liked the perennial plant known as **hens-n-chicks** but my new house has a bed filled with them. What should I do?

Many areas have perennial exchanges or plant sales sponsored by local garden clubs. This may provide you with the opportunity to trade them for something else you'd really like. The usual procedure is to dig up your offering and divide it into pots or flats and identify the plants clearly with a tag. If the plant is diseased or insect-ridden, just get rid of it. Other gardeners don't want or need this. As long as the plants are in good shape, you might try offering them to neighbors and friends as well. Backyard perennial giveaways are a time-honored tradition. Finally, if you can't find a home for these happily spreading succulents, you can compost them.

PREPARING THE SOIL AND PLANTING

The directions on my seed packet tell me that the peas I've purchased can be planted "as soon as the soil can be worked." How can I tell when the soil is **ready to be worked**?

The soil is ready for planting if when you pick up a handful of soil and squeeze it, no water comes out. When you loosen your grip, the soil should still be moist enough to stay together. If you poke at the clod of soil, it should break apart into smaller clods. If you have clay soil and

The frost-free date in my area is still two weeks away, but it's been really warm for a week now. Can't I just go ahead and stick my plants in now?

You've got to ask yourself one question: Do you feel lucky? The frost-free date is arrived at using an average of the dates of last freezes over previous years. Sometimes the last freeze arrives earlier, sometimes later. But the possibility for cool nights still exists. Even if there isn't a freeze, nighttime temperatures really need to be well-established above the 50 degree Farenheit mark in order for warm-season crops like tomatoes to thrive. Its also important to remember that while air temperature is one thing, soil temperature is another. Many plants don't do anything until the soil has warmed up sufficiently for growth to occur. It's probably best to wait until after the frost-free date to plant.

work the ground too early, your soil will harden and remain compacted the rest of the season. If you have sandy soil and plant when it is too dry, the soil won't be moist enough to germinate direct-seeded plants or hold newly planted seedlings.

After three days, it just stopped raining and the garden is wonderfully wet. Isn't this the best time to add a flat of **impatiens** to my flower bed?

Actually no. A prime time to spread disease is when the garden is wet. Besides, soggy soil is more difficult and heavy to work with. It's best to wait a day or so to let things dry out.

How can I **protect my vegetable garden** from frost?

In order to minimize the impact frost has on your garden, it is important to site your garden on high ground. Frost and cold air settle into

A gardener plants some bulbs in his backyard plot.

low portions of the landscape (also known as frost pockets). If you are setting your plants out prior to the frost-free date, be sure to use season extenders such as row covers or cloches to protect your plants from frost. You can also use plastic sheeting or newspaper as protection.

Okay. The **frost-free date** has passed and my garden is dry. Should I just dig a hole and stick my plants in?

Although different plants have different needs in terms of spacing and planting depth, all plants need to be pampered at this time. Once they've

41

> **I started my tomato plants from seed but I didn't transplant them to larger pots right away so the plants got too leggy. Can I still save them?**
>
> You can save leggy tomato plants by using a deep transplanting technique. Dig a small trench, angling one side of it . Strip the plant of its lower leaves and lay it in the trench on the angled side. New roots will grow along the buried stem of the plant. Other plants that take well to this treatment include lettuce and cabbages.

been hardened off, plant your plants according to their needs and water thoroughly. Water them every few days until their roots have taken. If they're planted in an area with lots of sun or wind, monitor carefully for leaf scorch and provide a little shelter in the form of row covers, cloches, or other devices if they show any signs of this. Mulch well to retain water around the root system. A kind word or two couldn't hurt either.

How deep should I **plant my seedlings**?

A basic rule of thumb is to set seedlings into the soil at the same height as they were growing in their pot. Tomatoes, however, should be placed on their sides and planted in a trench so that the stems will grow roots, providing the weighty fruits with additional support.

What is meant by the term **"double-digging"**?

Double-digging is a strenuous method of preparing the soil by digging down about one foot, setting the soil aside, working in organic soil amendments to the sublayer as well as your topsoil, and then replacing the topsoil. While it is considered by some gardeners as a badge of honor, you must be careful to keep the topsoil and subsoil separate and ensure the topsoil remains on top. Otherwise you may end up with rockier, heavier soil than you had planned on.

What does it mean to **"broadcast" seed**?

Broadcasting seed means scattering the seed from your hand using a kind of sweeping motion over the ground. After broadcasting, you need to rake the soil gently and water using a fine mist or a watering can.

My packet of carrot seeds tells me they need to be **thinned** after growing a few inches. What does that mean?

Seed that is tiny or has a low rate of germination is usually planted more thickly than needed initially to ensure enough seedlings come up. Once they're up, seedlings that are too close together or are weaker than other plants need to be removed. To avoid damaging other seedlings in the process, use a small pair of scissors to snip the unwanted seedlings at ground level.

CARE AND FEEDING

WATERING

When is the **best time of day to water** my garden?

The best time to water is in the morning, before the sun is full in the sky. Watering in midday can cause leaf scorch from the sun burning the leaves. Mostly it's just plain inefficient as the water evaporates quickly before doing its job. Late evening is the worst time to water, as it leaves the foliage damp at night when molds and fungi are most active. However, remember that even watering at the wrong time of day is better than not watering at all.

I live in an area where drought and water shortages are common. What are some methods of **water conservation** in the garden?

A major source of heavy water usage is the all-American traditional lawn. By reducing the size of your lawn and switching to a more drought-resistant grass or groundcover, you can drastically reduce the amount of water you use. Selecting drought-resistant native plants and mulching all plantings ensures the plants you have stay healthy and look good. Using a drip irrigation system to water your garden will maximize the impact of the watering you do. You can also conserve water by

Can I use my sprinkler to water my vegetable garden?

You can but it's really not recommended. Plants absorb most of their water through their roots. Water from sprinklers mostly hits the foliage which can encourage disease and mold, along with being inefficient. A better, though labor-intensive method is to water plants individually using a cup and a pail. Soaker hoses and drip irrigation systems are other options. Sprinklers work best for lawns. If you must sprinkle your vegetables, try to do so in the morning, before the sun is full in the sky in order to maximize the effect of the water. Avoid evening sprinkling which leaves foliage wet and ripe for disaster.

watering deeply and less frequently and spacing plants closer together in your vegetable garden.

What are **wet feet**?

The term wet feet refers to plants whose roots are immersed in water most of the time. Plants that like their feet wet such as river birches (*Betula nigra*), willows (*Salix*), ferns, goatsbeard (*Aruncus dioicus*), monkshood (*Aconitum*), yellow flag (*Iris pseudacorus*), sweet flag (*Acorus calamus*), blueberries, spice bush (*Lindera benzoin*), witch hazel (*Hamamelis*), sweet woodruff (*Galium odoratum*), and summersweet (*Clethra*) can be planted in moist areas. However, since plant roots require oxygen in order to go through the process of respiration, most plants prefer to be in drier conditions.

What are the advantages of a **drip irrigation system**?

Drip irrigation uses low water pressure to move water through pipes to precise points in your garden. It delivers water where the plants need

An example of a typical watering can.

Are there any kinds of plants that don't need frequent watering?

There are a number of plants from lamb's ear to cactus that will tolerate some drought. Drought-tolerant plants tend to have one or more of the following characteristics which enable them to survive with less water. Look for plants with smaller leaves (a rule of thumb being that the larger the leaf, the more water it requires). Plants with gray or fuzzy foliage tend to retain water better than others. Low-growing or mat-forming plants are not affected by drying winds. Herbs and other scented plants produce an aromatic oil which prevents them from drying out.

it—directly to their root zone. Water isn't wasted in runoff or evaporation. Less water at the surface also means drier soil with less likelihood of weeds taking root. Soil doesn't erode as quickly and plants stay free of diseases caused by soil and water splashing onto their leaves. Nutrients stay put, rather than leaching out of the soil. Plants also appreciate the regular attention—they aren't stressed by over- or under watering. Finally, for busy gardeners, drip irrigation systems save time and effort spent moving hoses and monitoring water uptake. While they are expensive to purchase and install, drip irrigation reduces water and energy costs over the long run.

What is a **soaker hose**?

A soaker or seeper hose is a hose made from old tires, canvas, or plastic which oozes or weeps water through tiny holes or pores along its length. Like a drip irrigation system, they conserve water by placing it directly at a plant's root zone. However, they don't have the precision of a drip irrigation system and so are best used for long beds of plants.

> ## What is green manure?
>
> A green manure or cover crop is a crop that is sown for the purpose of being turned under to enrich the soil. A cover crop also prevents weed seeds from taking root and soil from eroding.

FERTILIZING

What is an **organic fertilizer**?

Technically speaking, organic fertilizers contain the element carbon. More commonly, however, organic fertilizers are made from once-living organisms.

What is a **foliar fertilizer**?

A foliar fertilizer is, of course, a fertilizer applied to a plant's leaves. Plants absorb nutrients and water through their root hairs and their leaf pores. If a plant is unable to absorb nutrients through its roots due to compacted soil or stress, foliar fertilizing may be a good alternative. Foliar fertilizers can perk up fast-growing plants and some are thought to work as catalysts in plants, increasing their uptake of nutrients through their roots. Some organic foliar fertilizers include fish emulsion, compost tea, and seaweed extract.

What are some **organic fertilizers** and their uses?

Bonemeal is high in nitrogen and commonly used when planting tulips and other bulbs. Cottonseed meal is also high in nitrogen but is very acidic and should only be used on plants that thrive in acid soil. Cattle and chicken manure in large amounts are good sources of nitrogen but

51

should be composted first. Fish scrap is another good source of nitrogen and is also high in phosphorus. Although fish emulsion is commonly sold as fertilizer, it is relatively weak in nutrients.

When do I **turn my cover crop under**?

Most cover crops should be turned under before they're half a foot tall. Once they're taller than that, or worse yet, have gone to seed, they're harder to work into the soil. You can mow the crop with a mulching mower first if you'd like to chop up the green matter more thoroughly.

COMPOSTING

My neighborhood offers curbside pickup of leaves and grass clippings, and my kitchen is equipped with a garbage disposal. Why should I bother with **composting**?

There are two main reasons to set aside those modern conveniences and build a compost pile: what it can do for the earth; and what it can do for you. A large percentage of curbside waste is compostable organic matter, and the landfills where this material goes are filling up at an alarming rate. Rather than disposing of things like leaves, grass clippings, and kitchen waste, why not recycle them and conserve all the plant nutrients they contain? At the most basic level, composting is a responsible and efficient way to manage your home and garden. It allows you to not only return something to the earth, but also to create a valuable product to improve your garden or landscape. Compost improves soil texture and structure, helping it to retain nutrients and moisture and improving its aeration. It also moderates the pH levels of soil and helps control weeds, reducing the need to purchase expensive soil improvements, fertilizers, and pesticides. For the little bit of effort that composting requires, you get a healthy garden and a lot of satisfaction.

What sorts of materials make good compost? Is there anything I shouldn't put in my compost pile?

Just about anything organic will decompose eventually in a compost pile, but what goes into a pile does affect the quality of what comes out. The key is to use a wide variety of materials in order to encourage quick and complete breakdown and to create a finished product with high nutrient value. Some common compostable materials include: grass clippings (but not those treated with chemical fertilizers or weed killers); flowers and other garden refuse (but be careful of weeds that have gone to seed and diseased plants); dead leaves; manure (but not human or pet waste, which can contain organisms that cause disease); hair—both human (unless chemically treated) and animal; feathers; sawdust; straw; corn stalks; soil; shredded paper; wood ashes; dried blood; and bonemeal. Kitchen waste—including fruit and vegetable peelings, eggshells, bread products, coffee grounds and filters, and tea grounds and leaves—is another important source of compostable materials. When adding kitchen scraps, be sure to chop or shred large pieces, mix them into the pile well, and add sawdust, leaves, or another dry, brown material to offset their moisture. There are also a number of things that you should avoid putting in your compost pile. Don't use dairy products, meat or fish, fatty foods, or bones because they are hard to break down and may attract critters. It is also best to avoid using cat litter, charcoal briquets, and coal ashes because they are often chemically treated. Finally, never compost anything that may have been treated with a chemical pesticide or herbicide.

What goes on **inside a compost pile**?

Some people are a bit squeamish about the decomposition process. It may be helpful to know a bit more about the intricate community of organisms that convert complex compostable materials into a useable form for plants. Decomposition occurs in a compost pile thanks to microorganisms

53

A compost pile with a healthy supply of red earthworms to aid in decomposition.

(invisible things like bacteria and fungi) and macroorganisms (visible things like earthworms and insects) that break down organic materials to release the nutrients plants need. Several types of bacteria participate in the decomposition process. Aerobes are an efficient type of bacteria that handle decomposition when plenty of oxygen is available (this process is known as aerobic decomposition). Another, less efficient type called anaerobes take over when not enough oxygen is available (this process, which is much slower, is known as anaerobic decomposition).

Different types of bacteria also prefer different temperature ranges. The first wave of aerobic bacteria to hit a new compost pile, psychrophiles, prefer cooler temperatures, down to 28 degrees Fahrenheit. They break down carbon materials and release nutrients and heat. As the pile begins to heat up, another type of bacteria called mesophiles take over. The mesophiles like temperatures of 70 to 90 degrees, but as they continue the work of decomposition they release even more heat. When the temperature of a pile reaches around 100 degrees a type of bacteria known as thermophiles take over. Thermophiles maintain a high level of activity and may raise temperatures up to 160 degrees for a time. All these types of bacteria also release enzymes that continue to aid in the breakdown of organic materials long after the bacteria have died.

There are also a variety of fungi at work during the composting process. Their main job is to break down cellulose and lignin—the tough materials in woody stems and paper. Macroorganisms—visible creatures like earthworms, mites, grubs, centipedes, snails, spiders, beetles, ants, and flies—are another important component of decomposition These guys mainly chew, digest, and mix compost materials to make the work of bacteria and fungi easier. Sometimes they eat each other or bacteria and fungi. Earthworms are particularly important in an efficient composting system because they do a lot of the preliminary digesting for bacteria, munching their way through the pile and producing fertile excrement known as castings. Overall, decomposition is the most natural of processes, and all of these creatures are simply links in the chain of life.

What are **brown and green materials**? What proportion of each should I put in my compost pile?

The microorganisms that control the decomposition process need both carbon and nitrogen—as well as air and moisture—in order to do their work. Materials that provide high levels of carbon are known as brown materials because they are generally brown, dry, coarse, and bulky. These materials include dried leaves, wood chips, sawdust, and cornstalks. Carbonaceous materials give mass to a compost pile, aid in aeration, and provide energy to microorganisms. Materials that provide high levels of nitrogen are known as green materials because they are generally green, moist, and dense. These materials include grass clippings, fresh garden weeds, manure, and blood meal. Nitrogenous materials mainly aid in the reproduction and growth of microorganisms. Ideally, composters should aim for a ratio of brown to green materials between 25:1 and 30:1. Some common compostable materials—such as clover, food scraps, and manure mixed with bedding—will already have a ratio near the ideal range. At any rate, there is no need to take precise measurements, because piles with very different ratios will decompose eventually.

What's the difference between **hot composting and cold composting**?

The many different methods of composting can be placed on a continuum from hot (fast) to cold (slow). The best method of composting to

55

choose depends upon the space you have available, your need for compost, the amount of time and energy you're willing to commit to the project, and the sort of equipment and compostable materials you have on hand. Hot composting methods require more effort and attention but also produce finished compost quickly—generally in less than eight weeks. But in order to maintain the temperatures needed for fast decomposition to occur (113 to 158 degrees Fahrenheit), you must provide the right combination of brown and green materials, control moisture carefully, and aerate frequently. Hot composting methods are recommended for those who have a large garden or a strong need to improve their soil conditions. Cold composting methods are considerably less trouble but also produce finished compost slowly—generally in six months to two years. Cold piles require little maintenance and allow you to add materials a little at a time. However, due to the low temperatures, they may also allow weed seeds to survive and later sprout in your garden. Cold composting methods are recommended for those who have lots of room for composting but little time to spend.

How do I know when my **compost is finished**?

Finished compost should appear dark and crumbly, with no large, readily identifiable chunks of the original source materials left over (although traces of fibrous materials, like straw, are okay as long as they can be easily crushed between your fingers). The consistency will usually be a bit more porous and fluffy than regular dirt. Finished compost should also smell rich and earthy rather than moldy or rotten. When compost is ready to be used, the temperature of the pile should be the same as the air around it. If the middle is still warm, more decomposition time is needed.

I've had a **compost pile** going for a couple of months now and nothing seems to be happening. How come?

With the right combination of materials, your pile should begin to heat up and show signs of decomposition within a few weeks. If your pile is just sitting there, with all the materials you've added still intact, there are several possible causes. For example, it may be too dry. Microorgan-

My compost pile smells bad. What's the problem?

A good compost pile, even in its early stages of decomposition, should smell mildly earthy. An unpleasant odor emanating from a compost heap usually indicates some sort of imbalance. For example, an ammonia smell means that the pile is too heavy on nitrogen (green) materials. To correct the problem, add carbon (brown) materials such as leaves or wood chips and aerate the pile with a pitchfork. Another common cause of odor is a lack of oxygen, either due to compaction of the pile or excess moisture (ideally, a compost pile should be about as moist as a damp sponge). If your pile is a wet, clumpy mass, add carbon materials and aerate. To prevent bad smells in the first place, aerate your pile on a weekly basis and remember that too much of any one material is never a good thing when it comes to composting.

isms require evenly moist, but not really wet, conditions to do their best work. If this seems to be the problem with your pile, poke holes in several locations, insert a garden hose, and water. If the moisture level seems okay, the problem may be a lack of nitrogen. Try mixing in green materials such as grass clippings, fresh manure, or blood meal to get things started. Another way to speed up the process is to add oxygen to the pile by turning it with a pitchfork. Finally, if nothing else seems to work, your pile may simply be too small to maintain heat effectively. Gather more materials until it reaches dimensions of at least one cubic yard.

What is **compost tea**?

It is definitely not something to be consumed in the afternoon with scones . . . but it is an easy, organic alternative to chemical fertilizers and pesticides. Compost tea can be used to give a quick fix to unhealthy plants, to promote growth of transplants or seedlings, or even to help get a new compost pile started. For a small batch, put equal parts finished compost and water into a watering can, stir, and let the mixture sit

57

for a day or so. For a larger batch, place compost in a burlap bag or old pillowcase, tie it at the top, and suspend it in a large bucket or barrel full of water for a week or so. The resulting nutrient-rich, tea-colored liquid can be poured on the roots of plants as a fertilizer or sprayed on leaves to discourage pests, mold, and mildew. Use the same compost for a few batches of tea, then return it to the compost pile or dig it into the garden (it will still have value because not all nutrients in compost are water-soluble). The same methods can also be used to make manure tea or weed tea, which are similarly high in nutrients.

What types of **bins or containers** are used for composting?

Although nature eventually will take its course when compostable materials are just dumped into a pile on the ground, many people choose to contain their compost to give it a more aesthetic appearance, to conserve space, or to speed decomposition. Compost containers range from simple enclosures of chicken wire to elaborate, three-bin wood structures. Perhaps the simplest container to make is a circular pen of woven-wire fencing. You just fasten the two ends of the fencing together to form an upright cylinder large enough to hold the compost heap. Then add compost materials in layers almost to the top of the fencing and drive a stake into the middle to help maintain the shape of the pile and direct water into its center. Whenever the pile needs turning, simply disassemble the enclosure, reassemble it a few feet away, and shovel the compost back in. Similar pens can be made by attaching chicken wire to a rectangular series of wooden tomato stakes placed about one foot apart. Although wire pens are slightly less attractive and create finished compost more slowly than some other containers, they are affordable and allow for good air circulation.

A more permanent type of compost container is a bin made of wood, plastic, or concrete. One well-known version is a Lehigh bin, made of alternating horizontal two-by-fours held together by vertical 3/8-inch rods through the corners. Lehigh-style bins are attractive, portable, adjustable, and allow for good ventilation. Another common type of bin is a chimney-like structure made of stacked cinder blocks or bricks. In most cases, the blocks are stacked with some space between them to allow for air circulation, and they are not mortared together so they can be moved if needed. Other simple, inexpensive compost containers can be made using shipping pallets, wooden snow fencing, prefabricated picket fence sections, or even old window screens assembled into a square around fence posts. Smaller composting systems can be created out of a metal garbage can or 55-gallon drum. A wide variety of commercial compost containers are also available. The best type of compost container to use depends upon the space and materials you have available, your need to protect the pile from critters or hide it from irritable neighbors, and your personal preference.

WEEDING

What is a **weed**?

A common layman's definition of a weed is a plant that is in the wrong place.

What are some methods of **weed prevention**?

By spacing plants closer together, you eliminate space where weeds can land and limit the amount of sunlight existing weed seeds may receive. Using mulch also keeps weeds from taking root in the soil and can smother any weeds that already exist in the bed. Plastic, metal, or wood edgings around your beds help prevent grass and other weeds from taking root in your garden.

What are some **perennial weeds**?

Perennial weeds include dandelions, bindweed, burdock, goldenrod, ground ivy, poison ivy, bentgrass, quack or couch grass, smoot bromegrass, timothy, tall fescue, zoysia grass, bermuda grass, creeping bellflower, plantain, stinging nettle, wild strawberry, and wild garlic. Perennial weeds are usually more difficult to pry from the ground due to their stubborn root systems or sneaky reproduction. A mature dandelion's taproot runs deep and has a tendency to snap if not dug to the bot-

59

If I'm only going to weed once a season, when is the best time to do it?

Weeding done during the first few weeks of spring before the weeds set seed will help keep their weed children from colonizing your yard. Don't forget to attack the areas surrounding your garden or beds too. Ideally, however, weeding should be done at least weekly to keep on top of them.

tom. Quack or couch grass spreads via stolons and by seed, making it difficult to eradicate. Ground ivy creeps through your grass and garden by sending off runners.

What are some **annual weeds**?

Chickweed, crabgrass, jewelweed or snapweed, lamb's quarters, ragweed, and shepherd's purse are some annual weeds. Annual weeds are usually easier to pull from the ground since they have shallower root systems. However, many of them go to seed quickly in order to increase their numbers. Try to nab these guys before that happens and you'll save time later.

MULCH

What is **mulch**?

Mulch is any material laid around the crown and root system of a plant in order to retain moisture around the roots and prevent weeds from forming. Mulching materials range from cocoa hulls or pea gravel to white rocks and black plastic.

A lawn spreader that can be used to distribute weed control or fertilizer.

What are some **organic mulches** I can use?

Compost, grass clippings, shredded leaves, shredded cocoa hulls, pine needles, straw, and shredded wood or bark chips all make fine organic mulches.

What are the benefits of using **compost as a mulch**?

Compost biodegrades over time and adds humus to the soil. It fertilizes at the same time that it suppresses weeds, and actually warms the soil. It should be applied when you plant your garden and periodically throughout the growing season to feed and mulch your plants.

I used **grass clippings** to mulch my vegetable garden but it began to smell quite nasty. How can I avoid this in the future?

Grass clippings provide a good source of mulch, if you are not already mowing your clippings back into your lawn. Used on your vegetable and

61

What is the purpose of mulch?

Mulch keeps weeds down by preventing weed seeds from taking root in the soil and blocking existing weeds from light and air. It also retains water, keeping plant crowns and roots moist. Mulch reduces soil erosion and compaction by protecting the soil from water runoff and the effects of weather. From a design point of view, mulch improves your garden's appearance by providing texture and a uniform backdrop for your plantings. Organic mulches also improve the soil as they decay.

flower beds, grass clippings should be spread thinly and allowed to dry somewhat before being used so that they are not decomposing on your beds. Don't use lawn clippings that have been treated with herbicides for at least a month and a half since being sprayed. Otherwise, the herbicides may begin to work their black magic on your garden.

Is it safe to use **newspaper as a mulch**?

Most newspapers today use soy-based, biodegradable inks and solvents as opposed to the metallic inks and toxic solvents of the previous generation so go ahead. You might consider soaking the paper first and placing another type of mulch on top in order to keep it in place, however.

I live in North Carolina and have heard of using **tobacco stems as mulch**. Are there any problems associated with this?

Tobacco stems can provide an additional source of compost to the soil and may help in repelling rodents and many insects. However, tobacco needs to be cured or weathered prior to its use as a mulch since it gives off an offensive odor as it decomposes. It should also be used with care

Mulches conserve moisture, hold down weeds, and, as they break down, improve the soil. Available at landscaping suppliers, mulch can be made from a variety of materials—hay, bean hulls, grass clippings, stone or, as pictured here, tree bark or ground pallets.

on the vegetable garden since the tobacco may be a carrier of tobacco mosaic which can affect tomatoes and other plants.

Why do I need to **remove mulch** from my Michigan garden in the fall if I'm only going to put it back on again in a few months?

It is a common belief that mulch keeps plants warm in the winter. However, mulch actually keeps plants cold. You need to remove mulch from your planting bed in order to allow the ground to freeze. Once that has

63

I just love the use of black plastic covered in white rock as a mulch! Is there any place I can't use it?

Black plastic can be very effective as a mulch as it heats up quickly and provides a barrier to weeds. Although it retains any soil moisture, it also prevents any rainwater from getting in, forcing the gardener to use either a drip irrigation system or to place a hose underneath it to bring water to plant roots. You can slice holes in the plastic in addition to your planting holes, but this does defeat its purpose as a weed barrier somewhat. In places where water conservation is required or needed, it might be wise to think twice about using black plastic.

Black plastic also should not be used under shrubs and trees. Since moisture (and air) are unable to penetrate the plastic, plant roots grow close to the surface in order to find water and oxygen. Roots are then exposed to extremes in temperature brought on by the plastic or can become girdled, causing the plants to decline and eventually die.

occurred, place the mulch back onto the bed. This prevents the ground from thawing and freezing which can heave tender plant roots out of the soil, exposing them to damaging frigid air.

GARDEN TOOLS

What is a **garden cloche**?

No, it's not a trendy garden hat—at least, not worn by the gardener. Garden cloches are small plant coverings that raise the air temperature around a plant or group of plants by trapping the sun's heat. Traditionally, they are lovely bell-shaped glass objects, treasured by collectors. But

What is a dibble?

A dibble is a tool shaped like a "t" which is used for planting small bulbs or making holes for large seeds. It is more commonly found in England although there are U.S. dibble fans as well.

even the ubiquitous Wall O' Waters are modern versions of the cloche. The Wall O' Waters uses narrow plastic tubes filled with water to trap the sun's warmth. You can make your own cloche by cutting the bottom from a plastic milk jug and placing it over the plant (small side up). Be careful to remove or prop up your cloches on sunny or warm days. Otherwise, you may cook your plants.

What is a **homi**?

A homi is a garden gadget adopted from Korea where it has been in use for hundreds of years. Homi, loosely translated from Korean, means "little ground spear." It is short-handled, with its blade at a curving right angle to the handle. The narrow and triangular blade ends in a point which can be used to make holes for planting or break up soil clods. The flat edges of the blade can be used for weeding, similar to a hoe. When used to dig small holes, the homi's tip is worked into the ground and the tool is pulled back, saving a gardener's wrists from the strain of pushing and lifting.

What is a **cold frame**?

A cold frame is a small garden structure which, like a garden cloche, uses the sun's warmth to heat plants. They are essentially bottomless boxes with slanted lids made of glass or translucent plastic that normally sit partially underground. A gardener can either place pots inside the cold frame or prepare the soil in the frame for planting. By opening or closing the lid, a gardener regulates the temperature inside the frame. During the heat of the day the window is opened to vent the frame and

An example of a gardener using a homi.

ensure seedlings don't burn in the high heat. In the late afternoon, the window is closed to trap the warmth for the cool night ahead. In early spring, cold frames can be used to start seeds. The combination of warm sun along with slightly cooler temperatures will result in seedlings that are strong and sturdy.

You can build your own cold frame using old storm windows and lumber or concrete blocks. Choose a site preferably facing the south and close enough to your house that you'll remember to monitor the temperature of the cold frame. Dig a hole 12 inches deep and slightly larger than your window. In order to prevent weeds from wending their way into your frame, place plastic or even an old sheet on the bottom and cover it with gravel and sand to provide drainage. Using either concrete blocks stacked a foot-and-a-half high or lumber cut the dimensions of your window and several boards high, frame the window and place it in the hole. The top of the frame should slant down at a 45 degree angle so stack your blocks or cut your lumber accordingly. Fix the window to the higher side (if you're using blocks you'll need to build another frame to secure the window to) with two hinges on the inside to keep the frame closed. Shovel soil back around the finished frame and pack it around to insulate the frame from drafts. Add a rope or chain to ensure the win-

How does a spading fork differ from a pitchfork?

A spading or digging fork has thick, flat tines and is used for loosening soil or prying perennial clumps from the ground. A pitchfork has three or four slender tines, making it useful only for light loads like hay or straw.

dow doesn't blow open on a windy day and use a dowel to prop it open when the temperatures heat up midday.

What is the difference between an **anvil set of pruners and a bypass set of pruners**?

Anvil pruners have just one moving blade that closes against the material being cut. They tend to be less expensive and readily available at your local garden center. They work for most garden jobs (cutting open a bag of peat, minor pruning) but tend to crush stems which can be a real problem when you're working on a prized ornamental. Bypass pruners have two moving blades (similar to a pair of scissors) and cut much more cleanly and closely. However, a quality set tends to run around $40–50 through mail order (although with the gardening boom, more and more local stores carry them).

What is a **rototiller** and why would I use one?

A rototiller is a gas-powered machine that has a wheel with triangular blades on it. As a rototiller is pushed or pulled across a planting bed, the blades dig into and turn over the soil or turn under organic matter. The larger ones can also be used to turn under sod. They make quick work of gardens that can take hours to turn by hand. They can be rented from tool rental shops or garden centers or you may choose to purchase one. Some of the newer rototillers have additional blades you can purchase to convert the tiller into an edger or aerator as well.

67

Hardening off plants in a cold frame built against a greenhouse.

What is the difference between a spade and a shovel?

A spade has a fairly flat, rectangular blade while a shovel has a curved blade that usually ends in a point. A spade is a more precise tool that makes a clean cut in the earth. It can be used to edge beds, dig up perennials and ornamentals, and divide plants with a large root ball, among other things. A shovel is best for lifting and digging large quantities of soil or manure since the size and curve of the blade allow it to carry more weight, though it can also be used to dig up perennials and ornamentals.

What is a **trowel**?

A trowel or hand digger is a short-handled tool with a small blade similar to a long-nosed shovel. It is used to dig small holes, transplant, lift plants, mix soil, weed, and cultivate. In short, it's the one tool you can't live without.

What should I do to **prepare my hand tools for winter**?

Begin by thoroughly cleaning and drying them (something you should do after every use!). Then polish the blades and metal parts of your tools using steel wool and oil them thoroughly to prevent any rust from forming. Place a few drops of lubricating oil on any moving parts and sharpen the blades. Store tools in a dry place.

I've never gardened before. What are the **top ten garden tools I should have**?

Everyone has their favorites but the following items come in handy just about every time you step into your backyard paradise:

Trowel You'll be using this often for tasks ranging from planting bulbs to mixing soil. Be sure to find one you like.

Spade See discussion above.

Pruners See discussion above.

Bucket My former next-door neighbor Henry gave me some large white buckets used by construction workers which come in handy during marathon weeding sessions, to haul water to an area, or to sit down on during gardening breaks. You can cart your hand tools around in them too. But you can also use buy a small bucket normally used for cleaning (of course, you can't sit on it).

Wheelbarrow or garden cart For hauling dirt and compost, moving plants, and major weeding (I certainly hope this isn't the case).

The above items are for me most crucial. The following are helpful, too, depending on where and how you're gardening:

Shovel See discussion above.

Gloves (unless you don't mind getting your hands dirty). You can go expensive and buy the yummy kidskin gloves that will fall apart by the end of the season and don't take kindly to washing (take it from me) or purchase a sturdy canvas or cotton pair and use them as rags (if there's anything left) every month or so. Purchase something heftier if you'll be pruning roses or picky ornamentals.

Watering can Buy one with a simple spout rather than a sprinkling head to aim water at the plant's root system. Useful for containers or your vegetable garden.

Garden hose To get water from your spout to where your garden needs it, of course. I have even seen mini-hoses that can be attached to a kitchen sink in order to water houseplants or a terrace garden.

Leaf rake If you have leaves that need to be raked. I buy plastic or rubber ones but they do sometimes break during overzealous raking on cold days.

Selecting garden tools is a highly personal decision but I would recommend purchasing the best quality trowel, spade, and pruners that you can afford as you will have them forever and use them constantly.

What are some garden tasks that should be done in the fall?

Compost all leaves, twigs, and debris in your garden. Remove mulch from beds. Once your beds are bare, dig in soil amendments such as compost or peat. Turn the soil over, digging half a foot where beds are empty and more shallowly near perennials and woody ornamentals. The goal is to expose any insects and weed seeds to the cooler temperatures. Let the soil lie for a few weeks then rake it gently again. Apply mulch once the ground has frozen thoroughly. The point of mulch in the winter is not to keep your plants warm but to keep them cold—preventing them from heaving out of the ground or starting new growth before the weather has stabilized. Fall is the best time to prepare new beds—there just isn't enough time in the spring. Fall is also a good time to aerate and reseed the lawn.

OTHER MAINTENANCE

What are some **garden tasks** that should be done in the spring?

Pruning and planting of trees and shrubs should be done in the spring. Spring is also a good time to divide perennials and plant them. Mulch should be removed from bulbs and perennials in order to allow beds to dry out and to disrupt any insects that have overwintered in your mulch hotel. Apply a fresh layer of mulch before the summer heat kicks in. Early spring is a good time to aerate and reseed the lawn.

What are some **garden tasks** that should be done in the summer?

Some garden tasks that should be done in the summer include: pruning spring-blooming shrubs and trees, deadheading and pinching back

71

annuals and perennials, shearing hedges, weeding, watering, harvesting, and planting extra crops for cooler weather.

What are some **garden tasks** that should be done in the winter?

Some garden tasks that should be done in the winter include: applying winter mulch once the ground has frozen but prior to snow if possible, watering (in dry winters), pruning all trees and shrubs except spring-bloomers and "bleeders", brushing heavy snow off tree limbs after a storm, tamping plants back into their spots if they've heaved out due to freezing and thawing.

PROBLEMS

FOUR-LEGGED PESTS

I live near a woods and a cornfield. It's a beautiful area but there are **deer** everywhere. I'd like to have a perennial garden. Are there any plants the deer won't eat?

> While a proper fit depends on the conditions of the area you'd like to plant (amount of sun received each day, soil pH and texture, your planting region), some plants that deer don't seem to care for include foxglove (*Digitalis purpurea*), blue monkshood (*Aconitum napellus*), and Jacob's Ladder (*Polemonium caeruleum*).
>
> There are various organic and chemical repellants on the market which claim to repel deer by changing the odor or taste of the plants. You can also throw fine netting over the plants although this can quickly become expensive. However, the best way to prevent having deer munch on your beloved plants is to build a tall (10 feet high) fence around them.

Every year I plant bulbs, and every year **squirrels** munch them up before they bloom. What can I do to discourage them?

> You can spray a repellant directly on the bulbs or place screening around bulb groups to discourage their digging. You might consider

domestic pets to discourage them as well—my dog loves to chase squirrels, although the cats seem less interested.

What's the difference between **a vole and a mole**?

A vole looks similar to a mouse and is active year-round. They will eat anything green and will also attack the base of trees, nibbling away at the bark. You can try wrapping the base of young trees in the winter to discourage this. Although moles create havoc by tunneling under your lawn and garden, they actually eat Japanese beetles and other grubs. If you get rid of your grub problem, you may well get rid of your moles.

I want to set out **live traps** for the moles in my yard. How do I know where to place them?

While trapping moles always involves a certain amount of luck, one way to improve your chances is to try to determine where they are most active. In the evening, go out to the spot in your yard where the moles have created their tunnels and flatten them down by walking on them. In the morning, you will find that some of the spots have become raised again. These are the tunnels that are most active. Set your traps near here and you may just catch a mole.

I seem to be having a problem with skunks in my garden. How can I keep them away?

Skunks will sometimes eat garden plants. If this is the case, you might try erecting a chicken-wire fence around your garden. Like moles, skunks also love to munch on grubs. Check your lawn for grubs (see Japanese beetle question below) and apply beneficial nematodes if feasible. Once the grubs have left the lawn, the skunks will most likely leave for grubbier pastures.

INSECTS

I live in a heavily wooded area in the Midwest and we just received a flier from the county notifying us that they will be **spraying for gypsy moth**. What is the gypsy moth and what will be sprayed?

The gypsy moth is non-native insect that feeds on the leaves of a number of hardwood trees such as oaks and aspens, and conifers. Egg masses (averaging 400–500 eggs per mass) are laid during late summer in protected areas such as woodpiles, underneath loose bark, and even under boat tarps and house eaves. After hatching, the larvae climb trees, dropping threads like spiders in order to be scattered by the wind. Once the larvae find a suitable host, they eat heartily and can defoliate a tree in a matter of days. Gypsy moth is commonly confused with eastern tent caterpillars which create silken tents in which they lay their eggs. Gypsy moths, however, don't spin webs or tents when they feed.

Gypsy moth defoliation itself does not kill a hardwood tree; it causes stress as the energy a tree uses to generate a new set of leaves weakens it. Conifers on the other hand are unable to completely recover from a complete loss of needles and therefore may die as a result.

If your county is heavily infested, it is probably doing aerial spraying of Bacillus thuringiensis (Bt). Bt is a biological pesticide made from a com-

Slugs are active by night and consume low-lying parts of many crops. They are attracted to stale beer, and will drown in baited saucers.

My roses have yellowed, curled leaves and I've seen swarms of tiny soft-bodied bugs clustered on the rosebuds and new leaves. What are they and how can I get rid of them?

It sounds like you have aphids. These pesky little bug-gers suck the juice from plants leaving them a little shriveled and stressed. An easy method of getting rid of them is to knock them from the plants with a strong spray of water from your hose. Keep it up over several days and you should dispel the population. Also, try to make your yard friendly to aphid-eating insects like ladybugs (see Special Gardens chapter).

mon soil bacteria. It is known to be toxic only to the caterpillars of moths and butterflies, with rare allergic reactions in some humans. While this makes it more selective than other controls, it is still generally only used when the gypsy moth population has grown large enough to be considered a major nuisance. In many heavily forested areas, the population is monitored but not actively combatted with spraying. This is to avoid interfering with a forest's natural defenses and possibly extending the outbreak.

The best thing a homeowner can do to discourage gypsy moths is to keep trees and shrubs well-watered and fertilized. A healthy plant almost always withstands outbreaks of disease and insects as it is not already in a weakened state.

My **hostas** appear to be under siege. They had lovely whole green leaves yesterday but this morning huge holes had been chewed in them. What should I do?

It sounds like you have slugs. These soft-bodied slimy creatures are the scourge of gardeners with lovely, shady, cool, damp beds and appealing

My lilac bushes have blotchy leaves that look almost burned. What's wrong?

Lilac leafminer larvae have infested your lilacs, burrowing between the upper and lower leaf surface and eating their way through them. Once they are mature, they will spin webs around the leaves and continue to eat until the leaves have been skeletonized. In order to get rid of them, you need to remove any infested leaves and burn them. Cut the branches back to unaffected areas. Finally, before the larvae matures in mid-summer, spray the shrub with an insecticidal soap.

green plants like hostas. Slugs generally feed at night leaving telltale holes and sometimes a sticky slug trail in their wake.

Try pulling any mulch back from the crown of the plant about 3–4 inches. Slugs love to hide in mulch and this will at least lengthen their trip to your plants. If this doesn't keep them away, place saucers of the cheapest beer you can find in the ground so that the lip of the saucer is even with the ground. Slugs will be attracted by the yeast and drown themselves (as one of my Master Gardener instructors said, not a bad way to die). Diatomaceous earth (made of the crushed bodies of tiny sea creatures) can also be spread around the plants. The slugs will scratch up their bodies as they attempt to scooch over it and will eventually die. Finally, you can also go on slug patrol at night—knocking slugs into a waiting pail of soapy water.

What is a **Japanese beetle**?

Japanese beetles are a rather pretty-looking beetle with a metallic green body and copper-colored wings. Their larvae spend their winters in your lawn, chewing on grass roots. If their population becomes large enough, you will notice large dead spots in your lawn. As adults, they feast on leaves and flowers with roses being a favorite delicacy.

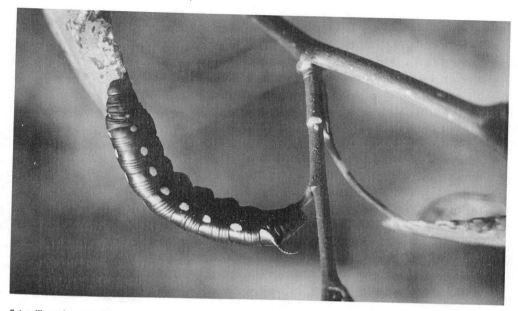

Caterpillars of most butterflies and moths can be hand-picked from a small garden as part of an integrated pest management system.

In order to get rid of the larvae, you can purchase beneficial nematodes (tiny wormlike organisms) which will burrow into the beetles, releasing bacteria which kills the grubs. You can also choose to pick them off of the affected plants, knocking them into a pail of soapy water.

Are there any plants that **Japanese beetles** won't eat?

In a study performed by a USDA scientist, Japanese beetles seemed to prefer other plants over asparagus, alfalfa, rhubarb, and red clover. And while they munched on the silks of corn plants, they tended to leave the foliage alone.

I noticed a canopy filled with **small caterpillars** turning up on a lot of my trees. What are they?

You have tentworms. These caterpillars are very destructive. They chew holes in the leaves of woody ornamentals, skeletonizing the leaves and even defoliating the tree. Remove the tents carefully now and destroy

81

When I brought home my new plant from the nursery and placed it on the table, I noticed a cloud of tiny winged insects flying away from it. What were they?

Unfortunately, they were whiteflies. These pests live outside in the South and in greenhouses up North and are frequently transferred from plant to plant when a new infested plant is introduced to others. They suck the juices from plants, leaving them yellow and dying. With serious infestations, the plant will weaken and die. You can spray infested plants with insecticidal soap but if the plant is new, I would return it to the nursery or compost it.

the tents by burning or smashing them. These worms are also sensitive to Bt, so if you have access to this, you might consider spraying your trees thoroughly.

I've discovered some prehistoric-looking beetles with horns on their heads and behinds underneath the mulch in my planting beds. Should I be concerned about my plants?

The insects you've described sound like earwigs. Earwigs are part of the scavenger insect population. They eat dead or decaying plant material and like to hang out in moist, cool areas such as mulched beds or under decks and stones. They've also been known to eat green plant material, but their innate shyness (actually they are normally active only at night) usually limits their impact.

Since they make mostly positive contributions to your garden in the form of munching up debris, it's best to leave them be. If you find they've been chewing up your prized hosta, consider moving your mulch back from the crown of the plant in order to make it harder for them to reach it.

What is rust?

Rust refers to a fungus whose different species infect a wide assortment of backyard crops such as asparagus, apples, beans, carrots, corn, and onions. A plant with rust has reddish-brown or rusty-looking spots on its leaves and stem. Eventually, the leaves turn yellow and the plant's growth is stunted. It thrives in areas with little wind so be sure your plants have good air circulation around them. If your plants succumb to rust, get rid of them or the affected part to avoid spreading it to other plants.

I just transplanted the tender little **pepper plants** that I had grown from seed into my garden. Now they all look like they've been knocked over. What happened?

Cutworms are to blame. These insects live in the soil of your garden waiting for a tender young stem to nibble on like that of your peppper plants. They feed at night, severing stems below the soil line. The best way to protect young seedlings is to place a barrier around the base of the stem—a collar cut from cardboard works fine.

DISEASE

My tomatoes have come down with a nasty case of something called **Verticillium wilt**. How can I cure it?

Verticillium wilt is a long-lived soil-borne fungus that affects a variety of plants in the nightshade family including tomatoes, potatoes, eggplant, and peppers. Infected plants wilt (hence, the name) and may turn yellow. There is no cure per se, but it can be controlled by regularly rotating your plants, watering at the base of the plant (in order to limit the amount of soil that splashes up on the leaves), and choosing wilt-resistant plant varieties. You can also try soil solarization on new plant beds. This entails loosening up the top layer of soil with a spading fork, then watering it heavily and allowing the bed to sit overnight. The following day, cover the soil with a layer of clear plastic, covering the edges of the plastic with soil so the bed is airtight. After the bed has sat for a month or so, you may remove the plastic and plant in the bed. The solarization process has been found to pasteurize the soil while leaving many beneficial organisms alone.

As for your current tomato plants, remove them from the garden and place them out with the trash to avoid infecting other plants in your garden.

My roses have funky **black and yellow circles on the leaves** and some of the leaves are turning yellow and falling off. What's wrong with them and what can I do?

Your roses have black spot—one of the major fungi that affect roses. Affected leaves have black circles with yellow edges. When the plant is heavily infected, it can lose all of its leaves and become weak and subject to other problems. Black spot is spread by water that remains on the leaves of the plant so be sure to water the root zone carefully to avoid splashing water up on the leaves. Also, provide roses with air circulation—keep them well-spaced and away from walls and buildings.

To decrease the impact of the fungus, remove any infected canes in the spring. You can also apply a fungicide (try one that is sulfur-based) once the leaves have formed, continuing to apply it weekly through the growing season.

My beautiful **spirea bushes** appear to be dying back—some of the leaves and twigs are dying and look like they've been burnt. What can I do?

Unfortunately, not too much. Your spirea has fallen prey to fire blight—a disease transferred by rain and insects. Caused by a bacteria, the blight

How do I get rid of the grayish-white powder-like substance on my bee balm?

You've described powdery mildew—a fungus that appears as white, powdery masses of spores on leaves. Bee balm or *monarda*, is highly susceptible to this fungus which can almost completely defoliate the plant by the end of the summer. It is spread through the air and can overwinter on leaves and infected plants. If the mildew is severe enough, you may have premature leaf drop. Be sure your plant receives a good amount of air circulation by placing it away from buildings and keeping its center open through pruning. Remove any infected leaves and stems and dispose of them. You may choose to spray a sulfur-based fungicide but I usually aim for proper cultural practices and ignore a few mildewed leaves.

causes leaves on affected shoots to die and droop. Dying branches look scorched. You can prune below the affected areas and hope it will pass or apply an antibiotic. In the future, try not to overfertilize your spireas as this makes them more susceptible to fire blight.

How can I prevent **potato scab**?

The fungus that causes potato scab is less likely to grow in an acidic soil. By amending your soil to a pH of less than 5.5 or allowing it to remain in its naturally acidic state, you can discourage this disease from affecting your potato crop.

DISEASE AND PEST CONTROL

What is the difference between **integrated pest management and organic pest management**?

Integrated pest management (IPM) is an approach to disease and insect problems in the garden that considers suitable and prudent solutions to keep these problem to acceptable levels with the least possible impact on the environment. Pesticides and chemical controls are considered, but only as a last resort. What is deemed an acceptable level may vary from area to area, from gardener to gardener, and from plant to plant! For example, while I will tolerate a certain amount of dandelions in my lawn (I do use one of those weed pullers to yank most of them), my neighbor on one side might be out squirting an herbicide on each plant while the neighbor on the other cultivates "dandies" for salads. Organic pest management (OPM) uses a purely organic approach to gardening with an emphasis on prevention by building up nutrients in the soil, proper plant culture, and preventative pest control. Organically acceptable chemical controls such as pheromone traps and insecticidal soaps are considered, but again only as a last resort.

How does a **botanical pesticide** differ from an organic one?

An organic pesticide is one which contains carbon. Contrary to the popular usage of the term, however, it is not "natural" but usually manmade or synthetic. Organic pesticides have been in frequent use in agriculture since the 1940s, and while inexpensive and fairly precise, they have been associated with a number of health and environmental problems as well as misuse. Inorganic pesticides (those without carbon) tend to be more expensive and are not nearly as precise in their action (which means they can be toxic to a wide range of things). A botanical pesticide is a type of organic pesticide that is derived directly from plants. Some examples of botanical pesticides include rotenone, nicotine, pyrethrum, and strychnine. Some botanicals seem to have less impact on the environment. However, just because a pesticide is derived from a plant does not necessarily make it less harmful to humans. Many poisons occur naturally.

A birch tree being treated with pesticide.

Is insecticidal soap the same thing as dish soap?

No. Insecticidal soap is a commercial product that was developed to kill certain insects while not harming beneficial ones. It is biodegradable, breaks down within a couple of weeks, and is safe to use with pets and people. In order to be effective, insects must come in direct contact with the soap.

What are **nematodes**?

Nematodes are microscopic parasitic worms that feed on plants and are always present in the soil. There are good or beneficial nematodes which burrow inside the grubs of some insect pests in order to reproduce, causing the host insect to die. The beneficial nematodes may be used to combat sod webworms, Japanese beetle grubs, flea beetles, gypsy moths, chinch bugs, and other insects. As an added benefit, they don't bother beneficial insects and earthworms in the process. Sold in packages, nematodes look like powder and are combined with water when applied.

The bad or pest nematodes which can weaken plants (sometimes forming galls on plant roots) or infect them with viral diseases. The pest nematodes can be combatted by topdressing plants with compost. The compost attracts organisms which will in turn attack the nematodes. Fish emulsion also repels or kills nematodes.

How can a **birdbath** help me solve my insect problems?

Birds are a natural predator of many garden insect pests. In luring birds to your garden for bath time, you can entice them to stay for lunch, dinner, and breakfast the following day!

What are some **disadvantages of insecticidal soap**?

Insecticidal soap breaks down quickly which means it is better for humans and the environment but bad if it breaks down before impacting the insect population. It is also more expensive and not as widely available as some synthetic insecticides. Finally, although it is less toxic than many synthetic insecticides, it is still toxic.

What is a **pheromone trap**?

A pheromone trap is an insect trap that releases an odor which appeals to insect sex hormones and lures them in. They are not particularly effective to get rid of insects and can indeed, lure insects which may not be in the area to your garden. They are mainly used by county extension offices and farmers to monitor insect populations.

ENVIRONMENTAL/CULTURAL PROBLEMS

What are the most common causes of **environmental or cultural problems**?

Physical damage to a plant's bark or roots, improper watering, improper fertilization, pH and mineral imbalances, and improper light intensity are the most common causes of cultural problems.

What is **desiccation**?

Desiccation refers to the drying out of plants, usually through wind. Evergreen plants such as rhododendrons and azaleas may be prone to this at the outer reaches of their hardiness zone.

What is **lawn mower blight**?

Lawn mower blight refers to the damage done by lawn mowers and weed whackers when they are used too close to the base of a tree. The blades or wire can cut into the tree trunk causing severe damage and eventually killing the tree.

What is girdling and how does it impact a tree?

A tree becomes girdled when a tree root wraps itself around a major root or even the entire tree trunk, slowly strangling the tree as it grows. Girdling can occur either above or below ground. It can also be caused by wrapping or staking a tree trunk too tightly or by not removing the wrap or the staking materials as the tree grows. Overzealous lawn mowing or weed whacking can also cause girdling. Symptoms of girdling include thin or skimpy growth at the top of the tree, underdeveloped bark, or even a slight discoloration of the leaves on one side of the tree. The trunk may appear to be concave on one side or swollen-looking. A tree trunk that appears to grow straight up from the ground rather than flared slightly at the bottom can also be girdled.

What impact does a **black walnut tree** have on tomatoes?

It can kill them. The roots of a black walnut produce a toxin called juglone which will poison tomato plants.

I planted azalea bushes near my house and they don't look happy—they haven't grown much and their **leaves are turning yellow**. What should I do?

The chlorosis or yellowing of the leaves could be caused by either winter injury or by an iron deficiency in the soil. Do a soil test to determine the pH of the azalea bed. Azaleas and other rhododendrons thrive in acidic soil; a more alkaline soil can cause an iron deficiency which in turn causes chlorosis. You may improve your soil's acidity over time by adding a couple of inches of compost a year but if you have another bed in your yard that is more acidic—say, under a stand of pine trees—it might make sense to move the shrubs to that location.

An example of how the roots of a tree can damage a lawn.

PROBLEM PREVENTION

What are the advantages of **crop rotation**?

Crop rotation is the practice of moving a vegetable crop to a different location in your garden from year to year. Because many diseases are soil-borne, this practice limits the effect of disease organisms on plants by not allowing them to build up in the soil. Crop rotation also reduces the number of insect pests which overwinter near a host plant, since you are moving their food source.

91

My friend offered me a clump of her bamboo stand. Should I take it?

If it's the spreading kind, rather than the clumping kind—be warned! Bamboo is a highly invasive plant which can take over your yard from almost all other plants. Invasive plants may be exotics like bamboo or innocents like tansy. In any case, these plants are very vigorous and beat out most other plants in the competition for resources. If you want to grow an invasive plant, be sure to take precautions like planting it in a container or placing an underground barrier around it to prevent it from overtaking your lawn.

What is **companion planting**?

Companion planting refers to the practice of placing plants in close proximity to each other based on the beneficial effects this will have. Actual scientific evidence of this is somewhat scarce but some research indicates that companion planting may attract beneficial insects by providing hiding places or food sources for the insects. Certain plants may also lure insect pests away from other plants or confuse a pest with its scent. Marigolds are thought by many to repel certain insects due to their strong scent. Nasturtiums may lure aphids away from other garden plants such as roses.

What is the benefit of **cleaning up my garden in the fall**?

Cleaning up your garden in the fall removes possible sources of disease or mold from your plants and disrupts or destroys areas for insects to overwinter. By removing diseased plant material along with your spent annuals and vegetables, removing mulch until the ground freezes, and composting or shredding leaves, you pave the way for a healthier garden next spring.

How can I prevent diseases in my garden?

Keeping plants healthy is a matter of good garden habits. Water your garden in the morning, at least before noon, in order to allow the garden plenty of time to dry out before night when diseases thrive in the cool, moist conditions. Also water your plants at their root zone to avoid transmitting soil-borne diseases to plants through soil splash. By the same token, stay out of your garden when it is wet to avoid spreading disease yourself. Mulch can also help keep soil-borne diseases down as well as keeping plants cool and moist. Keep your tools clean, wiping them with a weak bleach solution after removing any extra dirt to avoid spreading diseases between plants. While this may seem extreme, at least clean the tool after using it on a plant you suspect is not healthy. Carefully inspect a plant before introducing it and its troubles to your garden—avoid sickly-looking specimens when purchasing them. While nursing a plant back to health may sound noble, chances are good you won't be able to cure its ills and you'll just end up infecting the rest of your clan. The most important method of prevention is to make sure your plants receive the proper amount of fertilizer, water, and sunlight. A plant under stress or weakened from improper conditions is always more susceptible to problems.

What are **beneficial insects** and how can I attract them to my garden?

Beneficial insects are insects that contribute positively to the garden environment. Bees, wasps, and some flies pollinate plants. Lacewings, dragonflies, ground beetles, fireflies, and beloved ladybugs prey on other insects. Spiders and mites (I know, I know—not technically insects) are also predators. In order to entice beneficial insects to your backyard, avoid using chemicals altogether or use them only when a plant is under siege and only on that plant. Provide them with alternate food sources by leaving some weeds (only the prettiest, of course) and fill a large bowl

The ladybug is the best-known beneficial insect in the garden. Both adults and larvae are an important contribution to managing pests without the use of chemicals. Ladybugs, preying mantis and other beneficial insects can be purchased from garden centers and mail order sources.

PROBLEMS

I've discovered a million ants in my vegetable garden— should I be concerned they'll eat up my harvest?

Ants in your garden are a good thing—ants aerate the soil, allowing air and water to reach plant roots. Ants are also responsible for moving seeds from place to place (the rapid spread of violets in a garden is an example of ants at work). They generally don't mess with vegetables.

or birdbath with water. Plants such as dill and yarrow provide them with extra food in the form of nectar. A brick or rock-edged path provides beneficial insects with a place to lurk.

What are the advantages of **plant diversity** in the garden?

A greater variety of plants in the garden means you provide a diversity of habitats for wildlife including beneficial insects and animals throughout the year. In addition, by selecting plants from a variety of plant families, you will still have a few plants left standing when a scourge of pests or disease that attacks a whole plant family invades your neighborhood.

GARDEN
DESIGN

GARDEN MAKING

What are some characteristics of a **formal garden**?

Formal gardens are based on symmetry. The shapes of beds and features tend to be regular—rectangles or ovals—and the paths are straight. Plants of the same type are normally used to create symmetry—for example, two globe boxwood marking each side of a doorway. Small or urban gardens take well to a formal design.

What are some characteristics of an **informal garden**?

Informal gardens usually have irregularly shaped beds with curving edges and paths. They may be asymmetrical—using different plants with similar shapes to flank a path. Irregularly shaped lots, yards with an uneven slope or larger gardens may be shaped informally.

What elements do I need to consider when **designing my garden**?

First consider the function of your garden. Do the children need a place to play soccer? Are you looking for a corner for garden parties or quiet solitude? Then consider the existing conditions of the site. I would strongly advise a soil test in order to determine the pH of your bed and

An informal garden with winding paths.

What is a focal point?

The focal point is an interesting element where the eye comes to rest when viewing the garden. The focal point of a garden may be a bench, a striking Japanese maple, garden sculpture, or your neighbor's majestic oak.

which soil amendments (if any) are needed. Then look at other conditions such as amount of sunlight, wind, impact of buildings, slope or low areas, existing plants, moisture and texture of the soil, and the proximity of water and the compost pile. Finally, decide how much maintenance you are willing to do—frame this question to yourself in terms of hours per week to really nail this down.

What are the basic principles of **garden design**?

Garden design is founded on basic principles: balance, proportion, repetition or unity, and contrast. Balance consists of providing elements of similar size and weight to each side of a focal point. If these elements are the same shape (usually the same plant), it is symmetrical. Proportion considers the relationship between the size of one element in a garden with the size of another. Unity or the repetition of an element (shape, color, texture, or even the same plant) throughout a garden ties it together. Contrast provides an element of surprise or variation to your garden. Using two plants with similar sizes but different textures or placing a strong-colored element against a pale background can be appealing. It is usually important to keep some element of similarity between plants in order to provide unity to a garden picture but experiment!

How can I design my garden to look good **year-round**?

Begin by studying your garden in the winter. In the winter in most regions, the structure or bones of a garden are bared to the world. With-

Conifers arranged in a symmetrical landscape design.

out the buds of spring, blooms of summer, and rich foliage of fall, elements like trees, shrubs, fences, and buildings become more prominent. Even the demarcation between the lawn or groundcover and the planted beds becomes more pronounced. Start by balancing the scene between evergreens that provide year-round foliage and deciduous trees and shrubs with pronounced shapes, interesting growth patterns, or colorful bark. Then work forward through each season, following basic design principles to fill in the bed with perennials, annuals, and bulbs that bloom or provide foliage to complement each season. If you are starting from scratch, a good rule of thumb to follow for trees and shrubs is to plant one winter ornamental for each summer or spring-featured one.

Okay, I've figured out how I'm going to use the garden, I know my soil and other conditions of the area, and how many hours per week I want to work. How do I **design**?

Based on the conditions of your garden (hours of sun per day, soil pH and texture, slope, wind, and moisture), come up with a list of plants (trees, shrubs, perennials, and annuals) that suit those conditions. Use garden publications, plant encyclopedias, even pictures of other people's gardens for ideas but always choose a plant that fits the site, rather than trying to make the site fit the plant. You have a much better chance of healthy, happy plants this way and you won't need to spend your time and energy trying to improve conditions for a lagging plant.

Next decide whether you're interested in a formal or informal garden design (see questions above for description of each). If you're designing a large space, begin by breaking it down into areas based on function. Break this down even further by beginning with a visual focus for each area. This might be a wonderful old apple tree, the view of a pond, or even your freshly painted yardhouse or shed. If you can't find a great focal point (or even worse have something to hide!), consider "borrowing" a view from your neighbor or surrounding area. For example, I have a large utility pole that stands at the edge of my property but to the left of that in the distance is an old cemetery with a huge majestic linden tree. By focusing on that tree and planning my garden out from it, visitors to my garden see the tree, not the utility pole. If you still can't find a visual focus, create one using a plant from your list or perhaps a garden seat or interesting old pot. The plant should be a tree or shrub or a perennial that has some winter interest so that your focal point doesn't disappear when the cold weather sets in.

Using your plant list and the elements of plant design (balance, proportion, and repetition), add plants to frame your visual focus. Some ideas include using contrasting foliage to make the focus "pop" more, choosing colors that complement the focus, and using plants in odd (not even) amounts. Although smaller plants are usually placed in front of larger ones, mix things up a bit. Remember, too, the finer or "cooler" in color the plant is, the more of it you'll need in order for it to stand out. Before you ever put a shovel into the soil, do a dress rehearsal of your ideas. You can either sketch them out on graph paper, or use garden hose to mark the bed and various garden and household flotsam and jetsam (an overturned pail, a burlap bag over a tomato cage) to appropriate plants at their various heights. Be sure to plan for plants at their mature height and width so that you'll place them properly. This all takes some practice but relax and have fun. And remember, you can always move things around later.

Examine how your garden and surrounding areas will look in winter.

How do I design a **low maintenance garden**?

Start by getting rid of your lawn, or reducing it in size. Even if you're somewhat lax about fertilizing and weed control, lawns have to be mowed and watered frequently. When deciding on plants, choose those that fit your site conditions and narrow this list even further to those which "thrive on neglect" or don't mind going long stretches without being watered. Select plants that need little (if any) pruning, deadheading, pinching back, or coddling whatsoever to look decent. Try to strike a balance between plant diversity (keeps disease and insects down) and choosing too many plants (bound to have different maintenance needs). About a dozen varieties is plenty in the average yard.

Before you plant anything, prepare the soil! Turn it under to about a foot and remove all weeds and weed parts. Anything left will be back to haunt you later. Use mulch everywhere! It will keep down weeds, retain moisture around plant roots, and prevent soil erosion. Finally, keep it manageable by only taking on what you know you can keep up. As I've mentioned elsewhere, frame it in terms of hours per week to be realistic.

PLANT SHAPES, TEXTURES, AND COLORS

How does **color** impact garden design?

Colors can influence perspective when viewing the garden from a distance. Cool colors (such as blue forget-me-nots, green hostas) recede into a landscape while hot colors (pink geraniums, red-flowered cannas) come forward into a scene. Colors can also be used to create repetition or a theme in a garden or set a mood.

What are some **common shapes** of plants?

Some common forms or growing habits of plants include weeping (weeping cherry or willow), vase (forsythia or *Buddleia davidii*), columnar (poplar or gas plant/*Dictamnus purpureus*), round (red maple

A yucca is an example of a course-textured plant.

'Autumn Flame' or *Sedum* 'Autumn Joy'), pyramidal (red maple 'Gerling' or Colorado blue spruce), spreading (tupelo or Sargent crabapple), oval (sugar maple or paperbark maple), and mat-forming (creeping thyme or *Dianthus*).

What is a **coarse-textured plant**?

A plant that has large, widely spaced leaves is said to have coarse texture. Sometimes a plant's texture does not appear coarse unless placed with plants of finer texture.

What are some fine-textured plants?

Bleeding heart, various ferns, Japanese maples, *Miscanthus sinensis* 'Gracillimus' (a grass), bamboo, dogwood shrubs, artemisia, and witch hazels are some examples of fine-textured plants.

What are some **coarse-textured plants**?

Cannas, hostas, iris, rhododendrons, water lillies, *Ligularia dentata*, *Bergenia cordifolia*, peonies, hollies, daylilies, yuccas, camellias, nasturtiums, and *Sedum* 'Autumn Joy' are some examples of coarse-textured plants.

What is a **fine-textured plant**?

A plant that has small, closely spaced leaves is said to have fine texture.

What is a **variegated leaf**?

A variegated leaf has an irregular arrangement of color on it with the most common being green and white or ivory. Other color combinations include: green, white, and yellow; pink and green; brown and pink; brown and green.

What are some **plants with variegated leaves**?

There are a number of pelargoniums (also known as geraniums) with variegated leaves including *Pelargonium hortorums* 'Mrs. Henry Cox,' 'Caroline Schmidt,' and 'A Happy Thought.' Coleus is also available in variegated forms such as *Coleus blumei* 'Carefree Mixture.' *Euonymus japonicus* has a variegated form which is fairly common. Other plants

107

with variegated leaves include ribbon grass, hostas (undulata, crispula, and fortunei), pulmonaria, and *Lamium maculatums* 'Roseum' and 'Beacon Silver.'

What are some design elements of a **white garden**?

White gardens are most effective when they are comprised of green- and gray-leaved plants that serve to offset white flowers or plants with variegated foliage. In a white garden, contrasting foliage textures are important to provide interest in green-on-green areas. Garden structures in the form of walls, fences, or hedges are also important in order to frame a scene or provide a background for white blooms.

GARDEN DESIGNS

How do I plan a **perennial border**?

Begin by preparing the soil in the border, amending the soil to a pH of around 6.0–7.5. and digging in plenty of compost to provide plants with

How do I create a hedgerow?

Keep in mind that a hedgerow works best in a larger lot, removed from houses or outbuildings, so that the shrubs have the chance to achieve their mature size without impinging on the rest of the yard or eating the house. The key to a natural-looking hedgerow is using a mixture of varieties of shrubs. Think of a hedgerow as a border of shrubs (which is essentially what it is). Design the bed for year-round interest by including evergreens for density, early and late flowering shrubs for color, a variety of foliage texture and color, and a mixture of shapes to keep things interesting. Place plants of similar upkeep and site needs together to simplify maintenance and achieve coherence. Keeping the number of different plants small and repeating a few key plants throughout the border will also unify the planting. If your goal is to create a privacy barrier instantly, include shrubs such as forsythia which grow quickly. Complete the look by planting some bulbs or perennials to naturalize just under the hedgerow.

a good head start. Most perennials will show their appreciation by filling out quickly in such conditions. When creating the size of the bed, remember that borders look best if they are no smaller than five feet wide and at least twice as long. However, your ability to maintain the bed should be the overriding factor in your decision. A perennial or herbaceous border is usually plotted against a fence or wall (hence the "border" notation), but poor air circulation can lead to disease and bacteria problems. Leave a path of a foot or so between fence and plants in order to provide circulation as well as an "invisible" path from which to do maintenance tasks like weeding and watering.

Draw up a list of plants that thrive in your area, given the conditions of your bed. Then narrow the list down to about a dozen plants, making sure to include plants that flower at different times through the season. Use paper and pencil to place bubbles (indicating the plant's mature width) on a diagram of your border. Start with the tallest plants first, 109 placing these mostly at the back of the bed. Then, review the elements of garden design and consider how each plant you add will impact the previous one. Think of color and texture combinations, flowering times, and foliage. A symmetrical plan is nice to start with but feel free to mix things up a little. Work towards the front of the bed using plants in descending height. Don't forget vining plants to add height or to creep over the straggling foliage of early bloomers. Consider including annuals in your border as well, especially in the first few years as your perennials are growing (they usually take several years to reach mature, wonderful-looking status). Then go ahead and plant. If the effect seems too studied (two silver mounds on either side of two asters clumped around the shasta daisies), go back and move things around slightly until you're happy with it. Mind you, this will take the rest of your life. . . .

My property runs along the edge of a **woods**. I love the wildness, but how can I tame it without tampering with it too much?

Begin by taking stock of what you have: plants, trees, shrubs, and soil. Use a field guide to identify the major plants and watch out for poison ivy! Then take note of any plant that catches your eye. It doesn't have to be a majestic oak but it could be a small attractive dogwood. These plants will serve as focal points. In order to call attention to them, remove underbrush and possibly some lower limbs from taller trees around these focal points. Based on your knowledge of the site conditions, develop a list of native and exotic plants that will grow well in your woods. Check with your local native plant society for suggestions and lists of invasive exotics to avoid. Select a few plants to enhance your woodland focal points. Consider mowing or maintaining paths that lead to these features, but try to follow the makeup of the woods, rather than felling any trees. Your primary goal is to enhance the woods, not overshadow it.

What is **intensive gardening**?

The intensive method of gardening features vegetables planted closely together in broad, raised beds. Initial soil preparation builds up the organic content of the soil using compost, rock phosphate, and other materials. Compost is used throughout the growing season to maintain

Coneflowers surrouding this bluebird box gives a flowing look and attracts birds and other wildlife.

the fertility level of the soil. Crops are planted in succession with cover crops planted when the soil is not in use. Crops are also rotated to maintain soil nutrients. Types of intensive gardening include the biodynamic method, French intensive, and square foot gardening. If executed properly, intensive gardening can produce higher yields than traditional row planting. But it requires long hours and heavy labor at the outset as well as continual soil improvements in order to maintain it.

What other plants are traditionally planted in **rose gardens**?

A formal rose garden usually includes a hedge of boxwood, yew, hemlock, or false cypress. Lavender or rosemary (if you live in a warm enough climate) can also be used to create a hedge. Blowzy or airy old-fashioned flowers such as peonies, violas, foxglove, baby's breath, and veronica will enhance your roses with pale colors that echo their shades.

GARDEN HARDSCAPING

What is **hardscaping**?

The term hardscaping refers to non-plant materials in a garden that are used to provide structure such as walls, fences, terracing, paths and walkways, arbors, and pergolas.

What is a **ha-ha**?

A ha-ha is a radical slope—a trough really—placed at the edge of a garden. Its historical purpose was to keep farm animals from invading the house garden.

What is a **pergola**?

A pergola is a garden structure with an open, trellised roof for vines. Pergolas are usually fairly substantial in size, compared to an arch or

An example of a pergola at Henry Ford Estate, Fair Lane in Dearborn, Michigan.

arbor. They are sometimes attached to buildings to provide a shaded area of seclusion.

What kind of materials can be used to create **garden paths**?

A path needs to be easy to maintain and durable enough to hold up to foot traffic. Both the tone (formal or informal) and composition of the garden should be considered. Grass makes a simple, though maintenance-heavy, path which looks right at home flanked by perennial flower beds. It is also impractical in drought-stricken areas. Pea gravel provides a pleasant crunching sound when you walk on it and can be counted on to look good without too much effort. Brick—either pavers or classic brick, depending on your region—can be used to create a more permanent path that would hold up to foot and wheelbarrow traffic. Bluestone creates a lovely, though expensive look. If the path meanders through trees, consider using pine needles or finely shredded bark to imitate the forest floor. You might also consider changing materials as the path wanders from area to area or combining materials such as stones set into a background of shredded bark.

113

Garden paths should be permanent and are often made of brick, cobblestones, gravel, stone slabs, or concrete paving blocks.

What is a **drift**?

A drift is a large and usually irregularly-shaped mass of one type of plant. The concept, credited to Gertrude Jekyll, creates instant impact in a garden—much more than say, a dozen different plants in the same bed.

What is a **nursery bed**?

A nursery bed or holding bed is a plant bed in which smaller plants are held until they're large enough to go into the main garden. Nursery

What is an alpine bed?

An alpine bed is comprised of plants which grow naturally in mountainous regions. As such, they do not like their feet wet! Alpine plants thrive in rocky, well-drained soil that is high in organic matter and tend to be spreading or creeping in nature. Alpine plants include *Erinus alpinus*, Cranesbill geranium, rock jasmines, *Euphorbia myrsinites*, alpine poppy, and mossy saxifrage.

beds are also useful to keep plants you're unsure of what do to with until a permanent (at least as permanent as your own whimsy) place in the garden is found for them.

What is an **island bed**?

An island bed is a bed that is placed so that observers may view the plants from all sides of the bed. They are designed with taller plants in the middle of the bed (with the height of the plants no more than half the width of the bed) and smaller plants around the edges of the bed.

What is an **allee**?

An allee is a tunnel made of living plants. Roses scrambling up arches that jut over a path or nut trees trained to curve over a walkway are examples of allees.

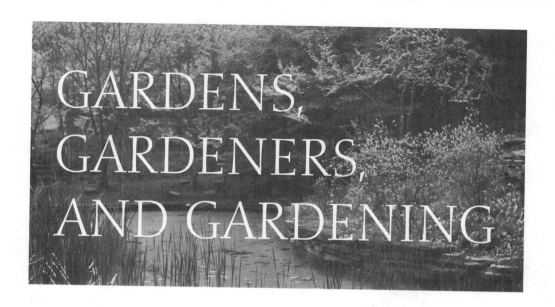

GARDENS, GARDENERS, AND GARDENING

FAMOUS GARDENERS

Which early **U.S. president** was known as an avid gardener?

The third president of the United States, Thomas Jefferson, was an avid gardener, landscape designer and naturalist. The genus *Jeffersonia* was named in his honor and features the wildflower *Jeffersonia diphylla* or twinleaf. It is a woodland perennial which bears white flowers in early spring, close to Jefferson's birthday on April 13th. Jefferson helped to popularize the idea of crop rotation and was a proponent of the use of native plants in the landscape. He sponsored Lewis and Clark's expedition which included botanical research and befriended many landscape designers and agriculturalists such as William Hamilton and Bernard McMahon. His estate, Monticello, served as his own botanical garden and outdoor laboratory. He documented all of his findings in a garden diary which was published in 1944 as *Garden Book*.

Who is known as the **father of American landscape architecture**?

Frederick Law Olmsted was responsible for coining the term landscape architecture, as opposed to landscape gardening, in order to better describe the foundation of the craft in architecture. He designed Central

Twinleaf (*Jeffersonia diphylla*), named in honor of Thomas Jefferson.

Park along with Calvert Vaux in the late 1850s. In the 1870s he designed the grounds of the U.S. Capitol. Olmsted founded a landscape design firm based in Brookline, Massachusetts and was known for his promotion of parks as functional green spaces in cities.

Who was **Jens Jensen**?

Jens Jensen (1860–1951) was a landscape architect known as the father of the Chicago Park System and for the movement towards native plantings in parks and gardens. He was born and received his training in Denmark, but came to the United States at the age of 24 to escape the "soulless" formality of European gardens. After working in the Chicago parks for several years, he planted an "American garden" featuring native shrubs and wildflowers in Union Park. He served as general superintendent and consultant to the Chicago Park System for nearly 30 years. Following his retirement from the park system, he designed private gardens for such famous families as the Fords and the Florsheims. Jensen also founded a school called The Clearing which served as a "school of the soil" for budding landscape architects and artists. He worked for the

> ## Which British father and son gardening duo have names synonymous with successful flower gardening?
>
> **A**lan and Adrian Bloom are famous for their 150-acre nursery, Blooms of Bressingham, which produces over three million pots of perennials every year. They have been responsible for plant introductions such as 'Moonshine' achillea, 'Franz Schubert' phlox, and 'Pink Panda' strawberry.

preservation of native landscapes as well as for the establishment of parks in crowded cities.

Who was **Gertrude Jekyll** and what were some of her gardening principles?

Gertrude Jekyll was a noted English landscape designer. She was born in London in 1843 and studied painting at the South Kensington School of Art. She was heavily influenced by the Arts and Crafts movement, collaborating with the architect Edwin Lutyens on a number of projects, including her own estate, Munstead Wood. Although she is often thought of as the mother of perennial borders, Ms. Jekyll contributed a number of ideas on landscapes such as:

- using grey-leaved plants to highlight sunny areas (those facing south and west) and green-leaved plants to highlight shadier areas (those facing north and east) in the garden

- designing wild gardens which connect formal landscapes to the country surrounding them

- planting in "drifts" or long, flowing groups similar to brushstrokes in a painting

- designing "hot" and "cool" areas of a garden, with hot areas featuring red, yellow, and orange flowers and cool ones with white, pale blue, and yellow ones

121

Who was Ellen Biddle Shipman?

Ellen Biddle Shipman was called the "dean of American women landscape architects." In the early 20th century, most women working in landscape design were relegated to the flower beds. Known for her heavily textured plantings that bloomed from April through October, Shipman began her career in 1912, working with an architect, Charles Platt. They worked on a number of projects through the 1920s when Shipman then began working with another well-known landscape architect, Warren Manning. Shipman and Manning did several jobs in the Midwest, particularly the Cleveland area. One of their commissions, a private estate outside of Cleveland known as Halfred Farms, remains almost the same as when it was first designed. Over her lifetime, Shipman designed over 600 gardens.

What are some trademarks of a garden designed by **Oehme and van Sweden**?

Wolfgang Oehme and James van Sweden are partners in a Baltimore-based landscape firm. They have been at the vanguard of the perennial gardening movement since the 1960s. Their gardens feature little or no lawn, drifts of hardy and bold perennials such as *Echinacea purpurea*, *Sedum* 'Autumn Joy,' *Eupatorium purpurem*, *Rudbeckia* 'Goldstrum,' and ornamental grasses, along with a few key woody ornamentals to create a garden that is inspired by nature.

FAMOUS GARDENS

What is a **botanical garden**?

A botanical garden is a collection of living plants, maintained and displayed for education and research. Botanical gardening groups may fea-

A view of beautiful Balboa park, located near San Diego, California.

Where is the largest bulb garden?

The Keukenhof Garden in Lisse, Holland is arguably the largest bulb garden. Previously an estate garden, Keukenhof was developed by Dutch bulb growers in 1949 as a showcase for their work. Keukenhof is comprised of 70 acres of lawns, ponds, and of course, bulbs. It is famous for its "rivers of bloom" including a river of blue muscari weaving through banks of red tulips and yellow daffodils, but the beds are redesigned every year. Between six and seven million bulbs are planted every fall, then dug up following their bloom and replanted the following year.

ture their research in publications or provide speakers on selected topics. Many botanical gardens also manage endangered native plant species and seek to educate others on these species. All plants, native and exotic, are clearly labeled for visitors and researchers. The garden may be affiliated with a university, a government, or a private group and may be comprised of a conservatory, research greenhouses, display and trial gardens, or an arboretum.

What is an **arboretum**?

An arboretum is a collection of trees established for education and research.

Where is the **Arnold Arboretum**?

The Arnold Arboretum is located in Jamaica Plain, Massachusetts. It is the oldest and largest arboretum in the United States. Since its inception, it has collected and introduced exotic plants. Although the trees at the Arnold are cataloged by genus and family, the grounds were designed by Frederick Law Olmstead, among others, so it looks like a natural landscape.

Which famous gardening event takes place in Chelsea, England?

The Chelsea Flower Show has been an annual international horticulture exhibition since 1913, except for temporary hiatuses during the First and Second World Wars. Sponsored by the Royal Horticultural Society, the show has traditionally marked the beginning of England's social season. The show holds a private viewing for members of the Society, followed by three days open to the public. It features exhibitions and competitions by nurserypersons as well as amateurs, scientific exhibits, tools and equipment, and flower arranging competitions. Members of the Royal Family have traditionally attended it during a private viewing as well.

Where is the **most famous white garden**?

The White Garden at Sissinghurst, England is probably the most famous white garden. It was designed by Vita Sackville-West and Harold Nicolson in 1939 but was not actually planted until 10 years later.

Which **famous golf course** is also the site of botanical gardens?

St. Andrews in Scotland, home of the British Open, can also boast of its botanic garden. The St. Andrews Botanic Garden was founded in 1889 to provide botanical specimens for teaching and research in the University of St. Andrews.

Which **French impressionist** established gardens at Giverny from which he drew inspiration?

Claude Monet settled in Giverny after a series of events including the death of his wife and the bankruptcy of his most enthusiastic collector

Which garden estate was designed in part by Henry Francis du Pont?

Winterthur, H.F. du Pont's birthplace which he inherited in 1928, had been occupied by the du Pont family since 1810. Du Pont collaborated with Marian Cruger Coffin, a landscape architect, to create 60 acres of garden surrounding his childhood home. Winterthur features a quarry garden, Azalea Woods, a reflecting pool, a sundial garden, and the Pinetum. In creating his naturalistic landscapes, du Pont was careful to preserve both native species as well as key specimen trees his parents had planted. Winterthur is located in Delaware and is open to the public.

forced him to seek a quiet place to care for his family and paint. He rented a pink stucco house and established plantings based on his artist's knowledge of color and proportion. He established the Clos Normand Garden which features three acres of flowers and the Grande Allee as well as a two-acre waterlily garden, inspired by Japanese woodblock prints. The gardens became Monet's living studio, featured in many of his paintings. Following Monet's death in 1926, the gardens were cared for by family members but became neglected with their passing. In 1977, they were restored and are today visited by thousands of art and garden lovers annually.

Which public garden has established a **catalog of U.S. landscape records**?

Wave Hill in the Bronx, New York is a 28-acre estate that features an alpine garden, a wild garden, woodlands, flower gardens, a conservatory, and a monocot garden. In its quest to educate the public on the history of gardening and landscapes in the United States, Wave Hill established a database called the CATALOG of Landscape Records in the United States in 1986. It logs information on the location and content of docu-

The sight and sound of water in the garden is attractive to humans as well as wild visitors.

ments such as maps, planting plans, nursery catalogs, personal or business archives, photographs, postcards, and real estate documents.

Where is the **first garden designed for the blind** located?

The Fragrance Garden is part of the Brooklyn Botanical Garden in Brooklyn, New York. It was designed by Alice R. Ireys in 1955 and features raised beds planted with fragrant flowers and plants with textured foliage, as well as culinary herbs. The BBG also houses the Cranford Rose Garden, the Osborne Garden (which imitates Italian gardens), a children's garden, the Discovery Garden, an herb garden, the Japanese Hill-and-Pond Garden, the Lily Pool Terrace, a native garden, a Shakespeare garden (featuring plants grown by Shakespeare), and a rock garden.

Where is the **Desert Botanical Garden**?

The Desert Botanical Garden is located in Phoenix, Arizona. It covers 145 acres and features over 20,000 desert plants representing 4,000 species, all planted in their natural habits.

Where can I go to see **collections or gardens of native grasses**?

The arboretum at the University of Wisconsin at Madison maintains a number of restored prairies. They include the Curtis Prairie which is the oldest restored tall-grass prairie in the world. Nebraska is also home to large grasslands including the Ogallala National Grassland in Sioux and Dowes counties. In Morris, Illinois, the Goose Lake Prairie State Park is the home of a remnant of the original tall-grass prairie which stretches from Minnesota to Texas.

Which national park is the only one to raise **water lilies**?

Kenilworth Aquatic Gardens in Washington, DC was formerly the largest commercial water gardening supplier in the U.S. The gardens were originally established by Walter Shaw in 1882, who transplanted water lilies from his former home in Maine to his property on the Anacostia River. He established over 40 ponds containing aquatic plants. The gardens were purchased by the East National Capital Parks system in 1938.

CAREERS IN GARDENING

What is a **Master Gardener**?

The Master Gardener program was first established by the Cooperative Extension Service in Washington state in 1972. The purpose of the Master Gardening program is to provide current information on horticulture and pest management to participants and to have them extend that knowledge into their communities. A certified Master Gardener is someone who has taken the Master Gardening certification program through the Cooperative Extension Service. A Master Gardener candidate normally attends classes and takes graded exams in botany, garden design, and lawns among other topics. In addition to this, a candidate must serve in a volunteer capacity for a certain number of hours in order to be certified. At least part of this time is usually tied to projects sponsored by the Extension Service such as answering questions at a Master Gardener booth at local nurseries or farmers markets. The remainder of volunteer hours can be fulfilled in a variety of ways, including speaking on gardening to groups and leading gardening projects for the elderly and children. After their initial certification, a Master Gardener must continue to pursue a set number of educational and volunteer hours in order to retain their annual certification. If you're interested in becoming a Master Gardener, contact your local Cooperative Extension Service for more information.

What is the **Cooperative Extension Service**?

The Cooperative Extension Service was established by the Smith-Lever Act of 1914. Smith-Lever provided an annual $10,000 grant to each state to develop a county-based Cooperative Extension Service. These Exten-

What is the difference between a landscape designer and a landscape architect?

Both landscape designers and architects may create plantings and garden structures. A landscape architect, however, has received formal training and is generally licensed in her state of practice. She may be proficient in aspects of landscape design such as exterior design and construction. A landscape designer may or may not have received training and tend to focus more on plantings than on buildings and structures.

sion Services work with land grant institutions (whose mission is to "promote liberal and practical education of the industrial classes in the several pursuits and professions of life") and the U.S. Department of Agriculture to communicate practical information on agriculture to their communities. Although agricultural agents initially worked primarily with farmers, the program eventually expanded to reach out to suburban and urban populations. The Master Gardener program is an example of this.

What is **horticulture**?

Horticulture is the study of cultivated plants such as ornamental trees and shrubs, flowers, vegetables, and fruit.

What is **olericulture**?

Olericulture is the study of vegetables.

What is **floriculture**?

Floriculture is the study of flowers.

Community gardens are an excellent way for gardeners with little space in their own yards to increase their harvest.

What is a **community garden**?

A community garden is a garden that is planned, established, and cared for by a group of people in that community. Individuals share time, space, and energy to make the garden fruitful. Community gardens have been around since World Wars I and II when neighbors shared land and water in victory gardens. According to *Rodale's Encyclopedia of Organic Gardening,* victory gardens grew 40 percent of the United States' produce during 1944, their peak production year. Community gardens have been established on vacant lots, in neighborhood parks, on private property, and in the middle of cities. Neighbors can choose to maintain the property as a group or subdivide it into individual plots for neighbors to maintain. In some areas, cities or neighborhoods set up lotteries in order to award individuals a plot, in other areas participants may pay an annual membership fee. Produce grown on these plots may be taken home by families or shared with the less fortunate. Although many community gardens feature vegetables, fruits, and herbs, some beds are designed for the sole purpose of neighborhood beautification.

SPECIAL GARDENS

CONTAINER GARDENS

What are some advantages of **container gardening**?

With containers, you can garden in small spaces—especially handy for apartment dwellers or those gardeners with more inclination than yard. Container planting also allows the adventurous gardener to experiment with plants ill-suited to her backyard environment or region. For example, a gardener with alkaline clay soil can grow acid-loving azaleas in pots. Plants in pots are also mobile—allowing the gardener to change her garden's look on a daily basis or to move plants indoors when frost hits. This mobility also means you can correct errors of placement—a plant can be easily moved from an area that is too shady or sunny. Containers are also wonderful for gardeners with physical difficulties which prevent them from working the soil. By placing containers on pedestals or tables, you can bring the garden to the gardener.

How do I select the **proper sized container** for my plant?

A good rule of thumb is to choose a container that is about two inches larger in diameter than the root ball of the plant (or group of plants). Plant roots need room to grow and breath. In order to provide proper support to the plant, the container should also be around one-third to one-half the height of the mature plant. If you select a pot that is too

An example of an outdoor terrarium.

large, the potting mix will tend to stay wet which can lead to fungal diseases or rotted roots. If the pot is too small, the plant's growth is stifled and it can become stressed, making it an easy target for disease and pests.

I'd like to **grow vegetables** but just have a small terrace off my apartment. What can I do?

Almost any vegetable can be grown in a container. Look for dwarf or "patio" varieties of plants and think vertical as well as horizontal. A salad garden could be created using a window box filled with a variety of cutting lettuces and greens such as Royal Oakleaf, arugula, and radicchio. Red and green chard in a crock would be lovely to look at and eat. "Patio" tomatoes such as "Superb Super" bush tomato or "Sweet Million" cherry tomato could be grown in deep pots. Try using a strawberry pot (a pot with "planting pockets" along its sides), filling it with annual herbs such as thyme, chives, and dill. Plant pole beans and peas in a pot with a trellis or allow them to scramble up a roof support. Bush varieties of beans, cucumbers, and squash as well as okra and broccoli also work well in containers.

How do I properly water plants in pots?

The best way to water container plants is to soak the potting medium thoroughly, allowing any excess to drain through the bottom (this means, of course that you need to provide proper drainage to begin with). This allows water to reach the roots, making them grow deeper and stronger and the plant more drought-resistant and less susceptible to problems. However, remember most plants are over watered, rather than under watered. You can check to see if your container plant needs water by sticking your finger in the soil an inch or so below the surface. If it feels dry, it's time to water.

When growing larger vegetables, be sure to use a large enough container for the plant's root system. Tomatoes like room to grow. If you're concerned about your terrace's ability to bear weight (and you should be), consider using some of the new "looks-like-clay-but-it's-not" pots. Made from polyethylene resin, these pots look great but weigh next to nothing.

What can I do to be sure my pot provides proper **drainage**?

Start with a container that has a hole (or holes, if it's larger) in the bottom. If there isn't one, you can use a drill and a masonry bit to drill one. If the holes are large, use shards from broken clay pots or a bit of screen over them to prevent soil from draining out of the container. If you're unable to drill a hole in the container, plant in another container that does have a hole in it (plastic works just fine). Line the original container with pebbles or broken pot shards to ensure the pot doesn't sit in water and place the potted plant inside.

Which **herbs** grow well in containers?

Herbs seem to be tailor-made for containers. If you only have room for a window box or pots on a windowsill, look for low-growing herbs such as

Can I grow plants in containers other than pots?

Growing plants in containers other than pots is very chic. Try recycling items such as old pails, a bathtub, a kitchen sink, or that backyard classic—the used tire! Almost anything can be used as a container as long as it is large enough for the root system of the plant you're planning on putting in it. You will also need to monitor the plant's moisture intake and ensure the roots don't get waterlogged. Plan on either drilling a hole in the base of the item or lining it with gravel or broken pot shards in order to provide proper drainage.

chives, basil, parsley, and thyme. If you have a terrace or balcony, almost any herb will do. A larger pot planted with herbs in the same culinary family works well. Try an Italian mix of oregano, parsley, basil, and rosemary or Asian specialties such as "Siam" basil, cilantro, and Chinese chives. You can even experiment with sweet bay trees or rosemary topiary in pots, moving them into the house when frost hits.

I've planted **annuals** in pots the last few years but they never seem to look as good as the nurseries. What am I doing wrong?

A common design mistake with containers is planting too few plants. Pack those pots full! By the end of the summer, you shouldn't be able to see any of the top edge of the pot. Try something different by planting a perennial in a pot such as lavender or even a variegated hosta. Or start with your basic pink geranium and jazz it up with one of the new cascading petunias, lamb's ear, a trailing ivy, and a trailing thyme for good measure. Even if you live in a cold climate, you can be both clever and hip by using containers to plant succulents and exotics.

You can also keep things interesting by changing the makeup of your pots through the year. Start with a large pot. Plant large bulbs such as

Chives (*Allium schoenoprasum*) in bloom.

tulips toward the bottom of the container and smaller bulbs such as crocuses just above those, following guidelines for bulb depth. Place a perennial plant or small woody ornamental at the center of the pot. Then, with each season, plant annuals. For spring, plant pansies or other cold-tolerant annuals. When the weather heats up, compost the pansies and switch to a summer palate of heat-tolerant annuals such as geraniums and petunias. As summer draws to a close, compost those heat-lovers and add fall-blooming mums or asters. In the winter, the perennial (if it is evergreen) or shrub will provide winter interest.

I purchased a lovely **wire planter** which hangs on my brick wall. How can I water it without losing dirt, soil, and plants in the process?

Be sure you've properly prepared the planter to begin with—lining it with plastic and/or peat moss to retain water, soil, and plants. Rather than using a can to water this fragile arrangement, try crushed ice. The ice will provide moisture to your plants without seeping out of the container. Since the ice is crushed, it will quickly melt without damaging the plants.

139

What kind of soil should I use in containers?

Do not use garden soil in your pots—it will be too heavy and filled with weed seeds. A light soil-less mix will ensure air and nutrients reach plant roots. Try a 1:1:1 mixture of soil, peat, and compost, with perlite or vermiculite thrown in to keep it loose or use a pre-mixed potting soil. Since these mixes tend to dry out quickly, be sure to monitor the moisture in your pots, especially if they are made of clay.

Can I **reuse the soil** I have in my containers from year to year or should I start fresh every year?

You can replant in the soil you have in a container for up to three years, unless the plants develop some kind of disease. I would start fresh if the plants become diseased or just aren't thriving.

WILDLIFE, WILDFLOWER, AND NATIVE PLANT GARDENS

I'd like to attract **butterflies** to my yard. Which plants should I use?

There are a large number of plants that can be used to attract butterflies. Among the most common are: yarrow (*Achillea*), pot marigold (*Calendula officinalis*), purple coneflower (*Echinacea purpurea*), blanket flower (*Gaillardia*), black-eyed Susan (*Rudbeckia hirta*), nasturtium (*Tropaeolum*), sweet alyssum, lupine, hollyhock (*Alcea rosea*), salvia, cosmos, thyme, *Sedum spectabile*, spider flower (*Cleome*), bee balm (*Monarda didyma*), and of course butterfly bush (*Buddleia davidii*).

A butterfly stops briefly on a blooming flower.

Which kinds of plants do **butterfly larvae** live in?

Spider flower (*Cleome*), asters, false indigo (*Baptisia*), columbine (*Aquilegia*), lupines, perennial pea (*Lathyrus latifolius*), hollyhock (*Alcea rosea*), and the Prunus (wild plum and cherry trees) and Oak species are among the plants which host butterfly larvae.

I'd like to attract **birds** to my backyard in the winter without a feeder. What kinds of plants can I grow?

Look for plants that retain their seedheads in the winter. These would include globe thistle (*Echinops*), purple coneflower (*Echinacea purpurea*), *Coreopis tinctoria*, golden orange safflower (*Carthamus tinctorius*), sunflowers (if left standing and uneaten by squirrels), European cornflower (*Centaurea cyanus*), cosmos, and marigolds (*Tagetes*). Evergreens or thickets of deciduous woody ornamentals provide cover and nesting material for birds. Don't forget to have a source of fresh water for the birds. While a birdbath is nice, even a shallow frost proof bowl sunk into the soil works wonders.

What is a **snag**?

A snag is a dead tree which is still standing. For wildlife gardeners, snags are important as they host beetles and borers which attract birds and other predators. Tree hollows also form nesting areas for birds and other mammals.

What are **beneficial insects**?

For the gardener, beneficial insects are those bugs whose presence assists the home gardener. They provide a number of positive functions such as pollinating flowers, eating other pest insects or killing them by means of a parasitic relationship, breaking down decaying material or serving as food for birds or other animals which provide additional benefit to the garden. Beneficial insects include bees, flies and some moths, parasitic wasps, yellow jackets, ground beetles, lacewings, and dragonflies.

What does my garden need to have to attract **wildlife**?

The basic elements of a wildlife garden are a source of water, a mixture of both sunny and shady areas for different types of wildlife to congregate, a wide variety of plants and habitats for different wildlife, and natural as opposed to chemical methods of pest and weed control. Although a small pond or creek would be ideal, a birdbath or even a shallow mud-puddle creates an oasis for butterflies and birds. If your yard lacks trees, consider planting a few fast-growing evergreens or thick deciduous

Praying mantis (*Tenodera aridifolia*) egg cases can be purchased at garden centers and through mail order catalogs.

shrubs to provide cover and perches for songbirds and squirrels. With a smaller lot, even vines and trailing plants can create thickets for nesting. If your yard is shade-filled, try pruning or thinning some of the trees and shrubs to provide a sunlit area for butterflies and meadow birds. A diverse garden with a wide variety of plants (even exotic ones) and habitats will attract a diverse number of insects and animals. Most importantly, stop using chemicals of any kind in your yard. Fertilizers, fungicides, pesticides, and most herbicides can kill garden creatures. Use compost and mulch and learn to live with a few bugs. Many are beneficial and others at the very least provide food for birds and critters.

What are some **grasses** that are native to the United States?

The United States has a large and diverse population of native grasses. Grasses that thrive in sunny, dry areas include bluestem (*Andropogon* species), wild rye (*Elymus* species), purple love grass (*Eragrostis spectabilis*), Indian grass (*Sorghastrum avenaceum*), switch grass (*Panicum virgatum*), and ribbon grass (*Phalaris arundinacea* 'Picta'). Bottle-

143

brush grass (*Hystrix patula*) and wood millet (*Milium effusum*) prefer moist shade.

What is the difference between **a native plant and an exotic one**?

A native plant is a species that grows naturally in a region while exotics—like bamboo, for example—have been brought into an area where they were not originally found.

I have a large sunny bit of lawn that I'd like to convert to a **meadow**. How do I start?

Contact your local Extension Service to determine native plant possibilities, then select plants based on the type of soil you have as well as the site. Remember, meadows usually include both flowers and grasses. Grasses are important because they add movement and sound to your meadow, so plan on keeping the percentage of grasses higher than the percentage of flowers. Meadow plants include yarrow (*Achillea*), wild onion (*Allium*), anemone, pussytoes (*Antennaria*), columbine (*Aquilegia*), aster, Indian paintbrush (*Castilleja*), wild carrot or Queen Anne's Lace, coneflower (*Echinacea*), California poppy, Joe Pye weed (*Eupatorum*), Queen of the Prairie (*Filipendula*), Prairie Smoke (*Geum*), hairy

144

I live in the desert. What are some desert natives that I can grow in my landscape?

Saguaro cactus is a well-known American desert native but it is rapidly disappearing from its natural habitats due to collection by unscrupulous plant dealers. Other choices are the buckhorn cholla (*Opuntia acanthocarpa*), creosote bush (*Larrea divaricata*), various penstemons, and chuparosa (*Justicia californica*).

star grass (*Hypoxis*), Houstonia, oxeye daisy (*Leucanthemum*), Layia, blazing star (*Liatris*), wood lily, Texas bluebonnet, owl's clover (*Orthocarpus*), annual phlox, obedient plant, meadow beauty (*Rhexia*), black-eyed Susan (*Rudbeckia*), goldenrod (*Solidago*), eastern and western blue-eyed grass, plains or desert zinnia, atamasco lily (*Zephyranthes*), milkweeds, bluets, flax, sages (*Salvia*), sneezeweed (*Helenium*), and false indigo (*Baptisia*). Meadow grasses include paspy, little and big bluestems, Indian grass, dropseeds, panic grasses, and lovegrasses.

Your next step depends on whether you have more time or energy. If you have time, you can till the grass under. You'll need to do this several times every few weeks for as long as it takes (it could be a year) until there are no more grass seedlings sprouting. If you have energy, remove the sod and compost it. If you want, you can add more topsoil to restore the soil line. You can use either transplants or seeds to create your meadow. If you choose to seed your meadow, begin by raking the soil level, then broadcast the seeds evenly by hand, making sure to keep off of the bed to avoid soil compaction. Rake and water the bed gently, then wait for the seeds to sprout.

Another option would be to stop mowing the lawn and see what happens. If you live in a neighborhood, you may want to check city ordinances and alert your neighbors that you're planning a meadow. To keep the area from looking too wild, mow a wide grass border around it which gives it a maintained look. After a year of letting the lawn grow out, mow the soon-to-be-meadow in early spring and leave the cuttings.

Wildflowers growing in the wild often carpet the landscape. Gardeners often plant flowers in masses to recreate this striking image.

Then overseed or place plantings throughout the bed. Keep the new seeds or plants well watered so that they will germinate. In order to prevent woody plants from taking over, you must be vigilant in weeding out small seedlings. Also remove any other plants that don't meet with your approval.

Once the meadow is established, you will need to cut it (or burn it, if you're out in the country) every spring, followed by a raking. This assists the plants with reseeding and provides those sprouting with more access to sun and rain. Finally, remember that the "wild look" is in name only. A meadow requires regular maintenance to prevent it from becoming a forest.

I'm interested in growing **native plants**. Can I just go to the woods and dig them up?

No. Not only is digging up native plants unethical, it may be illegal depending on the plant you choose and the area you live in. These plants are also usually very particular about the environment they grow in and will most likely die when transplanted. Unscrupulous nurseries remove plants from the wild, drastically decreasing or even eliminating their populations. Finding more than one kind of wildflower in a pot or that a plant is loose in its container (indicating it may not have been grown in that container) may signify that the plant has been collected, rather than propagated. Choose instead to purchase plants that have been propagated by a reliable nursery. Doing a little research to discover which plants are most easily propagated will also help to determine whether a plant has been collected. Try to find plants that have been propagated and grown close to home. They will have adapted to conditions closest to your own backyard.

The exception to this rule is in areas where land development threatens native plant populations. Plant societies and interested individuals often band together to rescue plants from destruction by earthmover. In order to make these moves successful, try to move wildflowers when they aren't blooming. They're less fragile. Younger plants are also more likely to withstand the shock of transplanting. As with other transplanting, choose a cloudy, misty day to move plants and keep the plant roots moist in order to prevent them from drying out. Include lots of the orig-

Purple loostrife (*Lythrum salicaria*) has escaped from gardens and become a serious threat to native species in marshes, where it tends to crowd out cattails and other natural food sources.

inal soil around the roots when you dig up the plant so its new home feels like its old one and try to replant the specimen the same day that you've dug it up. Finally, keep the new plant well-watered in its new environment as it recovers from the shock.

What are some **invasive plants**?

Invasive plants are plants that tend to spread and take over in areas where they are planted due to their vigorous growth habits in ideal conditions. Oriental bittersweet, Japanese honeysuckle, kudzu, English ivy, poison ivy, violets, pink knotweed, mulleins, horsetail, evening primrose, sweet rocket, soapwort (Bouncing Bet), and spurge are some examples of plants that can become invasive when planted in ideal conditions. Purple loosetrife or *lythrum* is an example of an invasive plant that has escaped into the wild, wreaking havoc in the boggy areas it loves by nudging out native cattails. If you must have a certain invasive plant in your garden, consider planting it in an area where it won't thrive (dry soil if it loves wet and so on) or place it in a container so it will be unable to spread.

WATER GARDENS

What kinds of plants **grow in water**?

Water plants can be divided between those that need to be planted and those that float. Floating plants help to discourage algae and provide shade. They include water hyacinth, duckweed, and water soldier. Plants that need to be planted in a pond include waterlilies, as well as floating heart, cape pondweed, yellow pond lily, sweet flag, irises, flowering rush, and pickerel weed.

What is a **bog garden**?

A bog is a continually wet area whose bottom consists of peat, as opposed to a swamp whose bottom consists of mud and decayed plants.

I have a very small yard—how can I create a pond?

A pond or small pool can be created using a half whiskey barrel (found at most garden centers). Begin by removing any loose wood and clean the barrel thoroughly. Once it is dry, coat the inside with a water sealer that is not toxic to plants or fish. Once the sealant has dried, fill the barrel with water and let sit overnight. Empty out the water to get rid of any remaining residue, then fill with water. Select small water plants that don't tend to be invasive. Plant those that need soil in plastic mesh containers using a special soil mix for aquatic plants. Floating plants can be placed on top of the water. Maintenance is important in a pond. Keep it clear of weeds, algae, and dead leaves and divide plants as they outgrow their containers. If you live in a cold climate, you will need to empty the pond and store it for winter.

Due to the peat, bog soil tends to be more acidic. If you have a low-lying area on your property that never completely dries, try creating a bog garden. Add peat and humus to the area, then select plants. Plants such as marsh marigold, rose mallow, cobra lily, pitcher plant, Joe Pye weed, Japanese and Siberian iris, and even Venus's flytrap (in zones 8 and 9) will grow well in bogs. Be sure to keep the area moist.

What types of maintenance are required for an **established pond**?

An established pond needs to have its plants pruned on a regular basis, removing brown or yellow leaves. It also needs to be cleaned twice a year (spring and fall are good times) in order to remove decayed vegetation. Removal of foliage, even if it is dead, needs to be done gradually so as not to upset the fragile balance of your pond's ecosystem. Aquatic plants also need dividing on a regular basis to keep them healthy and ensure they refrain from taking over your pond paradise. In cold-weather areas, you may need to heat your pond in the winter to ensure plants and fish survive.

Fragrant water-lily (*Nymphaea odorata*) on a pond.

What is an **oxygenator**?

An oxygenator is a type of water plant that is used to absorb salts and release oxygen into the water, allowing for the healthy growth of water plants and preventing algae from forming. Oxygenating plants include *Elodea canadenis*, cambomba, willow moss, water starfwort, water violet, water crowsfoot, curled pondweed, water moss, and *Ceratophyllums*.

What is **hydroponic gardening**?

Hydroponics refers to the practice of growing plants without soil. Plants can be grown in water, aggregates, or even humid air, but the most important element is a nutrient solution. Crops such as tomatoes, squash, sweet peppers, hot chiles, lettuce, spinach, chard, cucumbers, broccoli, and beans, as well as herbs, flowers and house plants have all been grown hydroponically.

151

OTHER SPECIALTY GARDENS

What is a **potager**?

Potager means "kitchen garden" in French. It is a vegetable garden in which flowers and herbs intertwine with vegetables to create a colorful design. The plants are laid out in rectangular beds, adding an element of formality to the design. A potager features vegetables which are chosen for their appearance as much as their flavor such as scarlet runner beans or okra.

Which kinds of plants grow in a **moon garden**?

A moon garden is one that is planted to be viewed at twilight or evening. In the dusky twilight, white flowered and grey leaved plants tend to make the strongest impact. You might start by creating a moon-shaped bed. Grey-leaved plants such as lavender, rosemary, and stachys (lamb's ears) could be used as structure or edging, along with boxwood or even holly for daytime viewers. In the spring, white tulips could be featured. Later, night-blooming jasmine, sweet alyssum, evening stock, four o'clocks and even a small star magnolia tree will provide the garden with both scent and flowers, adding romance to your nocturnal strollings. *Nicotiana* or flowering tobacco, evening primrose, *Brugmansia* or angel's trumpet, evening stocks, moonflower vine, night-blooming cereus, and abronia all bloom in the late afternoon or evening. 'New

What is a cutting garden?

A cutting garden is one that is planted and laid with flower arrangements in mind. It might include plants for drying such as statice and sweet Annie. Annuals such as *Nicotiana*, *Calendula*, zinnias, and stocks stand up to cutting. Oriental poppies are beautiful but need to have their ends seared in order to last. Bulbs and corms such as tulips, narcissus, anemones, gladiolus, and allium are essentials in the early spring. *Rudbeckia*, asters, coreopis, dianthus, and roses of course are other possibilities. Try plants with unusual growing habits such as gallardia or blanketflower whose stems curl towards the sun for interesting arrangements.

Dawn' and 'Nevada' are pale-flowered roses that work well in the night garden, along with 'Pallida' which has a sweet fragrance. Stachys or lamb's ear, silver mound, artemesias, lavender, and senecio provide a finishing glimmer of silver in the dusk.

Another interpretation of a moon garden is rooted in feminist thinking. These gardens might include herbs and flowers traditionally associated with women such as pennyroyal and shepherd's purse.

What is a **jardin du cure**?

Jardin du cure translates as "priest's garden" and refers to a small, informal version of a potager.

How can a garden be adapted for **gardeners in wheelchairs**?

A garden can be adapted for gardeners in wheelchairs by raising a garden high enough above the ground so that a wheelchair can fit under it. Create or purchase planter boxes and place them on old card tables or a table created from plywood and sawhorses. Consider purchasing a light-

153

What is a Shakespeare Garden?

In his sonnets and plays, Shakespeare mentions several hundred different plants widely used in the rural society that was 16th century Elizabethan England. Shakespeare lovers everywhere have designed Shakespeare Gardens which feature plants such as wormwood (*Artemisia*), primrose (*Primula*), thyme (*Thymus*), violets (*Viola odorata*), honesty or money plant (*Lunaria annua*), and lavender (*Lavendula*).

weight hose set, similar to those used in greenhouses and locate the garden near a spigot. Garden supplies should be at the ready, placed on waist-high shelving. Follow guidelines for container gardening in order to successful maintain the garden. Gardeners with back problems could also use this type of garden, adjusting the height of the garden so that they could stand or sit while gardening.

What is an **alpine garden**?

An alpine garden is one that mimics the growing conditions above the tree line on a mountain. The soil is gravelly though fertile (a mixture known as scree) and the bed may even include larger rocks for plants to spread out on. An alpine garden may feature plants native to alpine environments (see question in Perennials chapter) or those that appreciate the same growing conditions such as hens-and-chicks, sedum, and even small cacti.

What is a **xeriscape**?

A xeriscape is a landscape that is water-efficient. It does not necessarily include cactus and yucca or exclude lawns and flowers. Instead, it makes the most of the natural rainfall or water sources in an area and keeps plants that need additional water to a minimum, siting them together for maximum efficiency.

PERENNIALS

PERENNIAL PLANT CARE

What is a **perennial**?

A perennial plant is one that flowers and sets seeds for two or more seasons. Perennials such as columbine only live for a few years. Others such as peonies may live for 100 years or more.

What is a **tender perennial**?

A tender perennial is a plant which is perennial in tropical or subtropical regions but that can't survive winter temperatures in other regions. A pelargonium (geranium) is an example of a tender perennial.

How do I prepare my **perennial bed**?

A perennial bed should receive careful preparation, since unlike annuals, you have only one chance to get it right! The bed should be dug deeply to at least a foot (if not deeper) with all weeds removed, clods broken up and the soil level. You might consider double-digging the bed to ensure loose soil which will enable your plants to develop strong root systems. A soil test should be done, with soil amendments added to bring the soil to 5.5–6.5 pH. Plenty of organic matter such as compost should be dug so that your plants will thrive.

What is a hardy perennial?

A hardy perennial is a perennial which tolerates frost. A chrysanthemum is an example of a hardy perennial.

What **growing conditions** are required for most perennials?

As a rule of thumb, most perennials need loamy, evenly moist soil with a pH between 5.5 and 6.5. The site should receive full sun (at least 6–8 hours) during the day. However, there are many exceptions to this rule because it is possible to find a number of perennials that will grow in drier or wetter soil, well-shaded areas, and clay or sandy soil.

How and when should I **plant perennials**?

Perennials can be planted throughout the growing season. The ideal planting time, however, is when the plant is first breaking its dormancy during early spring and the ground is ready to be worked. Fall would be next best as the cooler temperatures place less stress on the plants. As with other ornamentals, try to plant your perennials on an overcast or misty day or at least avoid overly hot or windy days.

Be sure you have your bed prepared before you purchase your plants. This will help you buy the right plant for the right site and will ensure the plant doesn't wither away on your deck awaiting your day off (though most of us are guilty of this). Loosen the soil in your perennial bed to at least a foot deep, breaking up any large clods and incorporate any needed soil amendments. The hole should be wide and deep enough to accomodate the root ball of the plant. If the perennial has fibrous roots, loosen these up and place the plant in the hole so that the crown or base of the plant is at the soil surface and the roots are spread out around it. Other plants vary in their needs. Plants with taproots such as Oriental poppies need a hole dug deep enough for the taproot to extend down. The rhizomes of bearded irises need to be placed just at the soil

Cardinal flower (*Lobelia cardinalis*) is one of the most familiar perennial wildflowers available at most garden centers.

surface, while peonies need to have their eyes or buds planted no lower than 1–2 inches below the surface. Fill the hole and add water immediately, adding a tad more soil if needed.

Remove any flower buds on your plant. During this first season, you want the plant to spend its energy building a strong root system. Monitor the plant carefully for the next few weeks, keeping it well watered. A one-inch layer of mulch applied a few inches away from the crown of your plant will help keep moisture at the root ball and weeds from competing with the new plant.

When is the best time to **divide my perennials** and how mature does the plant need to be to do it?

Generally speaking, most perennials are divided in the spring, just as the new growth is starting to emerge but before they begin to bud or are in full bloom. However some perennials such as Oriental poppies and herbaceous peonies like to be divided and planted in the fall. Other perennials that bloom very early in the spring such as bleeding heart should probably be divided and planted in the fall in order to preserve their flowers.

A perennial normally does not need to be divided for a year or two after being transplanted. There are some signs that indicate a plant might need to be divided. When my Shasta daisies have fewer blooms and begin to die out in the middle, it's time to divide them (usually every

Butterfly weed (*Asclepias tuberosa*) is a native perennial that is difficult to transplant due to its extremely long taproot. Although a milkweed butterfly weed's stems are not milky when broken.

other year). Dianthus (carnations or pinks) also tend to die out if they aren't divided every few years. Other perennials such as bergamot (bee balm) will quickly spread through your garden if they are not divided every two years or so. Hostas can be divided every few years (each new rosette forming a new plant), but they provide more visual weight to your garden if they are left to grow larger. In addition to encouraging more vigorous growth and bloom, dividing plants also ensures you will regularly check them for bugs and disease.

How do I **divide a perennial**?

It depends on the root system of the perennial. Bearded iris and other perennials with rhizomes should be cut apart so that there are buds (knobby-looking growth) on each new plant. Perennials with fibrous roots can be dug up and gently teased apart with your hands. Larger plants with tougher root clumps can be pried apart using digging forks or by making a clean cut with a spade. Chrysanthemums and other plants that become woody when they mature should be dug up with new plants created from the growth around the edges. Compost the remain-

161

How do I stake my perennials?

In staking soft-stemmed plants, it's important to remember to be gentle with them. The goal here is to provide support without mangling your plant. In your quest for a beautiful garden, you should also refrain from using any staking materials that are obvious or just plain ugly. In general, the plant support should be at least 3/4 as tall as the plant to provide proper support. For tall plants such as delphiniums, place a stake near the crown of the plant, being careful not to damage the plant roots. Using garden twine or other soft and inconspicuous material, loosely tie the plant to the stake. You can also purchase stakes that are flexible so they bend with the plant without letting it break, or stakes with a U-shaped end to hold the plant steady. Twigs can provide a rustic-looking support for smaller, lighter plants. For broader plants with weighty blooms such as peonies, plant rings or several stakes with twine wrapping around them and the plant, provide sturdy support. Remember to place plant supports early in the season before your perennials actually need them to avoid plant mangling.

ing woody growth in the center. Before dividing plants, it is best to know where you'll be putting the new plants so they can be back in the ground with their roots covered in soil and soaked well with water in no time.

I divided my **peony bush** but it hasn't bloomed since and it has been two years! What did I do wrong?

Peonies don't generally like to be disturbed, so it takes them a few years to get back to blooming. They can also be planted too deep. When planting your new peony division, be sure the eyes (pink buds on the root system) are planted just 1–2 inches below the soil surface. During the first few years after planting, you should consider removing any flower buds that do appear so that the energy of the plant goes into growing strong roots. Once the plant is mature and has healthy foliage, be sure the plant is receiving at least six hours of sun per day and that it isn't receiving too much nitrogen, which can also decrease blooms.

Why do **chrysanthemums** need to be pinched back?

Removing the top or apical bud from a stem, also known as pinching back, causes the mum to send off new branches below the bud. This results in a plant that is fuller-looking with better blooms. For more information, see the question on apical dominance in the Plant Science chapter. Generally speaking, mums should be pinched every month or so during the growing season up until the end of July.

How often should I **fertilize my perennials**?

Something to consider in fertilizing perennials is that they will be in the ground longer than annuals. While this sounds self-evident, it has implications for how often you want to fertilize them. While perennials need nitrogen to grow, you may want to consider fertilizing them only 1–2 times per season. Plants can become fertilizer-dependent—needing that quick fix of 15–15–15 in order to bloom at all. But if you properly prepare and regularly amend the soil and have chosen a perennial that appreciates your site conditions, it should do well and be better adapted to survive periods of your life where you don't feel much like gardening (I know, hard to believe that will happen . . .).

How do I **mulch my perennials**?

Perennials generally need a layer of 1–2 inches of mulch. If you use a mulch that decomposes quickly like grass clippings, you may consider a slightly thicker layer. Place the mulch around the plant, being careful to leave space around the crown to reduce the possibility of disease and damage from slugs. Perennials should be mulched after the soil warms up in the spring in order to keep the roots of the plant moist and weed-free. In the fall, remove the mulch until after the ground has frozen. Then replace it to keep the soil around the root ball from freezing and thawing which can damage the plant.

Jack-in-the-pulpit (*Arisaema triphyllum*) is a native wildflower that grows well in shady areas.

What is the advantage of **perennials over annuals**?

Although you might think perennials are cheaper in the long run, since you only purchase them once every few years, they do require more labor and cost more (in terms of soil amendments and compost as well as the price tag of the plant) at the outset than annuals do. The main advantage of perennials in cooler climates is that they can extend the growing season. Many annuals require temperatures above freezing in order to survive and thrive. Some perennials need cooler temperatures to flower and some remain green throughout much of the year.

Now that I've successfully grown perennial flowers, I'd like to cut a few for **bouquets**. Are there any guidelines I should follow?

The best time to cut flowers is in the early morning. Use a set of sharp scissors or pruners and cut the stems as long as possible down to a bud or leaf node that is facing the outside of the plant. By cutting flowers in a variety of budding and blooming stages, you make your bouquet more interesting and lifelike. Carry a bucket of lukewarm water with you and plunge the stems into the water immediately after cutting. For hollow-stemmed flowers like Oriental poppies, use a match or lighter to sear the end of the stem in order to keep water inside.

PERENNIAL SELECTION

Which perennials will grow in **dry and shady conditions**?

Perennials that will grow or thrive in dry and shady or partially shady sites include the celandine poppy (*Chelidonium majus*), candytuft (*Iberis sempervirens*), gas plant (*Dictamnus albus*), pinks (*Dianthus*), bishop's hat (*Epimedium*), lungwort (*Pulmonaria*), *Liriope muscari*, Solomon's Seal, and *Iris foetidissima*.

Which perennials will grow in **dry and sunny conditions**?

Think meadow flowers for dry and sunny areas: coneflowers, *Coreopis*, sages, golden rods, globe thistle (*Echinops ritro*), yarrows, blanketflower (*Gaillardia grandiflora*), daylilies, blue flax, and gayfeather. Artemisias, baptisias, *Scabiosa*, thrift, Golden Marguerites, veronica, lavender, lamb's ears, pinks, sedums, spurge, statice, torch lilies, and yuccas also thrive in these areas.

Which perennials will grow in **moist and sunny conditions**?

Think of swamps and wetlands: cardinal flower (*Lobelia cardinalis*), *Tradescantia*, white turtlehead, yellow flag, marsh marigold, mead-

165

Which perennials will grow in moist and shady conditions?

Ferns, primulas, comfrey (*Symphytum uplandicum*), columbines, astilbes, bergenias, bleeding hearts, hellebores, epimediums, and hostas are just a few of the perennials that thrive under moist and shady conditions.

owsweet, meadow rue, bee balm or monarda, sneezeweed (*Helenium autumnale*), spiderworts, loosestrifes (stay away from the invasive ones), and Virginia bluebells all thrive in moist and sunny areas. Goat's beard (*Aruncus*), Japanese and Siberian iris, hibiscus, Himalayan cowslip (*Primula florindae*), geums, and *Rodgersias* also love moist soil.

Which perennials will grow in **alkaline soil**?

Although gardeners with alkaline soil often curse it, a number of beautiful perennials will thrive in this type of soil. Butterfly bush (*Buddleia davidii*), foxtail lily, globe thistle (*Echinops ritro*), verbascum, oriental poppy (*Papaver orientale*), *Linaria purpurea, Perovskia, Salvia superba*, yarrow 'Cerise Queen' (*Achillea millefolium*), gas plant (*Dictamnus albus*), pincushion flower (*Scabiosa caucasica*), *Sedum* 'Autumn Joy', *Coreopis verticillata*, red valerian (*Centranthus ruber*), pinks (*Dianthus*), strawflowers (*Helichrysum bracteatum*), pasque flower (*Pulsatilla vulgaris*), and baby's breath (*Gypsophilia paniculata*) all love alkaline soil.

Which perennials will grow in **acidic soil**?

Primulas, Virginia cowslip, Gentian, toad lily, Himalayan cowslip (*Primula florindae*), lilies rubrum and lilies tigrinum splendens, lupines, *Calceolaria rugosa*, flame flower (*Tropaeolum speciosum*), heaths and heathers, *Helleborus foetidus*, and milkweed are among the perennials which will flourish in acidic soil.

Monarda or bee balm will grow well in moist and sunny conditions.

Are there any perennials with grey or silver foliage?

Grey and silver-leaved plants act as an excellent foil for bright or pastel colored flowers and can provide contrast to darker-leaved plants, lighting up areas of a garden. Meadow rue (*Thalictrum aquilegifolium*), *Hosta sieboldiana*, lamb's ear (*Stachys lanata*), plume poppy (*Bocconia microcarpa* 'Kelway's Coral Plume'), *Senecio cineraria* (used as an annual except in zones 8–10), silver mound (*Artemisia schmidtiana* 'Nana'), *Ruta graveolens* 'Jackman's Blue', yarrow (*Achillea* 'Moonshine'), *Verbascum bombyciferum*, wormwood (*Artemisia absinthium* 'Lambrook Silver'), *Helictotrichon sempervirens*, and *Buddleia fallowiana* are some of the perennials with grey or silver foliage.

Which perennials were commonly used by the English landscape designer **Gertrude Jekyll** in her plantings?

Lamb's ear (*Stachys*), *Bergenia cordifolia*, roses, *Clematis montana* and *Clematis* 'Jackmanii', Oriental poppy (*Papaver orientalis*), delphiniums, *Gypsophilia paniculata* (perennial baby's breath), a variety of ferns and epimediums, perennial candytuft (*Iberis sempervirens*), a variety of irises, and geraniums (both perennial and pelargoniums) are among the many Jekyll-favored perennials.

What are some perennials that could be used as **focal points**?

Yucca provides an exciting focal point to a garden—its knifelike leaves making an exclamation point in a garden. Plume poppy can also serve as a subtler focal point with its salmon-colored flowers rising from its large leaves. Any of the hostas, when large enough, can be used as a focal point in a low-growing bed. For the summer garden, consider using cannas with their large, tropical good looks providing emphasis to a perennial border or globe thistle for the wild garden. *Ligularia dentata* 'Desdemona,' sometimes known as golden groundsel, rises to three feet

I have a hard time growing delphiniums in my area, what else looks like it that is easy to grow?

Delphiniums are a demanding plant to grow. They want a fertile soil that is well-drained yet moist. Plus, it is important to stake them as they are beaten down quickly by rain and wind. They also appreciate full sun and bloom in early summer. Dwarf species of alkanet or *Anchusa azurea* will grow in rock gardens and don't necessarily need staking to preserve their spikes. Aconite or monkshood (*Aconitum*) will grow in cool and shady areas, although they'll tolerate full sun. Look for 'Bressingham Spire' and *Aconitum carmichaelii* 'Arends' to bloom in late summer or early fall. *Salvia*, also blooming later, will provide a tall, deep blue flower without staking for areas of your garden, though most salvias prefer warmer areas. In zones 8–9, the delicate blooms of Gentian sage (*Salvia patens*) resemble the delphinium. Larkspur, although a hardy annual, does a pretty good imitation of delphinium as well.

at maturity and has wonderful dark green leaves that are plum-colored underneath setting off its deep orange flowers. You might consider using a vining plant such as clematis on a tuteur or other upright support to create interest in the garden as well. In the winter, the tuteur could be left bare to provide something for the eye to rest on. In drier parts of the country, look for tall, native plants such as cacti in the *Opuntia* genus to provide focus in a desert landscape.

What are some perennials that have **fragrant flowers**?

Roses are the obvious choice, though considered shrubs. Other perennials with fragrant flowers include pinks (*Dianthus* species), *Iris graminea*, *Clematis recta* and *Clematis integrifolia* 'Hendersonii,' the perennial sweet pea, Sweet Rocket (*Hesperis matronalis*), Himalayan cowslip (*Primula florindae*), peonies, and violets all have fragrant flowers.

What are some **blue-flowered perennials**?

Taller blue-flowered perennials include delphiniums, the taller *Veronica* species, Stokes aster, *Perovskia* or Russian sage and other sages, Michaelmas daisy (*Aster frikartii* and *Aster novi-belgii* 'Marie Ballard'), Cupid's Dart (*Catananche caerulea*), hyssop (actually considered an herb), bellflower (*Campanula persicifolia* 'Telham Beauty' and *Campanula glomerata* 'Superba'), and false indigo (*Baptisia australis*). Lower growing perennials include *Geranium* 'Johnson Blue,' spreading veronica (*Veronica prostrata*), perennial forget-me-not (*Brunnera macrophylla*), *Gentiana septemfida*, ajuga (though usually classified as a ground-cover), and bellflower (*Campanula garganica*).

What are the different ways **vines** climb?

Vines such as wisteria, honeysuckle, and bittersweet twine their stems around trees, pillars, and posts. When a twining vine touches an object, its sensitive plant tissue reacts by growing more cells at that spot, causing the vine to twist and bend around the object. Other vines climb by means of tendrils, delicate structures that wrap themselves around things. Clematis, grape vines, and sweet peas all climb using their tendrils. Other vines produce plant structures that will cling to an object upon touching it. The structures are usually either small rootlets, shooting off either side of a stem, which burrow into the cracks of whatever they are climbing or adhesive disks which adhere to a building through suction. Many ivies cling using their rootlets, while vines like Virginia creeper attach with adhesive disks.

What are some perennials with **striking foliage**?

A design element of perennials that is often overlooked is their foliage. Perennials with variegated foliage include *Molinia caerulea* 'Variegata', ribbon grass (*Phalaris arundinacea* 'Picta'), *Hosta undulata*, golden balm (*Melissa officinalis* 'Aurea'), zebra grass (*Miscanthus sinensis* 'Zebrinus' and also *Miscanthus sinensis* 'Gracillimus'), *Iris kaempferi* 'Variegata' and *Iris pallida* 'Variegata', variegated Japanese Solomon's Seal (*Polygonatum odoratum* 'Variegatum'), lungwort (*Pulmonaria saccharata*), and snow-on-the mountain (*Euphorbia marginata*). For a dif-

Purple coneflower (*Echinacea purpurea*) is a native perennial that prefers rich, well-drained soil and full sun.

"Backyard" peonies or common peonies are herbaceous
perennials, meaning they die back to the ground each
year. A tree peony, is more shrub than tree, but is considered a
woody ornamental with its woody stems and slightly lax
branches. Common peonies do, however, retain their foliage for
most of the summer until it sadly shrivels in the fall. They are
also slightly more cold-hardy than tree peonies, surviving in
zones 3–8 as opposed to a tree peony in zones 4–8.

ferent effect, perennials such as the dead nettle *Lamium maculatum*
'Aureaum,' Bowles' Golden Grass (*Milium effusum* 'Aureum'), *Hosta fortunei* 'Aurea,' spurge (*Euphorbia polychroma*), common oregano (*Origanum vulgare* 'Aureum'), and lady's mantle (*Alchemilla mollis*) feature
yellow or acid green leaves. Some perennials even change colors later in
the season including the previously mentioned spurge, a number of
heaths and heathers, hardy plumbago (*Ceratostigma plumbaginodes*),
Bishop's Hat (*Epimedium niveum*), *Geranium pratense* 'Album' and
Geranium pratense 'Mrs. Kendall's Clarke,' and vines like Virginia
Creeper and Boston Ivy. See the previous question on grey and silver-
leaved plants for additional color ideas.

Finally, some perennials have foliage which is beautiful in form. Consider
any and all ferns, *Bergenia cordifolia*, *Rodgersia tabularis*, astilbes,
herbaceous peonies (for a short while), *Gunnera manicata*, plume poppy
(*Macleaya cordata*), and the bamboos such as *Arundinaria murieliae*.

What are **alpine plants**?

Alpine plants are those that are adapted to growing above the tree line
on a mountain. However, in the garden, they include any plant which
grows in a rock garden or trough garden. They like a gravelly, fertile,
well-drained soil similar to their natural habitat. Some alpine plants

include wooly yarrow (*Achillea tomentosa*), sea thrifts or pinks (*Armerias juniperfolia* and *Armerias maritima*), *Euryops acraeus*, *Aubrieta deltoidea* 'Variegata', *Hypericum olympicum*, and *Amur adonis*.

I love the look of **ornamental grasses** but I have very damp, moist soil. Aren't grasses suited only to dry areas?

As a matter of fact, there are dozens of grasses which will thrive in the moist soil you have. They include Japanese blood grass (*Imperata cylindrica* var. *rubra*), heavenly bamboo (*Nandina domestica*), snowy woodrush (*Luzula nivea*), ravenna grass (*Erianthus ravennae*), striped eulalia grass (*Miscanthus sinesis* 'Zebrinus'), maiden grass (*Miscanthus sinesis* 'Gracillimus'), and bottlebrush grass (*Hystrix patula*).

I live in an area that has been undergoing **drought-like conditions** over the past several years. Are there any perennials that can survive this?

With weather patterns shifting and more regions limiting the amount of water available for outdoor use, it is smart to consider making a switch to perennials that will thrive under these conditions. Drought-tolerant perennials include rock cress (*Arabis procurrens*), aster, *Baptisia perfoliata*, globe centaurea (*Centaurea macrocephala*), threadleaf coreopsis (*Coreopsis verticillata*), a number of the spurges or Euphorbia family including *Euphorbias corollata*, *Euphorbias cyparissias*, *Euphorbias epithymoides*, and *Euphorbias mysrinites*, prickly pear (*Opuntia humifusa*), stonecrop (*Sedums spectabile* and *Sedums spurium*), Iris Pacific Coast, blanketflower (*Gaillardia grandiflora*), hollyhock mallow (*Malva alcea*), bee balm (*Monarda fistulosa*), and lavender (*Lavandula angustifolia*).

BULBS

What is a **bulb**?

A bulb is a plant such as a tulip that comes up from a swollen underground stem that is made up of food surrounding a bud. This enables a

173

bulb to survive periods of cold/drought. Bulbs multiply by generating bulblets from the mother bulb. Growers often refer to plants that are actually corms and tubers as bulbs as well, but technically, they are different kinds of plant structures. See the question in Plant Science for more information.

What is **bonemeal** used for?

Bonemeal is an organic fertilizer derived from animal bones which supplies bulbs, fruit trees, and shrubs with a good source of phosphorus. It is most commonly used when planting or topdressing bulbs.

What is a **naturalizing bulb**?

A naturalizing bulb is a bulb that grows vigorously and will multiply itself, if it is planted in an area where it can hold its own against other plants such as grasses or groundcovers. When you want a bulb to naturalize, you usually plant them in drifts or large groups. If you plant them in a lawn, remember that you need to hold off mowing until the foliage has turned brown. Some examples of naturalizing bulbs include narcissus (daffodil) varieties, squills, glory-of-the-snow, snowdrops, crocuses, and winter aconites.

How do I **plant bulbs**?

On average, bulbs need to be planted three times their own depth. Although you can use either a bulb planter or a dibble to plant single bulbs, most bulbs look best when planted in groups or drifts. I use a spade or trowel to dig a small bed, placing a light dusting of bonemeal followed by a half inch of backfill at the bottom. Then, I scatter my bulbs (growing tip up!) through the bed, attempting to keep at least a bulb to two bulbs width between them. After backfilling with the remaining dirt, I water the area thoroughly.

How do I **plant bulbs in my lawn**?

You can plant bulbs singly (which is more time-consuming) or in groups. To plant them singly, sprinkle the bulbs across the lawn. Then

> ## My tulips are done blooming and look so straggly. Can I remove the leaves?
>
> If you'd like to have beautiful tulips next year, it's best not to. Removing the leaves disrupts the cycle of the bulb, preventing it from storing energy for the next year. If you wait until the leaves have shriveled and turned brown, you can help this process along. While some people place rubber bands over the leaves and various other contraptions, the most beautiful method of hiding the wilting leaves is by planting a spring-flowering plant or beautiful groundcover over the bulbs.

using a trowel or a bulb planter, lift up a core of sod to the depth required by the bulb, creating a hole for each bulb. Sprinkle a small amount of bonemeal into the hole and mix gently, then pop the bulb in with the tip up. If you plant a large group of bulbs, cut away a square of sod. Loosen the soil underneath to the depth required by the bulbs and scratch some bonemeal into it. Then place the bulbs at least a bulb's width from each other and replace the sod.

What are some good **bulbs to plant in lawns**?

When selecting bulbs to be planted in lawns, consider the fact that you will not wish to mow the lawn in that area until the bulb foliage has shriveled and browned. Choose early bloomers such as crocuses, daffodils, and early tulips or else your lawn may become tall enough to go to seed in that area.

How can I get my tulips to **reflower** every year? I'm tired of planting them again and again.

Tulips do have a shorter life expectancy, than say, narcissus, which all tend to be naturalizers. Planting tulips deeper (say to five times their

175

What growing conditions do bulbs require?

Most require a period of either cold or drought in order to break dormancy. They also require full sun, for the most part, but this is not normally a difficult requirement for spring-flowering bulbs as the leaves have yet to fill out on the trees. Bulbs planted in warmer parts of your yard will bloom earlier than cooler areas, so you may want to consider scattering them in different portions of your yard to extend the show or to provide a psychological boost a few weeks sooner than usual. Bulbs do not like being water-logged, so be sure the soil they are planted in is well-drained, if not sandy.

own depth) can help ensure the tulips will produce flowers for more years. Also, by refraining from removing the foliage before it turns brown, you allow the bulb to continue growing, putting its energy towards storing more food. Deadheading after the bulb has finished flowering prevents the plant from putting its energy into seed formation. Finally, plant species tulips sometimes listed as "naturalizers." Hybrids of *Tulipa kaufmanniana* tend to live longer than others.

How do I plant a mixture of **bulbs in containers**?

The best way to plant a variety of bulbs in containers is to plant in layers, beginning with the largest bulbs at the bottom of the container. All bulbs should be planted three to four times their depth. For example, start with tulip and narcissus bulbs at the lower part of the container, followed by hyacinths, then crocus.

Can **forced bulbs** be replanted?

The process of "forcing" bulbs does require more energy from a bulb than if it were planted in the ground. These bulbs won't successfully

Crocus bulbs ready to be planted.

"re-force" but they can be replanted in the garden, if they are properly treated in their container. This means deadheading and allowing the foliage to wither, just as you would outdoors. Keep them moist initially, but reduce your watering until the foliage has withered. After being replanted in your garden, it may take several seasons for them to recover.

What are some **summer-blooming bulbs**?

Summer-flowering bulbs include gladiolus, lilies, some cyclamens, tuberous begonias, alliums, dahlias, and ranunculus, cannas, agapanthus, and oxalis.

What are some **spring-blooming bulbs**?

Spring-flowering bulbs include tulips, narcissus, hyacinths, bulb iris, glory-of-the-snow (*Chionodoxa*), scillas, winter aconites, snowdrops, fritillarias, and anemones.

177

How do I force bulbs to bloom inside my house?

Some bulbs are easier to "force" than others. These include paperwhites and other *Narcissus tarzetta*, hyacinths, and crocuses. In order to have a bulb blooming at a particular time, you must consider both the time the bulb needs to spend in the dark (on average about three months but this varies from bulb to bulb), and the time the bulb needs to spend in the light (usually around a month). Count backwards from the desired bloom date to determine the "potting up" date. "Potting up" consists of filling containers with a 1:1 mixture of potting soil and topsoil (for its moisture-retentiveness), then placing the bulbs in the container with their tips just showing above the soil line. Fertilize lightly with a liquid fertilizer, then place the container in a cool, dark area that stays right around 40 degrees Farenheit. Once they have completed their "dark" phase, gradually bring the container into the light and water occasionally to keep the bulbs moist. Some bulbs like paperwhites, hyacinths, and crocus can be grown in water (these can be purchased in planting "kits" which include the bulb and container.)

Are there any **fall-blooming bulbs**?

Fall-blooming bulbs are less commonly offered by garden centers and usually need to be ordered by mail. The most common fall-blooming bulb is the autumn-flowering crocus. Hardy cyclamens also bloom in the fall, along with some alliums and colchicums.

What should I do with my **canna bulbs** in order to keep them for next year?

Wait to dig up your cannas from the ground or container until after the first frost. Then, carefully dig up the bulbs and remove any dirt from them. Inspect them carefully and discard or compost any diseased or

Grape hyacinth is a spring-flowering bulb.

unhealthy looking bulbs. Separate any bulbs that will do so easily. Take the remaining bulbs and place them in a paper bag packed loosely with paper and store them in a cool, dry place for next year.

I love **gladiolus** but they never seem to look right in my garden with other plants. What am I doing wrong?

Due to their distinctive shape and flower, gladiolus are one of those rare plants which look better in the vase than in the garden. They are best grown in a cutting garden where they can be planted far enough apart to yield nice-sized flowers. If grown in a flower border, they look better planted close together but this has an adverse affect on their bloom.

ANNUALS

ANNUAL PLANT CARE

What is an **annual**?

An annual is a plant that completes its life cycle in one year—germinating, growing, flowering, setting seed, and dying. However, in the nursery trade, many plants known as annuals such as pelargoniums and heliotrope are actually tender perennials. Others, such as foxglove and columbine, are actually biennials.

What is a **biennial**?

A biennial is a plant that doesn't bloom or set seed until its second year of life. It may actually survive another season or two, but its flowering isn't nearly as profuse. Biennials include foxglove (*Digitalis*), columbine, forget-me-not, larkspur, Canterbury bells (*Campanula medium*), hollyhock (*Alcea rosea*), and sweet William (*Dianthus barbatus*). Some biennials can be sown early in the fall season and spend winters as good-sized plants (foxglove is an example).

What are **half-hardy annuals**?

Half-hardy annuals can take light frost (usually as larger plants, rather than seedlings), but can't withstand continued exposure to temperatures

What are hardy annuals?

Hardy annuals are annual plants that tolerate a fair amount of frost, with the degree of frost-tolerance depending on the plant. They grow best in cool weather and with seeds surviving prolonged exposure to cold temperatures. Some examples include pot marigold (*Calendula officinalis*), Icelandic poppy (*Papaver nudicaule*), English daisy (*Bellis perennis*), money flower (*Mimulus x hybridus*) and bachelor's button or cornflower (*Centaurea cyanus*). Like biennials, hardy annuals can either be sown in the fall (though usually later than biennials), for flowering the following spring, or in the early spring, as soon as the ground can be worked.

below freezing. As a result, they can't be planted until the spring as they won't "winter over." Some half-hardy annuals include spider flower (*Cleome*), cosmos, and petunia. It should be noted, however, that in milder winters, these same half-hardy annuals may reseed themselves and survive.

What are **tender annuals**?

Tender annuals can't take any frost at all. These annuals can't be sown outdoors or planted outside until all danger of frost has past (the frost-free date for your area is the best indication of this). They are mainly started indoors, although a few, such as marigold (*Calendula*) and zinnias, grow so quickly that they can be direct-seeded outdoors. Other tender annuals include nasturtium (*Tropaeolum majus*) , sweet verbena (*Verbena officinalis*), ageratum (*Ageratum conyzoides*), moss rose (*Portulaca*), and red salvia.

What are **cool-weather annuals**?

Cool-weather annuals are those annuals that thrive in cooler temperatures and shorter days and tend to poop out in warm, long days. Gen-

Pansies (*Viola tricolor*), despite their name are extremely hardy, withstanding temperatures down to 15 degrees Farenheit.

When is the best time to plant annuals?

Hardy and half-hardy annuals that are direct-seeded can generally be planted as soon as the soil can be worked in the spring (see chapter on Seeding and Planting), although some can be planted the previous fall or even late summer for bloom in early spring. Annuals started from seed should be started according to the packet directions (usually several months before the frost-free date in your area). If you have started plants from seed or have purchased transplants, don't forget that they need to be hardened off before planting. Tender annuals should not be transplanted before the frost-free date in your area. Hardy transplants such as pansies (Violas) can usually be set out a month or so prior to that, if they have been hardened off.

erally speaking, these are half-hardy or hardy annuals such as bachelor's button. Others, such as pot marigold (*Calendula officinalis*), pansies (*Viola*), sweet alyssum (*Lobularia maritima*), lobelia (*Lobelia erinus*), sweet pea (*Lathyrus*), and nasturtium (*Tropaeolum majus*), thrive in that short period in Michigan known as early summer. In hotter areas, they may be grown in the winter. They can also be preserved through the heat in partially shaded areas that receive regular watering.

What do I need to do to prepare an **annual bed**?

Annuals are not as deep-rooted as perennials so they don't require a deeply-prepared bed. However, loosening the soil to about a foot will allow moisture to penetrate the roots and drain properly. Many annuals rot easily when their roots sit in water. Add any soil amendments to bring your pH to the average noted previously. Be sure to weed out any perennial or annual weeds to keep out competition for nutrients and water. Also, annuals grow at such a fast rate, weeds can easily be lost among them.

186

Why do some plants self-seed?

Self-seeding is a form of sexual reproduction. Most plants set seed after they bloom, but some plants because of the size of their seed (usually small) or the number of seeds they produce, tend to be more successful in finding a spot which receives enough water, sun, and nutrients to become another plant.

What **growing conditions** are required by annuals?

The most important requirement of annuals is full sun. Most annuals (with some exceptions noted under shade annuals), need at least six hours of sun per day to keep their blooms blooming. The soil needs to be fertile, moist, and friable with an average pH of between 6.0 and 7.0. Annuals also "feed" a little more heavily than perennials do, so you want to be sure to incorporate compost or manure into your bed.

What is meant by **"direct-seeding" annuals**?

Direct-seeding means to plant annuals directly in the ground. As noted previously, hardy annuals and some half-hardy annuals may be planted in this manner.

How do I **plant and space annuals** to look their best?

Another term for annuals is "bedding plants" which refers to their propensity for being planted in groups. Annuals planted singly just don't have the same impact on the landscape as the riot of color produced by a large grouping. Obviously, this does not negate planting a single annual in a container but even there, more *is* more. When planting your annuals, pay attention to the instructions on the tag which usually calls for spacing them anywhere from several inches apart to a foot apart, depending on their growth habit. However, if your particular favorite

187

As noted, annuals tend to be heavier feeders than perennials since much of their life is spent in bloom. If you apply fertilizer when planting out annuals, they shouldn't require any additional fertilizer for a couple of months. When the plants slow in their growth or develop yellow leaves, it may be time to fertilize again. Plants that need a great deal of moisture tend to need more fertilizer as well. Manure tea or a balanced (one that has an even ratio of nitrogen, phosphorus, and potassium) water-soluble fertilizer works well.

annual has a tendency towards powdery mildew or has a bushy growth habit, consider spacing them even further apart for air circulation and to enable them to reach their full potential.

What is **volunteer**?

A volunteer is a seedling that has grown of its own volition—self-seeded by its parent plant. Volunteers sometimes spring up in places you don't want them where they become weeds. But they can easily be dug up and carefully transplanted to an area where they will become a desirable plant again.

What is **deadheading** and why do I have to do it?

Deadheading refers to the removing of spent or faded blooms from a plant. When a plant blooms, it is preparing itself to reproduce or go to seed before it dies. This requires a great deal of energy from the plant. You can prolong the bloom (and the life of the plant) by deadheading it. Some plants, such as impatiens, do their own deadheading when flowers drop off the plant. However, most flowers require human intervention. The majority of annual flowers can just be pinched off from a plant

How do I pot an annual to spend the winter indoors?

It depends on the annual you are bringing inside. For all of them, however, bring them indoors before frost and select younger plants. Pot them up and leave them outside initially before bringing them in. For plants such as zonal geraniums, coleus, petunias, moss roses, and wax begonias you may either cut them back by half, fertilize, and plant in a pot or take stem cuttings and root them indoors in either a rooting medium or plain water.

using your thumb and index finger. With a large annual planting, you might consider using shears to remove spent flowers. Many perennials that need deadheading require pruners or small scissors to get through their woody stems.

How do I **mulch my annuals**?

Annuals need 1–2 inches of mulch in order to retain moisture. As with perennials, try to keep the mulch away from the crown of the plant to reduce the incidence of slugs and other garden pests. You might also consider using an organic mulch that decays and can be turned under at the end of the season, rather than an inorganic one which will need to be disturbed every year during planting and at the end of the season.

How do I **select annual plants** for purchase?

It's usually best to buy annual transplants without blooms or at least with just buds, rather than in bloom. Some plants such as pelargoniums, petunias, and marigolds can be purchased in flower, but look for transplants that are stocky and healthy. Although this makes a gardener more dependent on a nursery to properly tag and identify plants (this is why it's important to go to a good nursery!), non-budded transplants

189

have not wasted their energy on blooms while growing in their tiny plastic cells.

What are the advantages of **annuals over perennials**?

Annuals have an extended period of bloom (usually from the frost-free date to the last frost-free date), while perennials usually bloom for several weeks at a time. They also bloom quickly, going from bud to bloom in a few short weeks. Annuals are also good for the beginner—they don't take much effort to get growing and are rarely bothered by disease.

ANNUALS FOR PARTICULAR USES

What are some annuals that will grow in **dry soil**?

Salvias, globe amaranth, statice, sweet alyssum, calliopis, dusty miller (*Senecio cineraria*), creeping zinnia, moss rose (*Portulaca grandiflora*), California poppy (*Eschscholzia californica*), tithonia or Mexican sunflower, and four o'clocks all grow well in dry soil.

What are some annuals that will grow in **wet soil**?

Most annuals don't care to have their feet wet, but monkey flower (*Mimulus cupreus* 'Red Emperor') and forget-me-not (*Myosotis sylvatica*) thrive in humusy, moist areas.

Which annuals flourish in **full sun**?

Sweet alyssum (*Lobularia maritima*), livingstone daisy (*Dorotheanthus bellidiflorus*), moss rose (*Portulaca grandiflora*), rock purslane (*Calandrinia umbellata*), linaria (*Linaria maroccana*), nasturtium (*Tropaeolum majus*), California poppy (*Eschscholzia californica*), everlasting (*Helipterum manglesii*), and cosmos do well in hot, sunny areas with dry soil.

California poppy (*Eschscholzia californica*) will grow well in dry soil but are weak growers where summers are humid and rainy.

191

What are some annuals BESIDES begonias and impatiens that will grow in shade?

Try nicotiana (flowering tobacco)—its white flowers will light up a corner of your yard. Coleus has lovely multicolored foilage with varying patterns. Although lobelia is often placed with geraniums to accent sunny pots, it thrives in shade. The black-eyed Susan vine adds height to your shady garden. Pansies are another tried-and-true shade lover. Look for violet cress (*Ionopsidium acaule*), browallia or sapphire flower, forget-me-nots, Canterbury bells, honesty or money plant (*Lunaria*), *Asperula orientalis*, and foxglove as well.

What are some annuals that will grow in **acidic soil**?

Although most annuals prefer soil on the more acidic side of neutral, begonias and snapdragons thrive in acidic soil that contains plenty of moisture-retaining peat.

Are there any **blue-flowered annuals**?

Bachelor's button, 'Heavenly Blue' morning glory, and borage are old-fashioned annuals with blue flowers. Lesser-known blue beauties include 'Blue Skies' petunia, California bluebell (*Phacelia campanularia*), Chinese forget-me-not, *Felicia bergeriana*, and 'Sapphire' lobelia.

What are some annuals traditionally used in **cottage gardens**?

Annuals used in cottage gardens include love-in-a-mist (*Nigella damascena*), morning glories (*Ipomoea* species), honesty or money plant (Lunaria annua), annual forget-me-not (*Myosotis sylvatica*), cosmos, shirley poppy (*Papaver rhoeas*), bachelor's button or cornflower (*Centaurea cyanus*), pot marigold (*Calendula officinalis*), sweet alyssum

> ## What are some spring-flowering annuals?
>
> **W**allflower (*Cheiranthus cheiri*) and forget-me-not (*Myosotis*) provide a lovely contrast of orange (*Cheiranthus cheiri* 'Golden Bedder') and blue in the spring garden. Wallflower has a wide range of colors to choose from including cream, red, and crimson to complement spring-blooming bulbs.

(*Lobularia maritima*), browallia, sweet pea, sweet William, and spider flower (*Cleome*).

What are some **summer-flowering annuals**?

Most annuals flower in the summer. Some used less frequently in back-yard plantings include nasturtium (*Tropaeolum majus*), Icelandic poppy (*Papaver nudicaule*), ferny-leafed love-in-a-mist (*Nigella damascena*), heavenly-scented stock (*Matthiola bicornis*), Canterbury bells (*Campanula medium*), small blue-flowered California bluebell (*Phacelia campanularia*), unspectacular but fragrant migonette (*Reseda odorata*), and bedding dahlias. These can be more difficult to find at your local nursery and are often grown from seed.

What are some **vining or climbing annuals**?

One of the easiest ways to beautify a mailbox or a fence post is by sowing some annual vining seeds at its base in the spring. Vining annuals include morning glory (*Ipomoea purpurea*), sweet pea (*Lathyrus odoratus*), black-eyed Susan vine (*Thunbergia alata*), and hyacinth bean (*Lablab*).

What are some annuals that bloom in the **late summer or early fall**?

It is always a sad time in the garden when the plants and flowers you've come to love begin to fade as winter approaches. Some annuals, however, seem to reach their peak at the end of summer, giving one last shout before frost hits them. Sunflower, spider flower (*Cleome*), cosmos, China aster (*Callistephus chinesis*), pot marigold, zinnia, red salvia, moss rose (*Portulaca grandiflora*), *Nicotiana alata*, and impatiens all bloom or retain their bloom in late summer and early fall.

Which annuals will work best for **dried flower arrangements**?

Globe amaranth (*Gomphrena globosa*), annual baby's breath (*Gypsophila elegans*), strawflower (*Helichrysum bracteatum*), cockscomb (*Celosia cristata*), starflower (*Scabiosa stellata*), Bells of Ireland (*Molucella laevis*) all dry well to provide fragile bouquets for the winter months.

What are some annuals that are grown for their **foliage**?

Licorice plant (*Helichrysum petiolare*) and dusty miller (*Senecio cineraria*) have silvery gray foliage. Coleus, annual fountain grass (*Pennisetum*), celosia, and sweet potato vine (*Ipomoea* 'Blackie') have lovely, dark leaved varieties. Asparagus fern (*Asparagus densiflorus* 'Sprengeri'), the knife-like "spikes," and *Vinca major* (along with licorice plant and dusty miller) are commonly used in container plantings. Snow-on-the-mountain (*Euphorbia marginata*) and hypoestes have beautiful variegated leaves. The elephant-ear leaves of Caladium (a tuber) come in a wide variety of stunning colors. Although love-in-a-mist is mainly grown for its delicate flowers, it also has handsome hazy foliage.

What are some annuals with fragrant flowers?

Heliotrope, mignonette (*Reseda odorata*), sweet pea (*Lathyrus odoratus*), *Asperula orientalis*, stock (*Matthiola incana*), sweet verbena (*Verbena grandiflora*), petunia, moonflower (*Ipomoea*), Swan River daisy (*Brachycome iberidifolia*), *Bartonia aurea*, and wallflower (*Cheiranthus cheiri*) are all scented annuals, with fragrance that ranges from delicate (stock) to overpowering (heliotrope).

What are some annuals that can be used as **focal points**?

Many annuals need to be planted in groups in order to provide enough visual weight in the landscape. For this reason, they are often unlikely candidates to be the focus of a planting. Cannas, ornamental cabbage (*Brassica oleracea*), foxglove (*Digitalis purpurea*), and of course, pelargoniums, however, shine as focal points.

Which annuals are **drought-tolerant**?

For cooler weather, annuals such as forget-me-not (*Myosotis sylvatica*), California poppy (*Eschscholzia californica*), Icelandic poppy (Papaver nudicaule), Swan River daisy (*Brachycome iberidifolia*), blue marguerite (*Felicia amelloides*), and Star of Texas (*Xanthisma texana*) all thrive in drought conditions. Spider flower (*Cleome hasslerana*), cosmos (*Cosmos bipinnatus*), portulaca (*Portulaca grandiflora*), and desert evening primrose (*Oenothera deltoides*) are warm-weather annuals that will survive drought.

Are there any annuals that can be **wintered indoors as houseplants**?

Many annuals can be kept as houseplants for either planting out the following summer, or to provide a bit of color during the winter months.

195

What is a pelargonium?

A pelargonium is commonly known as a zonal geranium or just plain geranium by most folks. It is a tender perennial much beloved by most gardeners and planted in clay pots and painted tires from Poughkeepsie to Potero. Actually, however, a true geranium is a perennial that is low-growing and spreading in habit, with smaller leaves and blooms than the pelargonium. Due to the misnomer of the pelargonium, a true geranium is sometimes known as a hardy geranium.

Wax begonia (*Begonia semperflorens cultorum*), coleus (*Coleus hybridus*), impatiens (*Impatiens wallerana*), zonal geranium (*Pelargonium hortorum*), pansy (*Viola*), petunia, moss rose (*Portulaca*), and verbena all take to indoor planting.

What is **heliotrope**?

Heliotrope (*Heliotropium* species) is an old-fashioned tender perennial, known to most gardeners as an annual. It has wrinkled, dark green leaves and beautiful violet-blue flowers that have an amazingly sweet fragrance.

VEGETABLES AND FRUITS

PLANTING AND CARING FOR A VEGETABLE GARDEN

What are the proper **growing conditions** for a vegetable garden?

The most important consideration for a vegetable garden is sunlight. Be sure the location you choose receives a minimum of six hours of direct sunlight per day. If you live in the north, you should choose a southern exposure. If you live in the south, you may want to choose a northern exposure to provide protection for your plants during the heat of the summer. If you are able to do a soil test on the site, the preferred pH of most vegetables is between 6.0 and 7.0. The ideal soil is a sandy loam. Be sure the area is properly drained (no standing water). A low-lying area in your garden could be more susceptible to frost. Finally, have a source of water, your compost pile, and your tools close by so that your garden will receive the attention it needs on a regular basis with little extra effort on your part.

How do I **plan my vegetable garden**?

Begin by deciding which vegetables you and your family enjoy. Unless you plan on growing extra vegetables for charitable organizations like Plant a Row for the Hungry (a worthy cause), stick to vegetables you

I'm going to a farmer's market next weekend to buy vegetable plants for my garden. What should I look for?

While it may be tempting to buy the biggest plants you find, look for transplants that are short, small and dark green. This means they are sturdy and well-nourished. Taller, paler spindly plants may have been under- or overfed or have received an inconsistent amount of light. Try to select plants which don't have any fruit formed yet, or if the healthiest-looking plants have buds, remove these before planting. Vegetables grow most vigorously before they set fruit and transplants need to spend their energy on growing new shoots and sturdier limbs during their first few weeks in your garden. Finally, carefully inspect the plants roots—be sure they are white and healthy-looking. Mushy or darker roots mean the plant has been in its pot for too long. Plants are healthiest when their growth is not hindered by lack of nutrients, proper temperatures, or growing room.

know you'll eat fresh or will process right away. If you've never grown vegetables before, start small and expand as you become more proficient or interested. You could even consider planting a theme vegetable garden like a salad garden or an all-Italian garden.

Next, decide on how you'll plant your crops—intensively (good for small gardens and growing organically), in rows, or another configuration. If you have a small plot or are growing your vegetables in containers, don't forget to think vertical. Even in larger plots, cucumbers, squash, and melons can all benefit from being trellised—it keeps fruits/vegetables off the ground and away from pests and disease. In planning your garden, it is important to keep track from year to year where you have planted your crops. To minimize disease and insect infestations, crop rotation (see chapter on Plant Troubles) is a must. You also need to consider the sun's angle in relation to your garden. For example, tall crops such as

A cucumber plant

corn can shade smaller crops. This can be a problem for peppers, but will provide shade for lettuces which tend to bolt in hot weather.

I'm planning my **first vegetable garden** but don't have much space. Are there any vegetables I should avoid?

Broccoli, corn, potatoes, and globe artichoke take up a great deal of space. Cucumbers, melons, peas, and winter squash also require large amounts of space but these plants can be grown vertically (on trellises and poles) in a small garden. Better choices for a small garden are beans (both bush beans and pole beans), carrots, eggplant, lettuce and greens, peppers, tomatoes, turnips, and onions.

What are the advantages of planting vegetables in **raised beds**?

You can preserve your soil's tilth with raised beds since you won't be stepping on the soil and compacting it. Raised beds also warm up more quickly in the spring—a boon in northern climates. They improve drainage or fertility problems. They tend to be easy to weed, water, and fertilize because of paths placed around these beds. Crop rotation is also easy—you just move your crops from bed to bed.

What are the disadvantages of planting vegetables in **raised beds**?

Double-digging, adding soil amendments, and building boxes (if you choose to) can make the initial creation of raised beds labor-intensive. It is probably too much bother and work to dig raised beds for large crops such as potatoes, corn, and beans. Raised beds also tend to dry out faster than flat ones.

What are the disadvantages of **planting vegetables in rows**?

For backyard gardeners, rows take up more space and produce less vegetable per square foot. When working in rows, you also stand the risk of compacting your soil through repeated stepping in to weed, water, and harvest.

What are the advantages of planting vegetables in rows?

Planting in long, straight rows is a time-honored practice which works well with the farm equipment and rolling acres this method was originally designed for. Mounded rows warm faster in the spring and improve drainage.

What are the advantages of **planting vegetables intensively or in squares**?

Intensive vegetable gardening produces greater yields from a smaller space. It also minimizes weeds, since they have no place to grow.

What are the disadvantages of **planting vegetables intensively or in squares**?

An intensive garden requires a great deal of work to establish and requires regular soil improvements. It is also more difficult to find space for large, aggressive growers like squash in these spaces unless you trellis them. Due to the close proximity of the plants, an intensive garden is hard to mulch, although technically, the plants should serve as a "living mulch" for each other by shading out weeds and keeping roots cool.

Should I **mulch my vegetable garden**?

Yes. Using a light mulch such as straw reduces watering and cuts down on weeds. Begin mulching once the soil has warmed up in the garden. You can also mulch by hilling up soil around the base of a vegetable plant. Vegetables such as corn, potatoes, and tomatoes appreciate this treatment.

203

Your vegetables generally need about an inch of water per week. They should be watered early in the day to keep down both the incidence of disease and fungus which occurs with evening watering, and the evaporation that occurs in warmer climates when watering at midday. Be sure to water the plants to their root zone in order to ensure the plants receive the maximum benefit from the watering.

Why should I **weed my vegetable garden**?

Weeding a vegetable garden is crucial to prevent weeds from competing with the plants for nutrients and water. Start with a clean bed—remove all perennial and annual weeds from the bed—then keep it up throughout the season. Although you can use a hoe or trowel, you should be careful not to injure tender vegetable plant roots.

How should I **fertilize my vegetable garden**?

Preparing the soil carefully at the beginning of the season by digging in compost and other organic matter will get you off to a good start. Quick-growing crops such as lettuces and bush beans probably won't need additional fertilization. Longer-season vegetables like tomatoes and peppers should receive an additional boost of compost or manure tea once they've set flower.

What does it mean to **"cage" a tomato plant**?

Tomato plants have a tremendous rate of growth but lack a strong stem to support the weight of its fruit. If left to sprawl on the ground, the tomatoes are more susceptible to soilborne disease. By placing wire mesh around the plant and staking the plant in the center, you provide

An example of a tomato cage.

Last year, I saved seeds from my pumpkin and zucchini plants. When I planted them this year, they grew strange-looking vegetables that weren't quite pumpkins and weren't quite zucchinis. What happened?

The cucurbit family is a cross-pollinating one. This means that when they are planted near each other, they pollinate each other. The resulting seeds/new plants do not maintain their identity. In the future, try to avoid planting them near each other or don't try to save seeds in order to start new plants.

support to the plant with room to grow. Be sure to select a mesh with holes large enough to harvest the fruit through!

Why don't all of my **cucumber flowers** result in a cucumber?

A cucumber plant is monoecious which means it has both female (pistillate) and male (staminate) flower structures. However, the pistil and stamen are found on different flowers. Since only a female flower can produce a fruit, the flowers you see which don't result in cucumbers are male flowers.

In the seed catalog I order from, it lists both **determinate and indeterminate tomatoes**. What's the difference?

Determinate tomato plants bear all of their fruit at one time and die after they reach their mature height. They are usually smaller, more compact plants. Indeterminate tomato plants grow and produce fruit throughout the season until frost kills them. As a result, they can grow quite tall. Gardeners who have a shorter growing season or who plan on processing or freezing their harvest might choose to grow a determinate plant.

I've had a hard time getting carrots to grow in my garden. What can I do to improve my chances?

Mix the carrot seed with radish seed. Carrot seed is very tiny and notoriously slow to germinate. By mixing them with radish seed, they are easier to broadcast. In addition, the radishes break through the soil surface, providing an easy path for the carrots to follow.

My **lettuce** has grown tall and leggy and has developed flowers. Is it still good to eat?

You have just described lettuce that has "bolted" or gone to seed. Most lettuces thrive in the cooler temperatures of spring and tend to bolt once hot weather hits. Once they've begun to flower, lettuces take on a bitter flavor and are best composted. Next time, plant your lettuce earlier or choose a bolt-resistant variety.

I'd like to minimize **water use in my vegetable garden**. Are there any vegetables which can get by with less water?

Tomatoes, peppers, and beans can get by with less water than vegetables like lettuce, onions, corn, cucumbers, and celery which have a higher water content.

I'm interested in **extending my vegetable garden** into the fall. Which vegetables survive some frost?

Root crops such as beets, carrots, and radishes survive early frosts. Peas, spinach, Swiss chard, lettuce, and parsley can also take some frost. Brussels sprouts and cabbages benefit in flavor and color from a light frost before being harvested.

207

I want to grow an enormous pumpkin for Halloween this year. What can I do to help it grow large?

Begin by digging in plenty of organic matter into your bed. Provide the pumpkin plant with a lot of growing room as pumpkin plants are notorious for their sprawling habit of growth. Thin down the number of pumpkins per vine to just a few to ensure the energy of the plant is focused. Finally, be sure to water the plant abundantly.

How do I plant and harvest **asparagus**?

Asparagus is usually started from crowns bought from a local or mail-order nursery. It should be planted in the spring, as soon as the ground can be worked. Make sure your bed is free of any weeds and is well-fertilized with compost. A soil test might be a good idea as well, since this planting is "forever" due to the perennial nature of asparagus.

Start by digging a foot-deep trench, placing a cup or so of compost at 12-inch intervals and set the crowns out on the compost hill, making sure the roots are spread out and the buds in the center are facing upward. Cover the crowns with a few inches of the soil, then as the season progresses and the shoots begin to come up, gradually add soil to refill the trench. No asparagus should be harvested the first year after planting. At the second year, a few spears thicker than a pencil may be harvested for around two weeks. Snap the spear off near the soil line, being careful not to injure the crown. The third and consecutive years, harvest larger spears for a period of a month to a month and a half, stopping when the spears are thinner than pencil width.

Once the season is over, let the asparagus ferns grow until they are dead, then compost them. In order to limit competition for nutrients and water, try to keep the bed weed-free by picking weeds by hand or using mulch. Using tools to pull weeds may damage the crowns. Fertilize asparagus using a fertilizer high in phosphorus and potassium, applying it when growth starts and at the end of the season.

208

What can I do to ready my vegetable garden for the **winter**?

Begin by composting all spent plants. Any plants that were diseased or insect-ridden should be placed with the trash in case your compost pile isn't hot enough to kill these organisms. Next, turn the soil over—leaving large clods on the surface to be broken up during the heaving and thawing that occurs during winter. Lastly, sow a cover crop to prevent soil erosion and keep weeds from taking over your bed. In the spring, a quick turn of the soil and you should be ready to plant again!

VEGETABLE FAMILIES

Which plants provide **nitrogen** to the soil in a form that is usable by other plants?

Members of the legume family such as beans and peas have a symbiotic relationship with a form of soil bacteria. Legumes work with *rhizobia* bacteria to extract nitrogen from the atmosphere and convert it to a usable form. The bacteria live on the roots of the beans or peas forming nodules which draw nitrogen out of the air and store it as nitrate.

Which vegetables are members of the **nightshade family**?

Vegetable members of the nightshade or solanaceous family include tomatoes, potatoes, eggplants, and peppers. With the exception of potatoes, they generally need warm temperatures to germinate and grow. Pests include the potato beetle. Raspberries and strawberries are the fruit cousins of this family.

Which vegetables are members of the **cucurbit family**?

Cucurbits or gourds include squash, pumpkins, melons, and cucumbers. They are vining crops which thrive during the summer (warm season crops).

Which kinds of vegetables grow underground?

Root vegetables include beets, carrots, parsnips, radishes, rutabagas, and turnips. Rutabagas and turnips are also part of the brassica or cabbage family. Vegetables that grow as bulbs include onions, garlic, shallots, and leeks.

What is the difference between **a squash and a pumpkin**?

Botanically speaking, a pumpkin has a hard stem attached to the fruit while a squash has a soft and somewhat spongy stem.

What are **cole crops**?

Cole crops are part of the cabbage or brassica family and include broccoli, Brussels sprouts, cabbage, kale, and cauliflower. They are generally cool-season vegetables and are susceptible to problems such as cabbage worm and clubroot. Research has shown that cole crops contain chemicals that seem to play a role in preventing certain types of cancer.

I was told the more you abuse your **peppers**, the hotter they get. So last year, when I planted peppers for the first time, I watered them only as they started to droop but the crop just didn't meet my expectations. What did I do wrong?

Peppers like a well-drained soil of average fertility and like to be sited in full sun. While they will tolerate drought, they can turn bitter if they go for extended periods without water.

Are there any **perennial vegetables**?

Vegetables that are perennial in all 11 U.S. growing hardiness zones include asparagus, rhubarb, and the Jerusalem artichoke.

A squash blossom.

What are some varieties of **heirloom or open-pollinated vegetables**?

Heirloom beans include 'Blue Lake,' 'Great Northern,' 'Scarlet Runner,' and 'Kentucky Wonder.' 'Early Pearl,' 'Black Aztec,' and 'Shoepeg,' are heirloom varieties of sweet corn. 'Nantes,' 'Danvers Half Long,' and 'Chantenay' are heirloom carrots. 'Oak Leaf,' 'Salad Bowl,' and 'Butter-crunch' are better-known varieties of heirloom lettuce. 'Brandywine,' along with 'Ida Gold,' and 'San Marzano,' are good-tasting heirloom varieties of tomatoes. Finally, 'All-Blue,' 'Yukon Gold,' and 'Acadia Russet,' are some of the heirloom potatoes.

PLANTING AND CARING FOR FRUITS

What are the proper growing conditions for **ground and bush fruits**?

Ground and bush fruits require a site in full sun that receives some wind to provide good air circulation around the plants. Most do best in light,   211 sandy soils of an average pH (with an exception below) but with plenty of organic matter dug in.

What are the proper growing conditions for an **apple orchard**?

Apple trees should be grown in a warm and sunny spot, ideally on a slight slope that faces south or southeast. This provides the trees with the benefit of a sheltered, warm home and protection from frost (as long as the trees aren't planted at the base of a steep slope). They need a deeply dug soil that has had all major obstructions (tree roots, old trees, rocks) dug from it and lots of organic matter dug in to provide drainage while retaining some moisture.

How do I plant a **peach tree**?

Review the tree planting question in the Trees and Shrubs chapter and follow those instructions. In addition, peach trees are usually grafted and therefore need to have the bud union placed 2–3 inches above the soil surface to eliminate suckering. If the union is planted below the soil line, the grafted tree may develop its own roots which will eliminate the benefits of the rootstock. Be sure to gently but firmly tamp the soil while filling the planting hole and provide a balanced, water-soluble fertilizer to the soil immediately after planting.

What are the proper growing conditions for a citrus orchard?

A citrus orchard requires a location in full sun and heat (obviously only the warmer regions should apply), although oranges will take some cold temperatures. Citrus fruits appreciate being kept out of wind and like a moist but well-drained soil with a slightly acid pH. Oranges like sandy soil while lemons will manage in heavier soils.

How do I prune my **grape vines**?

Young grape vines are pruned in order to encourage them to fill out a two-wire trellis quickly. Pruning is done in the early spring, before growth starts. The planted vine is cut back to 2–3 buds which will grow into canes. The longest of these canes will form the trunk and should be secured to the trellis. All other canes should be removed in the second year, with two buds left to branch horizontally from the trunk along the top wire, and a strong sucker left at the bottom to create a second trunk at the lower wire. The following years, the top cane should be pruned down to its wire, with growth encouraged along the top and bottom wires. Any fruit that develops during these early growing years should be removed as well. With mature grape vines, select four healthy canes with previous season's growth on them and remove all other growths.

How do I plant **strawberries**?

Strawberries need to be rotated, so be sure the bed you choose is large enough to accommodate this. You can choose from a number of different ways to plant your berries, depending on how much time and effort you want to devote to your berries.

If you want a minimum of effort, use the matted-row system. Berries need to be planted about a foot and a half apart in a row with 3–4 feet

How do I prune my peach tree?

After planting, cut back the young peach trees to 18–24 inches leaving 2–3 vigorous-looking branches close to the cut that have a wide angle between the branch and the main trunk (the angle is known as the crotch), are fairly long and thick, and are of similar size to one another. Thesewill become your scaffold branches. If the branches are thin, cut them back to short stubs with a few outward facing buds and the following year, choose scaffold branches from these. If there are no branches with these characteristics, cut back all branches to short stubs. A month later, lightly prune to remove any shoots that appear. Monitor for several weeks and remove additional new growth from the trunk. The following spring, choose additional branches to keep so that the tree develops a nice, rounded shape and cut the scaffolds into equal lengths. This pruning method is known as the open center method.

between rows. As runners develop, they root themselves where they'd like with the gardener composting daughter plants (see below) when they are less than a half foot apart and keeping the width of the row at around a foot by moving or composting plants. This system tends to result in smaller berries but by getting rid of daughter plants first, you can stave this off somewhat.

If you're willing to work a little more and like things neat, try the spaced runner system. Berries are planted about at least a foot and a half apart with around two and a half feet between the rows. Keep only half a dozen runners spaced half a foot apart and compost older plants to keep this spacing.

If you don't mind keeping a close watch on your strawberry patch, the hill system is one for you. The berries are planted 1–1 and one-half feet apart in all directions and any runners that form are cut. This works best with berries that are poor runners.

How do I prune my **everbearing raspberry bushes**?

Raspberries are produced on new canes. Everbearing raspberries will produce two crops on the same cane—one in the late summer or early fall and one in the late spring of the following year. Once the cane has produced its crop, remove it. If you are renovating a raspberry patch, use a sharp, clean pair of pruners to remove all weak, spindly canes, retaining only 4–5 strong central canes. If the patch appears to be diseased, get rid of it and start again with new plants.

How frequently should I water my **apple orchard**?

If it is a young orchard, the apple trees should be kept evenly moist with the root system soaked thoroughly when it becomes dry. Mulch can help this process. A more established orchard still needs water, but receives most of it from nature. It should receive additional water if a check of the soil around a tree's root system indicates it is dry. Apples should not need or receive additional water after the early fall in order to prepare for winter dormancy.

How should I **fertilize my brambles**?

Bramble fruits (see question below) should be fertilized in early spring. Compost or manure can be used to topdress brambles or you can apply a   215

Blueberries require well-drained peaty soil of a pH from 5 to 5.6, which is quite acid.

balanced fertilizer. If growth is out of control, consider reducing the amount of fertilizer you're using.

I have an old **apple tree** on my property that's in need of some TLC. What do I do?

Take on this project in the early spring so that the tree will have time to recover during the summer. First, determine if the tree can be saved. The trunk and major limbs should be in good shape (not hollow or rotted). Then look for younger sprouts in the lower part of the tree. The bark on these branches will be very smooth, indicating its youth. These sprouts will be encouraged to create a new structure for the tree. Remove all old, larger limbs to about half a foot above the new growth. This is best accomplished through the use of a chainsaw and a professional in order to ensure the removal doesn't damage the younger shoots, the older tree, and any people nearby. The tree will undergo a tremendous amount of new growth that year. During the following spring, remove most of this except those limbs that can be trained or will grow outwardly and horizontally. These limbs should be cut back

216

What are the bramble fruits?

Bramble fruits are fruits which grow on thorny canes. They are mostly perennial plants which bear fruit on biennial canes. Red, black, and purple raspberries and blackberries are brambles.

half a foot or so. Additional vigorous growth should result, with most of this removed the following spring. Any desirable branches left should be cut back slightly to encourage outward, rather than upward growth. During these first few years of renovation, don't fertilize the tree as it is already expending energy on new growth.

What's the proper method for **harvesting berries**?

All berries should be picked in the cool of the morning to maintain fruit quality. Bramble berries (see question below) should be picked when they have full color, with any overripe or inferior fruit composted. Blueberries should be harvested by running your hand over a cluster and letting any ripe berries fall into a pail. This is because they need to sit on the bush a little longer to ripen after they've turned blue. Strawberries should be harvested when they're fully red. Pick them by the stem to avoid bruising and place them in a shallow basket so that the weight of the topmost berries will not damage those on the bottom.

FRUIT FAMILIES

What is the difference between **pomme fruit and stone fruit**?

Pomme (which means apple in French) fruits, such as apples and pears, have many seeds. Stone fruits, as their name might suggest, have one hard pit. Peaches, plums, and cherries are stone fruits.

217

Which native fruit grows in acidic soil?

Blueberries thrive in acidic soil. Native to North America, blueberries appreciate full sun and soil with a pH between 4.0 and 5.0. In the wild, some varieties of blueberries grow in swamps, while others grow on barren, rocky mountaintops. In the garden, however, they need moist, well-drained soil around their roots.

Which types of trees are in the *Prunus* species?

Trees in the *Prunus* species include both ornamental and edible fruit trees including almond, cherry, peach, and plum. They are stone fruits.

Which types of trees are in the *Malus* species?

Apple and crabapple trees are member of the *Malus* species. They are pomme fruits.

Which kinds of **grapes** will grow in the U.S.?

American grapes (*Vitis ruscana*), European grapes (*Vitis vinifera*), hybrids between the two, and muscadine grapes (*Vitis rotundifolia*) are all grown in the U.S. American grapes tend to be more disease-resistant and hardy than European grapes, but are grown mainly for eating and juice. European grapes area also known as wine grapes. Muscadine grapes are grown in warm regions and used mainly for jelly, juice, and wine.

What is a **dwarf fruit tree**?

A dwarf fruit tree is a fruit tree that has been grafted onto a rootstock which provides the tree with its size characteristics. Dwarfs generally

What is an everbearing plant?

An everbearing fruit is one which bears fruit throughout a season, as opposed to a June-bearing variety which bears all of its fruit at one time. For canning and preserving, a June-bearing plant might be preferable.

mature at around 8–10 feet in height. Genetic dwarf fruit trees have their own ability to remain small (they are not grafted onto a different rootstock).

What are **strawberry daughters**?

Strawberry plants reproduce themselves by developing runners. Daughter plants are the first series of plants to develop from a runner, forming about a month or so after a strawberry has been planted. While they provide a constant supply of new plants, retaining every daughter (and granddaughter) plant that "runs," can weaken your strawberry patch. Therefore they need to be carefully managed, with the weaker plants being composted, in order to retain high yields and flavor.

TREES
AND
SHRUBS

WOODY ORNAMENTAL TYPES

What is a **woody ornamental plant**?

A woody ornamental is a perennial plant such as a tree or a shrub that does not die back to the ground each year. Even though a plant may be commonly called a bush or a shrub, such as buddleia or butterfly bush, it may not be a woody ornamental.

What are **deciduous ornamental plants**?

Deciduous ornamentals are plants such as burning bushes, dogwoods, and maples that lose their leaves in the fall and remain leafless until the spring. They are used in the landscape for their flowers, their changing foliage color, and the shape and color of their leafless silhouette in the winter.

What are **narrowleaf evergreens**?

Narrowleaf evergreens are ornamental plants that have long, slender, needle-shaped leaves that remain green throughout the year. Pines, firs, junipers, and cedars are some examples of narrowleaf evergreens. Larger varieties are used in landscaping to screen out unsightly views and noise. They also provide shelter, reducing the effects of wind and sun on buildings.

What is a **conifer**?

Conifer means "cone-bearing." This term refers to primarily evergreen trees and shrubs which have either true cones (such as pines) or arillate fruits (yews).

What are the **layers of a forest**?

A forest can be divided into vertical layers. The canopy or top layer is comprised of all of the tree crowns in an area. The understory is comprised of smaller trees that grow under the canopy. The shrub layer is made up of woody vegetation (shrubs as well as seedling trees) that grows under the understory. The ground layer is made up of small plants such as wildflowers, ferns, and mosses that grow on the forest floor.

What types of shrubs can be kept as **hedges**?

A number of shrubs can be planted to form a hedge. If you would like to create structure in your garden year-round, try using a shrub that is

A common hedge.

evergreen. A classic hedge may be created using a variety of boxwood such as *Buxus sempervirens*. Box requires annual trimming to retain a formal shape. Other evergreen shrubs that make nice formal hedges include common yew (*Taxus baccata*) and common holly (*Ilex aquifolium*). An evergreen hedge also creates immediate privacy and can be used to provide shelter from the wind.

Deciduous shrubs create a more informal-looking hedge which can also be quite lovely in the garden. Some deciduous shrubs that take well to hedging include roses (the rugosa variety grow nicely as informal hedges), berberis, spirea, viburnums, and forsythia. As its branches weave together, a more established deciduous hedge can also provide privacy.

What are some trees or shrubs that will grow well in **alkaline soil**?

Some woody ornamentals that will grow in alkaline soil include the golden-rain tree (*Koelreuteria paniculata*), the American smoketree (*Cotinus obovatus*), Japanese cherry (including 'Tai-Haku' and *Prunus serrulata rosea*), lilac bushes, and mock orange shrubs (*Philadelphus* varieties).

225

What are some trees or shrubs that have year-round interest?

Barberries (*Berberis*) have beautiful foliage that changes color in the fall as well as ornamental fruit year-round. Burning bush (*Euonymus alata*) has an interesting, corky shape in the winter and clear scarlet leaves in fall that give it its common name. Crape myrtle (*Lagerstroemia indica*) looks outstanding all year long with its beautiful flowers and fruit and stunning bark. Harry Lauder's walking stick (*Corylus avellana* 'Contorta') is a slow-grower that provides a distinctive silhouette in the winter with its spiraling branches. For its beautiful haze of purple leaves and interesting shape, the common smoke tree (*Cotinus coggygria*)is also a four-season winner.

What are some trees or shrubs that will grow well in **acidic soil**?

Woody ornamentals that will grow in acidic soil include most varieties of heaths and heathers, rhododendrons and azaleas, camellias, *Magnolia virginiana*, serviceberry or Juneberry (*Amelanchier arborea* or *grandiflora*), sourwood, mountain ash, and Carolina silverbell.

Are there any trees that will stand up to the **punishing environment** between my street and sidewalk?

The area you describe has a number of factors that can make it difficult to grow trees in: exposure to wind and weather; exposure to salt (in cold weather areas); exposure to pollution from vehicles; limited amount of room for root system due to space considerations and generally compacted soil. In addition, these stresses make the trees much more vulnerable to insect infestations and disease. Trees such as the Bradford pear (*Pyrus calleryana* 'Bradford'), honey locust (*Gleditsia triacanthos* var. *Inermis*), and green ash (*Fraxinus pennsylvanica*) can survive these stresses.

What are some trees or shrubs with **plum-colored foliage**?

Burgundy or plum foliage can provide a distinctive accent in the sea of green that comprises many landscape plantings. The common smoke tree (*Cotinus coggygria*), Eastern redbud (*Cercis canadensis*), Japanese maple (*Acer palmatum atropurpureum*), barberry (*Berberis thunbergii atropurpurea*), purple-leafed plum (*Prunus cerasifera atropurpurea*), and purple beech (*Fagus sylvatica* 'Purpurea') all have beautiful plum colored foliage.

What are some trees or shrubs with interesting **bark or branches**?

For the winter months, the stark beauty of trees with unusual bark or branches gives a landscape that needed "winter interest." River birch (*Betula nigra*) has lovely peeling pink bark while the coils and twists of Harry Lauder's walking stick (*Corylus avellana* 'Contorta') and the corkscrew hazel (*Corylus avellana* 'Contorta') provide comic relief to the barren and staid canopy trees of winter. Dogwoods (*Cornus*) and willows (*Salix*) are colorful additions to a winter yard.

What are some trees and shrubs with **variegated foliage**?

Trees and shrubs with variegated foliage can serve as focal points in mixed borders. *Weigela* 'Florida Variegata', *Buxus sempervirens* 'Aureovariegata', variegated box elder (*Acer negundo* 'Variegatum'), variegated holly (*Ilex aquifolium* 'Argentea Marginata'), and *Euonymous fortunei* 'Silver Queen' are a few of the woody ornamentals with variegated foliage.

I've just moved into a new house that has a full acre of property but no trees! Are there any trees that will provide me with instant **privacy and shade**?

There are a number of trees which grow quickly, but some of them such as silver maple (*Acer saccharinum*), Tree of Heaven (*Ailanthus altissima*), and weeping willow (*Salix babylonica*) have other less desirable characteristics which make them a poor choice for most homeowners.

227

The bloom of a magnolia.

Better choices include the *Magnolia* species, corktree (*Phellodendron amurense*), silverbell (*Halesia*), blue ash (*Fraxinus quadrangulata*), and yellow-wood (*Cladrastis lutea*).

What are some **white-flowering trees**?

The Japanese pagoda tree (*Sophora japonica*), Japanese tree lilac (*Syringa reticulata*), star magnolia (*Magnolia stellata*), serviceberry (*Amelanchier*), sourwood (*Oxydendrum arboreum*), some crabapples (*Malus*), Callery pear (*Pyrus challeryana*), and Carolina silverbell (*Halesia carolina*) all have lovely white flowers.

I'm interested in **growing native trees and shrubs.** Which grow well in moist soil?

Sourwood (*Oxydendrum arboreum*), white fringe tree (*Chionanthus virginicus*), summersweet (*Clethra alnifolia*), red-osier dogwood (*Cornus sericea*), winterberry (*Ilex verticillata*) and inkberry (*Ilex glabra*),

I live in an area where water for landscaping has been rationed. What are some trees and shrubs that will tolerate drought?

Gray birch (*Betula popuifolia*), native hackberry (*Celtis occidentalis*), *Amelanchier canadensis*, ash (*Fraxinus* species), Amur maple (*Acer ginnala*), silver fir (*Abies concolor*), Kentucky coffee tree (*Gymnocladus dioica*), Rocky Mountain juniper (*Juniperus scopulorum*), pine (*Pinus* species), ginkgo, and the golden-rain tree (*Koelreuteria paniculata*) are some trees which tolerate drought. Black chokeberry (*Aronia melanocarpa*), sumacs (*Rhus* species), crape myrtle (*Lagerstroemia indica*), Longacre potentilla (*Potentilla fruticosa*), common lilac (*Syringa vulgaris*), Oregon grape holly (*Mahonia aquifolium*), and yucca (*Yucca filamentosa*).

highbush blueberry (*Vaccinum corymbosum*), and swamp azalea (*Rhododendron viscosum*) are all American natives which thrive in moist soil.

PLANTING

When is the **best time of year to plant** trees and shrubs?

It depends on the region you live in. In colder regions with early and late freezes, it is best to plant trees and shrubs between April and October. In warmer climates, ornamentals can be planted throughout the year. For all areas, however, if the site selected is exposed to heavy wind, the plant is marginally hardy, or the soil is too moist or too dry, then spring is the best time to plant.

229

I planted a ginko tree this year and I love its beautifully shaped leaves that turn yellow in the fall. Unfortunately, a virus or something has attacked its fruit because they smell horribly. What can I do?

Ginko trees are lovely but you need to choose a male (non-fruiting) tree for your landscape. Female ginko trees produce healthy but foul-smelling fruit that is quite messy as well. Next time, purchase your tree from a reputable grower who will work to ensure the tree you plant is a male one.

I'd like to purchase some trees and shrubs for my backyard. How do I **select healthy ones**?

For any type of plant, be sure to examine the root system. Don't buy plants whose roots are growing out of their containers or that have black or discolored roots. Healthy ornamentals have firm white roots, good leaf color (beware of yellowing or curled leaves), and strong branches. While shape doesn't necessarily impact health, look for a specimen with a single, straight central leader branch and a symmetrical shape.

What factors should I consider when deciding what **type of tree to plant** in my yard?

When choosing a tree or shrub, one thing you must be sure of is that the environmental conditions of the site match the environmental requirements of the plant. Environmental factors include your region's hardiness zone, the conditions of the soil, the light available, and the wind and air circulation. Most ornamentals require well drained and evenly moist soil with a pH in the mid-range of 5.5–7.0 and some light to grow. However, they vary in their specific light requirements. It is important to know both the ornamental's requirements as well as the

> ### I'd like to plant a tree near my house to provide shade in the summer and keep it cool in the winter. How close to the house can I plant it?
>
> **A** good rule of thumb to follow is to plant the tree at least half of its spread or width at maturity away from a building. Also, in order to be sure the tree is proportional to the house, be sure it won't get larger than twice the height of your home.

light conditions in your landscape. An inappropriate amount of light can cause leaf scorch (too much light), spindly growth (too little light) or impact the amount of flowering/fruiting and leaf color. While most plants require good air circulation to reduce the possibility of fungus, some ornamentals can suffer from desiccation or wind scorch if planted in an area that is too windy.

It is also important to consider the growth habit and physical traits of the tree. Physical traits include such characteristics as mature size, form or shape, color, texture, maintenance, and growth habits such as size and nature of an ornamental's root systems and overall speed of growth. Too many gardeners select plants based on their color, texture, and current size, only to find themselves pruning away to keep a shrub in check or hacking a tree down that has been planted too close to the house. Since woody ornamentals tend to be priced more expensively than other landscape plants and make an immediate impact on the landscape, most gardeners would do well to plan their purchases carefully.

What is a **bareroot tree** and when should it be planted?

As its name would imply, a tree packaged for sale as bareroot is not potted nor does it have any soil around its roots. Instead, its roots are covered by peat moss or newspapers and then wrapped in plastic to preserve moisture. Because of this, they are highly perishable and need to be

231

planted soon after they have been shipped. They are usually planted during the spring or fall when the plant is dormant. When purchasing these plants, examine the root system to be sure the plant has retained moisture around the roots and that bud break hasn't happened yet.

I'd like to **plant a tree in the corner** of my yard but I think the area might be too wet. Can I still plant there?

Yes, but with some caution. Trees and shrubs that are planted in areas that are too wet can die quickly as a result of a lack of oxygen to the roots. You could plant shallowly or on a berm (see instructions for planting a tree). You could also install a drainage system to carry away excess water. This would require placing an agricultural drain tile in the bottom of the hole. If the hole is less than six feet across, one tile should do it. If the hole is larger, you may need two lines of tile. The tile should lead away from the tree to a storm sewer or dry well (a hole filled with gravel where the water may drain). Your best bet is to select a tree that grows naturally in wet conditions, such as a river birch (betula nigra).

What is a **balled-and-burlaped tree** and when should it be planted?

A tree that has been balled-and-burlaped (B & B) has had its roots and soil ball covered in burlap and wrapped with rope or wire. Larger trees are usually shipped in this manner. These trees can be planted any time during the growing season although extra care should be taken during hot weather to protect the root hairs from exposure. When purchasing B & B trees, examine the root ball to be sure it is solid and that it doesn't

A crab apple tree in bloom.

wiggle at the trunk (indicating the root system may have been loosened from the plant).

How do I **plant my tree**?

You've begun, of course, by selecting the proper tree for the site. Next, dig a planting hole approximately 2–3 times the width of the tree's root ball and only as deep as the root ball. If you are unsure how deep to dig the planting hole, it is always better to dig the hole too shallow. Most of the strong, healthy roots are actually in the top 10–12 inches of the root ball. By planting a tree too deep, the roots can suffer from a lack of oxygen or too much moisture which kills the tree in the long run. If you have heavy clay soil, you can actually plant the tree or shrub with the top of the root ball slightly higher than the existing soil.

Remove any inorganic materials from around the root ball such as burlap, metal, and rope. If the root ball is contained in a wire basket, use cutters to loosen or remove the wire from the top 8–10 inches. However, if the root ball begins to break apart while you are removing burlap or cutting off wire, then stop. With root-bound container ornamentals, cut and spread

233

the roots slightly in order to prevent the roots from girdling the plant. For bareroot ornamentals, try to arrange the root system so that the roots are spread fairly evenly from the plant in its natural growing position.

Finally, don't add compost or any other soil amendments to the hole, just backfill with existing soil. If you have planted the tree in a site compatible to its growing requirements, the tree will thrive. In a clay soil, adding compost or peat to the hole may encourage water to collect in the area. Fill the hole half way up and water thoroughly to be sure any air pockets are eliminated. Then use the remaining backfill to fill the hole, water again, and tamp the soil slightly, making sure not to compact it. There is no need to prune the tree, except to remove dead, broken, or rubbing branches. Mulch the planting hole with approximately three inches of organic mulch, making sure that the mulch is several inches from the trunk. Staking is also unnecessary, unless the tree can't stand upright without support. Finally, don't forget to remove any tags or labels so that they won't girdle the trunk or limbs.

FERTILIZING AND CARE

How often do I need to **water my newly planted tree**?

If your woody ornamental does not receive an inch of rainfall per week, it should be watered to meet this requirement. As with most plants, however, you must be careful not to over water. Before watering, check the moisture in the root ball as well as the surrounding soil as these will differ. Using a soaker hose or a root feeder attachment (without fertilizer) on a slow trickle will allow the water to penetrate the roots of the tree.

How often do I need to **fertilize my tree**?

Newly planted trees should be fertilized carefully at planting time to ensure new roots are not burned by high nitrogen amounts. A small amount of slow-release fertilizer (no more than one pound of actual nitrogen per 1,000 square feet of planting—see Botany section) can be

When is the best time of year to fertilize my tree?

Fertilizer applications take best during the active growth periods of a tree—spring and fall. The worst time to fertilize is during the heat of summer through the beginning of fall as you run the risk of spurring new growth that won't harden off before a freeze. Once you've determined your tree's needs, apply fertilizer twice a year for optimum results.

mixed with the backfill. More established trees have varying needs. Begin by looking at the plant to see if it is growing as vigorously as it should. Next, check the coloration of the leaves. A common problem in trees is an abnormal yellowing of the leaves. Chlorosis, as it is called, is frequently caused by a lack of soluble iron or manganese in the soil.

In order to determine specific fertilizer needs for your tree, have the tree's soil tested by your local Extension Service and have a foliar analysis done at the same time. With a foliar analysis, leaf samples from the entire tree are analyzed to determine nutrient deficiencies. Nutrient levels in the soil and the leaves may be different due to the impact of the soil pH level. Between the two, you should be able to determine your tree's needs. All plants require nitrogen for growth so you will need to use a fertilizer high in nitrogen. Phosphorous and potassium needs are more rare and would be indicated by the foliar and soil analysis. Most woodys respond to fertilizers in the 3-1-2 or 3-1-1 ratio.

What is **topdressing**?

Topdressing refers to the application of fertilizer to the soil surface around a plant. It is the least expensive and time-consuming method of fertilization. Fertilizer can be placed by hand (wearing gloves) or using a lawn spreader to ensure an even application. If a woody plant is growing in a lawn, apply fertilizer when the grass is dry to avoid burning the grass. Water the area thoroughly and rinse any excess into the soil to avoid excessive lawn growth.

How do you fertilize a tree with **water-soluble fertilizers**?

The liquid injection method of fertilization injects water-soluble fertilizers into the soil. While professionals use a high-pressure hydraulic sprayer, homeowners (my husband included) use a lance with a canister attached for fertilizer. When attached to a garden hose, water runs through the canister, dissolving the fertilizer and distributing it through the end of the lance. Follow the same instructions for holes as the drill-hole method. The water helps to distribute the fertilizer more evenly and ensures the tree absorbs it. Without the fertilizer pellet, the lance can also be used with the garden hose to water the tree roots deeply.

What is the **drill-hole method** of fertilizing trees?

This method is most commonly used by commercial arborists. Holes are drilled 8–12 inches deep in the soil around the tree in concentric circles 2–3 feet apart from one another beginning approximately three feet from the main stem and extending at least three feet outside the tree's drip line. Fertilizer is then distributed equally between the holes. This places granular fertilizer below grass roots and can aerate heavy or compacted soils.

What are the drawbacks of **injecting fertilizer into a tree's trunk**?

Trunk implants and injections which inject nutrients directly into a tree's xylem layer (beneath the bark) also mask problems caused by iron, manganese, and zinc deficiencies. However, the act of boring a hole in a tree trunk is difficult, time-consuming, and can cause decay, so this method should only be considered when others have failed.

TRAINING AND PRUNING

Why are **ornamental plants pruned**?

Woody ornamentals are pruned for a number of reasons. Pruning can preserve the natural shape and size of a plant or can be used to limit it. It can also be used to train a plant such as a hedge or an espaliered tree. Pruning removes broken, diseased, dead, or undesirable limbs which keeps the plant healthy and removes any danger to humans or buildings. Pruning removes older growth, rejuvenating elderly plants by spurring new growth. Proper pruning enables proper air circulation and light penetration to the center of a plant. Pruning can correct or direct the growth of trees by eliminating poor branch structures or weak crotches and removing suckers or water sprouts.

What is a **tree sucker or water sprout**?

A tree sucker is a vigorous, upright branch that originates at the base of a tree. Water sprouts are similar growths that originate on the trunk or main branches of a tree. Both should generally be removed as they can interfere with the shape and proper growth of a tree. Sometimes water sprouts are left on to fill in an empty space on a tree, if they are at a proper height and crotch.

What is a **central leader**?

The central leader is the central trunk or axis of a tree. A straight, tall central leader is especially important for certain types of fruit trees in order to maintain their shape and promote air and light circulation in the center of a tree.

237

An example of how to stake a tree.

Should I **stake my tree** and if so, how do I do it?

A tree needs to be staked when it cannot support itself, but staking should only be viewed as a short-term proposition. Newly planted trees generally don't need staking. However, if the tree is very large or is planted in a highly porous soil such as sand or in an area that receives a lot of wind, it may need extra support. In order to ensure minimum damage to the tree, use flexible stakes and soft material to attach the tree to the stakes. Use only one stake for a tree with a trunk diameter of less than two inches and two stakes placed on opposite sides of the tree for a trunk between two and four inches in diameter. Guy wires (wires inside protective hosing) are used to stake larger trees. These are placed around branch crotches (the angle where the branch meets the tree's trunk).

Stakes should be placed as low on the tree as possible. They should be placed in the ground approximately a foot away from the tree on the same side as the wind blows in order to provide proper support. Be sure to watch the tree carefully to ensure the stakes and attachment are not girdling the tree or overcompensating in terms of support. Most trees don't require staking for more than one season.

How do I **prune my woody ornamental**?

Before beginning to prune, consider what you are trying to accomplish and be sure it is within your ability and comfort zone to do so. Large-scale pruning of shade trees is something that is best left to professionals. For smaller trees and shrubs, keep the function and natural shape of the tree in mind when pruning. Forsythias, for example, are often pruned to a round shape like evergreens but their natural form is a more elegant vase-like shape.

Start with clean, sharp tools including hand pruners, loppers for larger branches, and pole pruners to reach high branches. All cuts should be made upward to an outward-facing bud with the main goal being to open up the plant. If you thin out deciduous plants rather than cutting them back, you will avoid excessive growth at the top of the plant. Begin by removing dead, broken, diseased and infested branches. Next, remove branches that cross each other or that are out of synch with the natural or desired shape of the plant. Prune branches that grow toward the crown or center of the plant in order to promote air and light circulation. Remove suckers and water shoots along with any old stubs to eliminate undesirable growth (suckers can grow from a plant's rootstock, resulting in a different shrub than the desired one).

Trees and shrubs have different growth habits and specific uses and therefore require different pruning. When pruning limbs from trees, be sure to retain only those with wide angles of attachment (called crotches) to the tree. These limbs are better able to withstand strong winds and storms. Be sure to leave room for lawn mowers and people underneath limbs. The position of a branch on the tree's trunk remains the

239

What is the difference between cutting back and thinning?

Both refer to pruning of shrubs and trees, but with different purposes and results. When thinning an overgrown shrub, you remove whole branches which allows air and light to reach the center of the plant. Some new growth may occur as a result. Cutting back stems to side buds forces new growth, encouraging the plant to branch out. Cutting back hard means removing a great deal of the branch while shearing just occurs at the tips of the shrub.

same throughout the growth of the tree but it might move closer to the ground as it widens.

Pruning should usually be done during the late winter or early spring, except in the case of spring-flowering woodys, pines, or trees that "bleed" or ooze sap heavily. Spring-flowering plants should be pruned after blooming in order so as not to disrupt their flowering (no harm done, just less of a show). When pine trees are pruned in order to encourage thicker growth, this should be done when their candles (new growth) are done growing but aren't quite firm. Trees that bleed can be pruned in late spring to early summer, after their first flush of growth. All trees and shrubs should be pruned in relatively dry weather, to limit the spread of disease.

How can I **force a forsythia branch into bloom**?

When the buds on a forsythia shrub begin to swell (in Michigan, this generally occurs in late March or early April), remove several branches by cutting them on a 45 degree angle. Place the branches in a container of warm water and place it in a sunny window. The branches should flower within the next few days. In general, the closer the shrub is to blooming when cut, the faster it blooms indoors. If you'd like to preserve the flowers as long as possible, keep the blooming branches in a cool room, away from direct sunlight. Other flowering shrubs or trees can be forced as well including the popular pussy willow, magnolias, apple trees and the *Prunus* genus which includes plums and cherry trees.

What is **espalier**?

Espalier is the practice of training trees or shrubs to grow flat against a wall or trellis. Fruit trees are sometimes trained this way in order to maximize yield from a smaller orchard.

How can I **create topiary** from my shrubs?

Before starting, be sure you understand and can execute the basics of pruning given previously. Topiary, or the practice of shearing plants into shapes or verdant likenesses of people and animals, requires a high degree of pruning skill to create elaborate shapes. Beginners can try their hand at shaping small globes of boxwood or even a woody herb such as rosemary. Choose an inexpensive plant specimen so that your pocketbook won't feel the heat of your early attempts. Shoot for a basic shape like a globe or one that isn't too far from the natural shape of the plant. Keep your desired shape in mind and review the plant from all sides as you work. Prune in early spring (or according to the plant's needs) but feel free to remove extra growth up until fall. As you become more confident in your pruning you can attempt more complex shapes.

ROSES

I ordered several **rose bushes** from a reputable catalog but when they arrived they just looked like a bunch of sticks. Why?

Bareroot roses have to be shipped in a dormant state since they aren't rooted in soil. Many plants, rose canes included, are shipped in their

241

dormant state so that they aren't damaged and don't perish in transit. A plant at the height of its growth would require water, sunlight, and food—all of which are difficult to come by in a cardboard UPS box. These roses should be planted as soon as possible.

My rosebush says that it is **"budded."** What does that mean?

This term refers to which root system your rose grows from. A budded rose joins a hardy rootstock (usually of a wild rose) to a more fragile hybrid tea or climber at a point called the bud union (swollen knob). Otherwise, a rose is grown on its own root system.

How can I achieve the largest possible blooms on my **hybrid tea rose**?

In order to produce large blooms on hybrid teas, you should remove all buds except the terminal bud (the bud at the end of the growing tip of the stem) when the buds are very small. This practice, known as disbudding, ensures the cane's energy is directed toward producing one beautiful rose.

How do I **plant my rose bush**?

Start by soaking bareroot roses in water for several hours. The planting site should be located in an area which receives at least four hours (six is better) of sun per day, plenty of air circulation, and good drainage. If you live in a colder region, you should consider placing the rose bush in a sheltered area to protect it from cold winter winds. Dig a hole slightly larger than the root ball.

The planting depth of a budded rose is determined by your hardiness zone. If you live in the colder regions (zone 6 and colder), the bud union should be planted just below soil level to provide protection to the plant from freezing temperatures. If you live in warmer temperatures (zone 8 and warmer), the bud union should be planted just above soil level in order to more easily prune any undesirable suckers which spring from the wild rose rootstock. Gently tease the roots apart so that they have access to the soil. Some gardeners add a small amount of bonemeal when planting but it is not necessary. If you do so, mix the bonemeal in with the soil at the bottom of the hole and avoid chemical fertilizers

I received several rose bushes as a housewarming gift. When can I plant them?

Bareroot roses (rose canes shipped in their dormant state) should be planted in the early spring in colder areas, early fall with milder winter areas, and in the winter in warm areas. They should be planted as soon as possible (within a week of receipt). If you can't plant them immediately, store the canes inside their packing materials in a cool but frost-free place and keep the roots moist. Roses planted in containers will establish best if planted in spring or fall, rather than the heat of summer. Potted roses should be soaked immediately and placed outside in a sunny area until you are ready to plant. If given your druthers, plant your rose bush on an overcast, misty day. Sun and wind can dry out the plant.

which may burn the roots. Mix in compost with the backfill soil to bring the rose to its proper depth. Water the bush thoroughly and add more soil as it settles. If the weather is still below freezing, mound compost around the base of the bush to protect it.

What is a **rose standard**?

A rose standard or rose tree is a cultivated rose that has been grafted on top of the tall, straight cane of a tougher rose. The result looks like a topiary. These types of roses require pruning of the top in order to retain a symmetrical shape.

How do I **prune my roses**?

The main goal of pruning is to promote a disease and mildew-free environment by allowing air to circulate freely in the center of the plant. A pruned plant also conforms to landscape standards of shape and size. While differ-

243

An example of roses that have been cut for display.

ent types of roses require slightly different approaches, the basic steps to rose pruning are the same. Begin with the right tools. You will need thick gloves, preferably to your elbow. You'll also need bypass pruners (which will cut the canes cleanly instead of crushing them) as well as a pair of loppers for thicker wood. All cuts should be made at about a 45 degree angle just above an outward facing bud. This will promote air circulation in the center of the plant by ensuring new growth is directed away from the plant. For most roses, you will also remove at least one third of the plant. Remember that most roses are underpruned, rather than overpruned.

Start by pruning any dead or diseased wood which will look black, brown or mottled. After pruning diseased wood, be sure to clean your pruners with a diluted bleach solution so that you avoid spreading the disease to other plants. Canes which cross each other should also be removed to eliminate injury caused by the limbs rubbing against one another. Any canes that have been damaged during the winter should be pruned just above the injury. Next, cut away rose hips and any blooms left from the previous year. Finally, remove any thin canes. Thicker canes produce the biggest blooms.

If you have a rose standard, be sure to prune the plant so that it remains symmetrical. On a hybrid tea rose, the largest blooms grow on new canes close to its base. So remove all canes except a few and cut these back to around a foot above the ground. Climbing roses should be tied to a trellis or fence with their canes bent downward in order to spur blooms all along the canes. Shrub roses should have all of their branches pruned by at least a third and be trimmed to retain their vase shape.

When do I **prune my roses**?

A good rule of thumb is to prune when the forsythia in your area are in bloom. If you don't have a forsythia or don't know what they look like, examine the branches of your rose bush. When the buds are slightly swollen and reddish colored, you may begin pruning them.

What are some plants that serve as attractive **companions for red roses**?

Weigela, butterfly bush (*Buddleia*), lavender, iris, nepeta, dianthus, and peony combine beautifully with red roses.

245

Should **miniature roses** just be used as houseplants?

Actually, although they may be grown inside with extra care, miniature roses are best grown outdoors where they can receive enough sun and air circulation to keep them happy.

Are there any **roses that are native to the United States**?

There are several roses that are native to the United States including Virginia rose (*Rosa virginiana*) which has rose-colored flowers and can grow up to six feet tall. Pasture rose (*Rosa carolina*) is a lower-growing shrub while prairie rose (*Rosa setigera*) has arching, far-flung canes.

What is the difference between **old garden roses and modern roses**?

Old garden roses are those that were in existence before 1867 and all species or wild roses. Modern roses are roses that have been introduced since 1867.

What are a **rose's thorns** used for?

The thorns on a rose (and those of other plants) are actually branches that have modified over many generations to deter plant-eating animals. The thorns on a cactus are another good example of this modification.

What do **strawberries and roses** have in common?

Both strawberries and roses are part of the *Rosea* family. Other members of this plant family include raspberries, blackberries, cherries, plums, apples, pears, peaches, and apricots. They are all highly favored by the Japanese beetle.

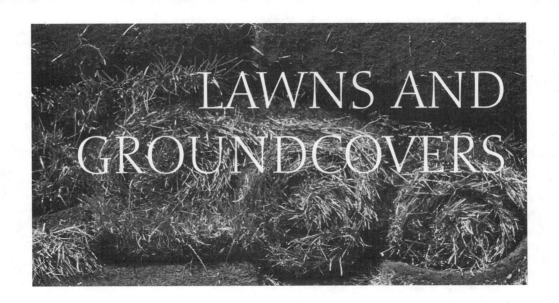

LAWNS AND GROUNDCOVERS

ESTABLISHING A LAWN

What is a **cool-season grass**?

Cool-season grasses are winter-hardy in regions north of zone 7. They remain evergreen for most of the year, but tend to become brown and parched during particularly hot weather. Cool-season lawns are usually mowed high and are planted as a mixture of different types of grasses. Cool-season grasses include Kentucky bluegrass, fine-leafed fescues, and perennial ryegrass.

What is a **warm-season grass**?

Warm-season grasses go brown and dormant in cool weather but are hardy enough to stand up to the heat in zones 7 and south. They are more coarse in texture than cool-season grasses and are usually mowed short. Warm season grasses include zoysia, bermuda, St. Augustine, carpet grass, and bahia.

Which are the most **durable types of grasses**?

New cultivars of tall fescue are hardy under heavy wear as well as drought. It will also survive some shade and stays green throughout the

How do lawn grasses reproduce?

Lawn grasses reproduce by setting seed, although in your lawn it will not produce viable seed (or seed that will germinate). They also spread through new plants that grow from the crown of the grass plant. These are known as tillers. Some lawn grasses spread determinedly through rhizomes which enables them to quickly fill in bare spots. Rhizomes are underground creeping stems. Aboveground creeping stems are known as stolons. Lawns that spread through stolons can also quickly fill in bare spots.

year. Improved (as opposed to common or unimproved) perennial ryegrass also survives wear-and-tear.

What is the difference between **a sprig and a plug**?

A sprig is an individual bareroot grass plant while a plug is a tuft of sod. Warm-season grasses can be sold as sprigs and plugs in order to start lawns. Cool-season grasses are only available as seed or sod.

What is **hydroseeding**?

Hydroseeding is a technique in which grass seed is mixed with mulch, fertilizer, and water. The mixture is then applied as a thick spray. Given the extra pampering, the grass seed tends to germinate more successfully and new seedlings thrive with more protection. However, the hydroseed still takes longer to establish than sod and can run into problems if not properly maintained.

What are the advantages and disadvantages of **seeding a lawn**?

Seeding a lawn is cheaper than sodding it. You also have a larger selection of grass types to choose from. Seeding a lawn, however is much

How do I care for my newly seeded lawn?

During the first several weeks after being seeded, a lawn should be kept evenly moist. Ideally, it should be lightly sprinkled a few times each day. Once the seedlings are between 1–2 inches tall, half of the straw mulch used to keep the seed in place and moist should be removed to allow more light and air to reach the young seedlings. After the lawn is 2–3 inches tall, it should be mowed for the first time using a mower with a sharp blade. The goal is to remove a little less than half of the grass blade. Just prior to this mowing, the lawn can be fertilized with a high nitrogen fertilizer applied at half rate and watered in well to prevent burning. Weedkillers should not be used until the lawn has been mowed several times. In the mean time, handpulling of broadleaf weeds is helpful.

more labor-intensive than sodding a lawn is. Seed also takes longer to establish. Newly sewn grass seed requires adequate moisture and a fine mulch to protect the seed and seedlings from birds, erosion, and heat. There is a small window of time in the year that seeding is done, to take advantage of moist soil and cooler temperatures. As a result, seeding a lawn can often have poor results, especially in areas that receive a lot of use or are subject to erosion.

What are the advantages and disadvantages of **sodding a lawn**?

Sod looks like a lawn immediately. It can also be put down at any time of the year that the soil beneath it can be worked. It can be walked on almost immediately and tends to "take" better on slopes. However, sod is much more expensive than seed and is not available in a wide variety of grasses.

How do I care for my **newly sodded lawn**?

A newly sodded lawn can be mowed as soon as it needs it, removing no more than 1/3 of the height at a time. It should be watered daily in order

253

Sod is delivered rolled or stacked flat. It is best to lay sod as soon as possible, since it will dry out quickly.

to encourage the roots to become established. Once the sod has taken root, it can be fertilized according to an established lawn maintenance schedule.

What kind of **lawn grass** is durable enough for my pets and kids to play on and still look good?

This depends on where you live. If you live in southern regions, zoysia grass is extremely durable and fairly easy to maintain (few problems). However, in the north, zoysia grass turns brown in the winter with some cultivars even dying in cold temperatures. In cooler areas, a mixture of different strains of Kentucky bluegrass, fine-leafed fescues, and improved perennial ryegrass results in a fairly durable lawn if your lot is sunny. With a shaded lot, a mixture of shade-tolerant cultivars is necessary.

My local hardware store sells **grass seed** by bulk and have a wide variety of grasses to choose from. Which one do I choose?

Actually, you might be choosing more than one variety of grass. Unless your lawn is uniform, with the same conditions of sunlight, moisture-retentiveness, and soil throughout it, you will probably select more than one type of grass seed.

LAWN CARE

When is the best time of day to **water my lawn**?

The best time of day to water a lawn is in the early morning. This ensures the lawn has enough moisture to make it through the heat of the day. The second best time of day to water a lawn is during the evening or night. Although this does make the lawn (like any plant) more susceptible to disease and fungi, most home lawns do not fall prey to these. Although you can water during the day, it is somewhat wasteful as the water evaporates quickly due to the sun and wind.

255

How frequently should I water my lawn?

The latest recommendation from agricultural schools and extension services is to water lawns lightly and frequently (read daily for a short period of time). In order to stay green, lawns require about an inch of water a week from human and heavenly sources. However, in deciding how frequently to water your lawn, consider water availability in your region (that precious water might prove useful elsewhere in your garden), how your lawn is used (lawns that receive heavy use usually need more watering), and how important it is to keep your lawn green. You might consider letting your lawn go dormant—it will usually revive with rain—or using drought-resistant grasses.

How often should I **cut my lawn**?

As often as it needs to be so that each time you cut it, you are not removing more than a third of it. Removing more than a third of the lawn at a time stresses it and can lead to problems with disease and weeds. Cool-season grasses should be kept around three inches high while warm-season grasses should be kept around an inch high.

When shouldn't I **mow the lawn**?

The worst time to mow a lawn is immediately following a rain. The mower has a tendency to "chew" the grass when wet and the clippings will clog up the mower.

I have a **mulching mower** but sometimes the clippings left behind seem so thick. Do I need to rake them up?

You have the right idea with the mulching mower, but consider mowing more frequently to decrease the amount of clippings. However, when

Typical lawn care includes mowing the lawn to an appropriate height.

you are unable to mow more frequently and the cut grass is very thick, you should collect it for your compost pile. Heavy clippings can kill the lawn.

What does it mean to **edge a lawn**?

Edging refers to the creation and maintenance of a fine edge between the sidewalk and the sod using a tool with a rotating, sharp blade. Edgers can be manual (quite backbreaking), electric, or gas-powered.

I just **edged my lawn** for the first time this spring and it was a lot of work! Is there an easier way to do it?

Unfortunately, no. There are gas- and electric-powered edges that can make it easier, but usually that first edging of the season takes a bit of effort since your lawn continues to grow over the winter. The best suggestion for maintaining a nicely edged lawn with the least effort is to keep at it. Edging every couple of weeks should keep that lawn at bay.

257

What is thatch?

Thatch is dead organic material that forms between the soil and the grass of a lawn. It develops when organic material accumulates at a higher rate than it decomposes. Some varieties of grass produce more organic material (resulting in thatch) than others do. Too much fertilizer, overwatering, and soil compaction can also cause thatch to accumulate. But a thatch layer of less than an inch helps protect a lawn from extremes in temperature and heavy use. If thatch has accumulated past this point, the lawn retains less water and fertilizer and becomes stressed, making it an easy target for disease and insect invasions.

When is the best time to **reseed my lawn**?

It depends on whether you have a cool-season lawn, or a warm-season one. Cool-season grasses grow best in cool weather, so it is best to plant these in late summer or early fall. Warm-season grasses become stressed in winter, so they are normally planted in the spring in order to have the summer to grow and thrive.

How do I **remove thatch** from my lawn?

Dethatching rakes or machines which have special tines to pull the thatch from the lawn can be used. The rakes are pulled across the lawn at different angles, but require a good amount of sweat equity for large lawns. However current research has shown that dethatching does not actually do much to reduce the amount of thatch. Core aeration is considered a better alternative.

What is **core aeration**?

Core aeration removes plugs of soil from the turf, causing grass roots to grow vigorously to replace itself which in turn spurs plant growth. This

> ## I've discovered brown spots on my lawn. What should I do?
>
> If you're a new dog owner or your lawn serves as a potty stop for neighborhood pooches, you'll find dark green patches where a dog has "watered" your lawn. If you catch it happening, immediately run water over the spot to dilute the ammonia which causes the burn.

also helps compacted turf. The plugs, when broken up and distributed, provide a topdressing to the lawn which aids in decomposition of thatch. There are aerating machines and some rototillers provide an aerating attachment.

I've just **aerated my lawn** and it looks pretty bad. Did I do it wrong?

No, it just has to look bad at first to look better. In pulling up cores or plugs of turf, the remaining turf can look a little rough. With water, fresh grass seed, a light topdressing of compost, it will look better than before in a few weeks time.

How do I **patch a spot of lawn**?

Begin by removing any dead grass or perennial weeds in the spot. Add soil if the spot is low to meet the soil level surrounding it. If soil isn't needed, scratch at the surface of the spot with a rake to loosen the soil. Then broadcast seed of the same variety or varieties as are in the lawn currently fairly thickly. Rake the seed in, apply a light mulch such as straw, and water thoroughly. Keep the spot moist until the seedlings are established. You may also have success with a new dry seeding medium composed of mulch and seed which can be purchased at nurseries and garden centers.

What are the pros and cons of letting a lawn go dormant?

A dormant lawn turns brown, signaling that growth has slowed or stopped. In allowing your lawn to go dormant, you eliminate or reduce water and fertilizer usage as well as the cost and time associated with watering and fertilizing. However, for many people, a brown lawn isn't as aesthetically pleasing as a green one. A dormant lawn can also fall prey to insects, disease, and weeds.

What are some non-chemical means of **reducing lawn weeds**?

If you are establishing a new lawn, you can reduce the number of lawn weeds be making sure all weeds are removed (via smothering or handweeding) prior to installation of the new lawn. Making sure you select a grass that is recommended for your area and planting it at the proper time of the year will also help reduce weeds since the grass should thrive in its desired environment, leaving less room for weeds. Cutting the lawn to its recommended height, making sure it is regularly fertilized and watered will also ensure the grass doesn't become stressed. A healthy lawn can beat out any weed competition.

What are some **organic methods of fertilizing** my lawn?

Many synthetic organic fertilizers such as ammonium nitrate, ammonium sulfate, and urea have a high potential for burning the lawn so they need to be applied at a low rate and watered in well. Milorganite is a natural organic fertilizer which is slow-release and has far less potential for burning. Other options are processed manure and sifted compost which can be spread evenly over the lawn just prior to a rain. Using a mulching mower or leaving your clippings on the lawn can also provide extra nitrogen to the lawn.

Why do I have moss in my lawn?

Moss will commonly grow in heavily shaded areas. But it will also invade areas where the soil is not fertile or is acidic. It can grow if there is poor drainage in an area, limited air circulation, or if the soil has become compacted. To reduce the incidence of moss, be sure you are using a shade-tolerant species of grass and mowing high enough to discourage competition. You should also do a soil test to check the pH level and aerate the lawn if it has become compacted. Finally, if you are unable to grow grass well in the area, consider planting a shade-tolerant groundcover.

When should I **fertilize my lawn**?

If you live in a region where cool-season grasses are predominate, fertilize in the spring and again in fall to take advantage of two periods when your lawn will be undergoing growth spurts. In warm-season areas, fertilize just as the lawn "greens up" (late spring), then again several weeks later.

Can I leave my **fall leaves** on the lawn to provide extra fertilizer over the winter?

No—leaves left on the lawn over the winter will smother and kill the grass as they become wet and matted down. Before the leaves become wet in the fall, run over them with your mower. The shredded leaves can be raked into the lawn, placed in the compost pile, or set under plants as a mulch.

How can I keep a **low maintenance lawn**?

Begin by reducing the amount of lawn you have to begin with. Lawns just require more upkeep than other parts of the garden. Then eliminate

261

What motor sport involves a basic backyard tool?

Lawnmower racing, billed as "The Alternative Motor Sport" by its fans, originally began in West Sussex, England in 1973. The mowers are self-propelled (including riding mowers, "run-behind" mowers, and towed seat mowers) that were all originally designed and sold to mow lawns. Participants maneuver them around grassy fields at speeds of up to 35 mph, according to the British Lawnmower Museum website, with various local and national championships culminating in the two-day international World Championships. As of this writing, it has not become an Olympic sport.

lawn in hard-to-mow spaces such as around trees and shrubs and on steep banks, use groundcovers or mulch rather than lawn. For other areas, eliminate as many difficult angles as possible by using broad curves around beds and employing the use of a mowing strip (bricks or other material laid side by side to create a strip for one wheel of the mower). Learn to live with a few weeds. Reduce watering in the summer or let the lawn go dormant.

LAWN TRIVIA

Which museum hosts the **largest collection of toy lawnmowers**?

The British Lawnmower Museum in Lancashire, England houses the largest collection of toy lawnmowers, along with a variety of adult-sized ones ranging from the original pushmowers from the 1830s to the modern, gas-powered beauties of today.

262

What are some advantages to substituting groundcovers for a grass lawn?

Groundcovers are easier on the environment than lawns since less fertilizer and water are required to keep it looking good and no power tools are necessary to maintain it. Groundcovers also provide a yard with a distinctive look. For shady lawns, groundcovers are the perfect solution.

What is the **world's largest grass**?

Bamboo is considered to be the world's largest grass. It is a large evergreen grass that produces a woody trunk. Reproducing via either clumps or runners, bamboo can live a long time.

GROUNDCOVERS

What is a **groundcover**?

A groundcover is loosely defined as any low-growing plant that will spread to cover the ground, looks attractive for at least a season, and keeps down the weeds. Any plant can be used as a groundcover including low-growing shrubs, perennials and annuals, and ornamental grasses along with the usual ivies.

Which is more expensive to maintain, **groundcover or lawn**?

Although groundcover can be more expensive to install initially, it does not require the same weekly upkeep as a lawn (mowing, edging, fertilizing, and watering).

What are some **disadvantages of groundcover**?

The initial investment in groundcover can be quite expensive, especially if you have a large area to fill. Groundcovers are also not as durable as grass—if you have children, you will most likely need to have at least a small grassy area for them to play.

How do I **plant groundcovers**?

Begin with a soil test to determine the pH level and ensure you have selected a groundcover that will thrive in the area. Remove any existing plants and loosen the soil to 1–2 feet, as with a perennial planting. Add any soil amendments and compost, then turn the soil to mix them in. Rake the area smooth and water well. Lay mulch down first, to reduce the labor required to mulch around so many small plants. Space plants according to their mature size and rate of growth, digging a hole large enough to accommodate the root system of the plant. Place the plant in the hole, letting the roots spread out, loosely fill with the dug topsoil, water well, and mulch. Using groundcovers in a large area can quickly become expensive. If you use a fast-growing groundcover, you can purchase smaller plants and space them far apart, with the plants filling in quickly. Remember, however, that you can always have too much of a good thing. A picture perfect groundcover this year may be a lawn invader the next.

How do I **maintain my groundcover**?

Newly planted groundcovers should be kept moist until they are established which can take up to a year with some plants. A light mulch can help the roots retain water. Weeding regularly ensures the groundcover is not competing for water and nutrients. Monitor for disease and insects and address problems promptly.

Which groundcovers are **evergreen**?

Evergreen groundcovers can provide a unifying theme to a yard planted in the northern regions. Try evergreen ginger, epimediums, hostas, some

Groundcovers are excellent alternatives to lawns, especially in areas where grass is difficult to establish or maintain.

I have a steep bank that I don't want to mow. Are there any groundcovers that are suited to these conditions?

You need to find a groundcover that has a deep root system in order to stabilize the slope. Some groundcovers that take well to slopes include daylilies, a low-growing form of yarrow (*Achillea tomentosa*), and creeping juniper (*Juniperus horizontalis*).

lamiums, *Astilbe chinensis* 'Pumila,' English ivy (*Hedera helix*), bearberry (*Arctostaphylos uva-ursi*), creeping juniper (*Juniperus horizontalis*), some cotoneasters, perennial candytuft (*Iberis sempervirens*), St.-John's-wort (*Hypericum calycinum*), *Euonymous fortunei*, periwinkle (*Vinca minor*), Allegheny foamflower (*Tiarella cordifolia*), and bergenias.

Which groundcovers have **variegated leaves**?

Groundcovers with variegated leaves can add visual interest to a yard. Some variegated groundcovers include *Pachysandra terminalis* 'Variegata,' *Pulmonaria saccharata*, *Ajuga reptans* 'Variegata,' variegated Japanese Solomon's Seal (*Polygonatum odoratum* 'Variegatum'), round-leaved mint (*Mentha rotundifolia* 'Variegata'), golden balm (*Melissa officinalis* 'Aurea'), *Hosta crispula*, *Hosta fortunei* 'Albopicta,' *Hosta undulata*, *Parthenocissus henryana*, *Vinca major* 'Variegata,' English ivy (*Hedera helix* 'Gold Heart'), and ribbon grass (*Phalaris arundinacea* 'Picta').

Which groundcovers grow best in **shaded areas**?

Shaded areas are difficult to grow grass in. But groundcovers such as ajuga (*Ajuga reptans*), bergenias, periwinkle (*Vinca minor*), bleeding heart (*Dicentra eximia*), English ivy (*Hedera helix*), lily-of-the-valley (*Convallaria majalis*), hostas, pachysandra (*Pachysandra terminalis*), wild ginger (*Asarum*), lungworts (*Pulmonaria*), and Chinese astilbe

I live in an area that receives less than 12 inches of rain a year. Are there any groundcovers that are drought-tolerant?

Groundcovers can be good problem solvers in regions such as yours that receive little rain. Drought-tolerant groundcovers include woolly yarrow (*Achillea tomentosa*), pussytoes (*Antennaria dioica* var. *rosea*), wormwood (*Artemisia absinthium*), cape weed (*Arctotheca calendula*), rock cress (*Arabis alpina*), wall cress (*Arabis caucasica*), snow-on-the-mountain (*Euphorbia marginata*), blue fescue (*Festuca ovina glauca*), candytuft (*Iberis sempervirens*), several of the cotoneasters, edelweiss (*Leontopodium alpinum*), creeping lilyturf (*Liriope spicata*), and creeping thyme (*Thymus serpyllum*).

(*Astilbe chinesis* 'Pumila') all thrive in shaded areas, pleasantly replacing a straggling lawn.

Which groundcovers grow best in **sunny and dry areas**?

Groundcovers such as lamb's ears (*Stachys byzantia*), cranesbill geranium (*Geranium*), chamomile (*Chamaemelum nobile*), moss pink (*Phlox subulata*), pinks or carnations (*Dianthus*), snow-in-summer (*Cerastium tomentosum*), catmint (*Nepeta mussinii*), thyme (*Thymus*), hens-and-chicks (*Sempervivum*), daylilies (*Hemerocallis*), and sedums grow well in sunny, dry areas. Crown vetch (*Coronilla varia*) also thrives under these conditions, but can be quite invasive.

Which groundcovers grow best in **wet areas**?

If you have areas of your yard that are too wet for lawn, certain groundcovers may be a good alternative. Chinese astilbes (*Astilbe chinesis*),

False Goat's Beard (*Astilbe taquetti* 'Superba'), Japanese primroses (*Primula japonica*), daylilies (*Hemerocallis* 'Pink Damask'), cowberry (*Vaccinum vitis-idaea*), comfrey (*Symphytum grandiflorum*), pulmonarias, and *Brunnera macrophylla* all grow well in wet areas.

I have large open areas underneath my trees where nothing will grow. Are there any groundcovers suited to these conditions?

Ajuga thrives in the dry shade under shallow-rooted trees like silver maples. *Gaultheria shallon* is more of a shrub and can become invasive, but it tolerates dry shade as well. Bethlehem sage (*Pulmonaria saccharata*), hostas, and pachysandra look right at home under trees.

HERB PLANTING AND CARE

What is an **herb**?

The textbook definition of an herb is a flowering plant that lacks a woody stem. However, in the popular sense, the term herb refers to plants which have aromatic, medicinal, or culinary properties and so include some woody perennials.

What **growing conditions** are required by herbs?

Although different herbs have different needs, in general, most herbs thrive in a well-drained soil with a pH between 6.0 and 7.0 that receives full sun. Choose an area that receives good air circulation and you will have little trouble with pests and disease. Herbs also need to be in an area free from competition such as tree roots. Some herbs that are Mediterranean in origin thrive in poor, dry soil. These include rosemary, lavender, and other grey-leaved plants. Otherwise, soil of an average fertility will keep most herbs happy.

What do I need to do to prepare an **herb garden**?

Begin by selecting the design for your garden (see question below). Herbs are planted in a similar fashion to perennials. Loosening the soil

Herb gardens are often formalized in design or have medicinal or culinary themes.

to about a foot will allow moisture to penetrate the roots and keep the bed properly drained, which is a must for herbs. Add organic matter and turn it under. Remove any weeds, along with old tree roots. If you come across new tree roots, move your herb garden to another site. Herbs can also be planted with flowers and vegetables, for their decorative and utilitarian qualities. Many herbs also do well in containers since they can be kept smaller and in peak flavor.

When can herbs be **planted**?

Like other plants, herbs may be hardy or half-hardy annual plants or perennial plants (see appropriate chapter for more information). Hardy annual herbs can be either sown in the previous fall or in the early spring, as soon as the ground can be worked. Half-hardy annuals are always planted in the early spring and tender annuals can't be planted until after the last frost. Perennial herbs are usually planted from seed or plant in the cooler weather of spring or fall in order to provide a gentle environment for the new plant or seedling to grow in.

How should herbs be fertilized?

Many perennial herbs such as rosemary, lavender, and sage prefer a poor soil to grow in. Fertilize these plants at the beginning of the growing season (topdressing with compost or a sprinkling of bone meal, watered in well) and no more than monthly after that. Annual herbs such as basil respond well to fertilizing, but select a liquid fertilizer such as fish emulsion or compost tea at half-strength and use it every 2–3 waterings. Your best bet is to keep adding organic matter such as compost to the soil regularly.

However, if you are planting your herbs in pots indoors, they can be started at any time.

How are herbs **started from cuttings**?

Herbs may be started from cuttings from perennial plants during their growth periods. Using a sharp knife or a set of pruners, remove a non-flowering shoot or woody stem around 3–4 inches long from the herb just below a set of leaves. Remove leaves from the bottom inch or so, press the cutting into a peat pot with moist compost and place it in a warm area. You can dab the end of the cutting in rooting hormone (available at nurseries and through mail order) before planting it in the compost, but it is not necessary. Once the herb has rooted, you may gently transfer it to another pot. Herbs such as rosemary, bay, and scented geraniums may be started from cuttings.

Which herbs may be **started from seeds**?

Annual herbs such as basil, anise, borage, chamomile, chervil, cilantro, cumin, dill, marigold, and savory are grown from seed. Some perennial herbs such as feverfew, fennel, hyssop, lovage, sage, salad burnet, valer-

273

Why is my basil wilting in the sun? I thought herbs needed full sun to thrive.

There could be a number of reasons why your basil is droopy. If you are growing it in a pot which is too small for it, the basil could be pot-bound with not enough room for its roots to receive nutrients and water. Turn the container over and check to see if roots are poking through the drainage hole. If so, it's time to change pots. Or your plant may be in need of water. Stick your finger into the container or soil around the plant and feel the moisture level a few inches down. If it's dry, you need to water.

Finally, you may live in a region or state such as southern California, and parts of the south and west in which full sun (six or more hours of light per day) is too much for the variety of basil you're growing. Some sweet basils can be heat intolerant. Try sheltering it with a larger plant, providing it with a few hours of morning sun but shielding it from the midday sun.

ian, and wormwood may also be grown from seed, though they generally need more than one season before being harvested.

How should herbs be **watered**?

Herbs grown in containers may need to be watered daily, as pots (especially clay ones) tend to dry out quickly. Herbs out-of-doors should be watered frequently, daily during hot weather. Since most herbs appreciate well-drained soil, be sure their roots do not sit in water for any length of time.

Do herbs require **pruning**?

Yes. Pruning woody herbs such as lavender and rosemary allows them to retain a neat and compact shape in the landscape. All basil, sage, and

When should herbs be harvested?

Herbs used fresh can be harvested at any time, although the flavor of some herbs change once they've set flower. Herbs used for drying should be harvested before the herbs set flower, on a day that is dry rather than rainy. Flowers for drying should be picked in the morning, just as the flowers have opened. Seed heads should be picked when the seeds have become ripe and brown.

scented geraniums have a tendency to become leggy or spindly without pruning. Harvesting itself is, of course, a form of pruning. All herbs are stimulated into new growth by pruning so shape them at least every month or so if they are just ornamental herbs.

How and when should I **prune lavender**?

Lavender looks best when it has a full, rounded shape. It should be pruned every year with its first flush of growth in the early spring. If it has been a while since you pruned your lavender, cut back every second or third stem to the base and trim the remaining stems by a third, shaping the entire plant into a rounded shape as you go. Your lavender should respond with a flourish of new growth and blooms.

Do herbs need to be **mulched**?

In areas with cold winters, herbs such as lavender, rue, and sage are said to benefit from a mulching of evergreen boughs over that season. However I have to confess that I leave these herbs uncovered and they manage just fine. Thyme will die out if covered in leaves or other wet mulch over the winter. During the growing season, all herbs with the exception of those native to hot and dry areas (such as rosemary, sage, and oregano) will benefit from a light mulch to retain moisture at their roots.

275

What are some traditional herb garden designs?

Aformal herb garden is usually square or circle with a focal point (such as a birdbath or urn) at its center. Brick or gravel paths edged with low-growing herbs such as chamomile, thyme, lamb's ears radiated from the center breaking the square or circle into pie wedges, each planted with a different herb. Medieval gardeners planted herbs in blocks with paths separating them. Herbs can also be planted in a border with the tallest herbs such as dill planted at back, medium height herbs such as basil in the middle, and low-growers like thyme at the front. Herbs also thrive in containers—strawberry pots with each pocket planted with a different herb (tall growers at the top, trailing plants at the sides).

How can herbs be **frozen for use later**?

Herbs should be picked fresh at the peak of their season. The leaves can then be rinsed and gently shaken to remove most of the water and stored whole in freezer bags. Another option is to place a leaf, flower, or finely chopped herb in each section of an ice cube tray. Fill the tray with water, and freeze overnight. You can leave the cubes in the tray if you'll be using them in the next several days or remove them and place them in a freezer bag for later use.

How can I keep herbs **fresh in the refrigerator**?

Pick the herbs in the morning and place them immediately in cool water (best to do this as you pick). If you have used any kind of pesticide (organic or chemical), wash them gently but thoroughly, and pat them dry. Wrap them in paper towels and place them in freezer bags in the crisper drawer of your refrigerator where they should last 1–2 weeks. You can also put large bunches into glasses or jars that have an inch of water on the bottom. If you keep them covered loosely in the refrigerator and change the water every few days, they should also last 1–2 weeks.

How do I **dry herbs**?

You can dry herbs either by hanging them or laying them flat. To hang herbs, pick them fresh and clean as above. Place them in small bunches and fasten their stems together with string and hang in a cool, dry space. Check often and compost any bunches that develop mildew immediately. Herbs and flower petals can also be dried by being laid flat on window screens in a cool, dry space. Gently move them around every few days to discourage moisture.

Which herbs are traditionally used in **knot gardens**?

Herbs in knot gardens are pruned or sheared regularly. Woody herbs that grow close to the ground such as lavender, lavender cotton, rosemary, germander, and hyssop are often used in knot gardens.

HERBS FOR PARTICULAR USES

What are some **fragrant herbs**?

Herbs and plants known for their aromatic qualities include bee balm (*Monarda didyma*), chamomile (*Chamaemelum nobile*), sweet marigold (*Tagetes lucida*), lavender (*Lavendula angustifolia*), fennel (*Foeniculum vulgare*), mints (*Mentha*), rosemary (*Rosmarinus officinalis*), roses (*Rosa*), scented geraniums (*Pelargonium*), lemon balm (*Melissa officinalis*), lemon verbena (*Aloysia triphylla*), sweet woodruff (*Galium odoratum*), artemisias, patchouli (*Pogostemon cablin*), sweet marjoram (*Origanum majorana*), sweet violet (*Viola odorata*), and sweet cicely (*Myrrhis odorata*).

Which herbs are **frost-hardy**?

Frost-hardy herbs include angelica (*Angelica archangelica*), anise (*Pimpinella anisum*), borage (*Borago officinalis*), catmint (*Nepeta* cataria), chives (*Allium schoenprasum*), fennel (*Foeniculum vulgare*), horseradish (*Armoracia rusticana*), lavender (*Lavendula*), lemon balm (*Melissa officinalis*), mint (*Mentha*), wormwood (*Artemisia absinthium*), sage (*Salvia*), parsley (*Petroselinum crispum*), yarrow (*Achillea millefolium*), thyme (*Thymus vulgaris*), sorrel (*Rumex acetosa*), rue (*Ruta graveolens*), and rosemary (*Rosmarinus officinalis*).

What are some **edible flowers** and how are they consumed?

Nasturtiums, daylilies, and violets—the whole flower or their petals—can be eaten in salads. Nasturtiums have a slightly sharp, peppery taste while violets are sweeter. The young leaves of daylilies can also be chopped finely and put in salads or eaten fried. Pot marigolds or calendulas (not the usual garden variety marigold) can be used to flavor and color dishes, similar to saffron. Chive flowers can be used in the same manner as garlic because their mature blooms have a pungent flavor. Rose petals are used to make jellies and syrups.

Which herbs may be used to **make tea**?

Herbs such as chamomile, anise hyssop, and lemon balm are traditionally used for tea. Monarda or bee balm is also known as wild bergamot, since its flavor is similar to that of the bergamot orange, which is used to give Earl Grey tea its distinctive flavor. Other herbs used for tea include the mints, tansy, sage, rosehips, ginseng, pennyroyal, lemon-

Oregano (*Origanum vulgare*) is a perennial herb native to Greece and the island of Cyprus. Its flavor is associated with Mediterranean cuisine.

grass, scented geranium, borage, lemon verbena, valerian, elderberry, rosemary, and thyme.

Which herbs can be trained into **topiary**?

It is possible to create a topiary from plants other than conventional shrubs. Rosemary, bay, lavender, lemon verbena, and other herbs which have woody stems can all be trained into topiary.

Which homegrown herbs are used in **Mediterranean cuisine**?

Thyme, oregano, marjoram, rosemary, sage, and winter savory are all used in Mediterranean cuisine. These plants thrive in poor, dry soil and do not care to be mulched.

Which homegrown herbs are used in **Asian cuisine**?

Basil, fennel seeds, coriander seeds and cilantro, and garlic can all be grown in most back yards and used to flavor Asian cuisine.

Are there any herbs that will thrive in acid soils?

Some herbs actually prefer slightly acidic soils. These include sweet woodruff, tansy, angelica, dill, basil, lovage, chervil, and mint.

Which herbs are members of the **onion family**?

Garlic and chives are both members of the *Allium* genus, whose plants are known as much for their beautiful blooms as their pungent qualities.

Which herbs (besides mint of course!) are members of the **mint (*Labiatae*) family**?

Hyssop, lavender, lemon balm, bee balm or monarda, basil, rosemary, sage, savory, thyme, germander, lamb's ears, and catnip all belong to the mint family.

Which herbs can be **grown inside**?

Although most herbs can be brought inside, some of them tolerate it better than others. These include scented geraniums (*Pelargonium*), rosemary (*Rosmarinus officinalis*), sage (*Salvia*), sweet bay (*Laurus nobilis*), chives (*Allium schoenoprasum*), and cilantro (*Coriandrum sativum*).

What is **lady's mantle**?

Lady's mantle or *Alchemilla mollis* is a dainty perennial with scalloped and pleated green leaves that are tipped in silver. It flowers in summer, with fragile acid-yellow blossoms. Lady's mantle received its common name for the shape of its leaves which are similar to a woman's cloak.

Lady's mantle grows best in a moist soil receiving light shade (although mine receives 4–5 hours of morning sun without ill effects so far) in zones 3–8. Some of the Alchemilla species were traditionally used to stop bleeding and as an astringent. In the garden, it functions as a groundcover or an edging plant—best in groups.

What is **santolina**?

Santolina is also known as cotton lavender or French lavender. *Santolina chamaecyparissus* is a hardy perennial that can grow up to three feet. Its leaves are a silvery grey and very fragrant, but the flowers are golden yellow rather than the lavender associated with the *Lavendula* species. Like lavender, it makes an excellent low hedge and is also sometimes used in herb mixtures used to discourage moths.

My herb garden has a **stepping stone path** through it. Are there any herbs that I can grow to creep up between the stones?

Any of the creeping thymes work wonderfully in paths as they will thrive in little soil and lots of sun. Although regular stomping on them will crush them, thymes are fairly durable and provide a wonderful scent when stepped on. In mid- to late summer, their blooms provide additional color to the garden.

What is a **woundwort**?

A woundwort is a healing compound made from an herb (or mixtures of herbs) which was believed to help stop bleeding and to serve as an astringent. Some herbs traditionally used as woundworts include yarrow, lady's mantle, St. John's wort, germander, selfheal (*Prunella vulgaris*), burnet, sage, betony (*Stachys officinalis*), comfrey, Solomon's Seal, and periwinkle.

Which herbs are **self-seeders**?

If you plant herbs such as borage, caraway, chervil, cilantro, dill, fennel, lemon basil, Roman chamomile (*Chamaemelum*), and sweet wormwood, don't be surprised to see their young seedlings poking up around your garden. They're prolific self-seeders.

Further Resources

Books

A-Z of Evergreen Trees & Shrubs. New York: Reader's Digest, 1998

The American Horticultural Society A-Z Encyclopedia of Garden Plants. New York: DK Publishing, 1997.

Ashmun, Barbara Blossom. *200 Tips for Growing Beautiful Perennials*. Chicago: Chicago Review Press, 1998.

Ashmun, Barbara Blossom. *200 Tips for Growing Beautiful Roses*. Chicago: Chicago Review Press, 1998.

Austin, Sandra. *Color in Garden Design*. Newtown, CT: Taunton, 1998.

Baker, Jerry. *The Impatient Gardener*. New York: Ballantine, 1998.

Baker, Jerry. *The Impatient Gardener's Lawn Book*. New York: Ballantine, 1998.

Ball, Jeff and Liz. *Rodale's Landscape Problem Solver*. Emmaus, PA: Rodale Press, 1989.

Bartholomew, Mel. *Square Foot Gardening*. Emmaus, PA: Rodale Press, 1981.

Barton, Barbara. *Gardening by Mail*, 4th ed. Boston: Houghton Mifflin, 1994.

Bennett, Jennifer and Turid Forsyth. *The Annual Garden*. Somerville, MA: Firefly, 1998.

The Big Book of Flower Gardening: A Guide to Growing Beautiful Annuals, Perennials, Bulbs & Roses. Alexandria, VA: Time-Life Books, 1997.

The Big Book of Garden Design: Simple Steps to Creating Beautiful Gardens. Alexandria, VA: Time-Life Books, 1998.

Bird, Richard. *Beds and Border*. New York: Stewart, Tabori & Chang, 1998.

Bisgrove, Richard. *The Gardens of Gertrude Jekyll*. Little, Brown and Co., 1992.

Boufford, Bob. *The Gardener's Computer Companion*. San Francisco: No Starch Press, 1998.

Bradley, Steven. *Keeping the Garden in Bloom: Watering, Dead-Heading, and Other Summer Tasks*. New York: Stewart, Tabori & Chang, 1998.

Brennan, Georgeanne and Kathryn Kleinman. *Backyard Bouquets: Growing Great Flowers for Simple Arrangements*. San Francisco: Chronicle Books, 1998.

Breskend, Jean Spiro. *Backyard Design: Making the Most of the Space Around Your Home*. New York: Bulfinch Press, 1991.

Brookes, John. *John Brookes Natural Landscapes*. New York: DK Publishing, 1998.

Brooklyn Botanic Garden handbooks.

Brown, Deni. *Garden Herbs*. New York: DK Publishing, 1998.

Campbell, Stu. *Let It Rot! The Gardener's Guide to Composting*. Pownal, VT: Storey Publications, 1990.

Caring for Your Plants. New York: Reader's Digest, 1998.

Cathey, H. Marc. *Heat-Zone Gardening: How to Choose Plants That Thrive in Your Region's Warmest Weather*. Alexandria, VA: Time-Life Books, 1998.

Clausen, Ruth R. and Nicolas H. Ekstrom. *Perennials for American Gardens*. New York: Random House, 1989.

Cooke, Ian. *The Pathfinder's Guide to Tender Perennials*. Portland, OR: Timber Press, 1998.

Coombes, Allen J. and Kim Tripp. *The Complete Book of Shrubs*. New York: Reader's Digest, 1998.

Coombes, Allen J. *Dictionary of Plant Names*. Portland, OR: Timber Press, 1994.

Cooney, Norma. *The Kitchen Garden: Fresh Ideas for Luscious Vegetables, Herbs, Flowers and Fruit*. New York: Friedman/Fairfax, 1998.

Coughlin, Roberta M. *The Gardener's Companion: A Book of Lists and Lore*. New York: Harper Perennial, 1991.

Courtauld, George. *An Axe, a Spade and Ten Acres*. London: Secker & Warburg, 1983.

Cox, Jeff. *Jeff Cox's 100 Greatest Garden Ideas: Tips, Techniques, and Projects for a Bountiful Garden and a Beautiful Backyard*. Emmanus, PA: Rodale Press, 1998.

Cox, Jeff. *Perennial All-Stars: The 150 Best Perennials for Great-Looking, Trouble-Free Gardens*. Emmanus, PA: Rodale Press, 1998.

Crandall, Chuck and Barbara. *Courtyards and Patios: Designing and Landscaping Elegant Outdoor Spaces*. New York: Friedman/Fairfax, 1998.

Crockett, James Underwood. *Annuals*. New York: Time-Life Books, 1971.

Cullen, Mark, and Lorraine Johnson. *The Urban/Suburban Composter: The Complete Guide to Backyard, Balcony, and Apartment Composting*. New York: St. Martin's Press, 1992.

Cunningham, Sally Jean. *Great Garden Companions: A Companion-Planting System for a Beautiful, Chemical-Free Vegetable Garden*. Emmanus, PA: Rodale Press, 1998.

Damrosch, Barbara. *The Garden Primer*. New York: Workman Publishing, 1988.

Dannenmaier, Molly. *A Child's Garden: Enchanting Outdoor Spaces for Children and Parents*. New York: Simon & Schuster, 1998.

Davis, Brian. *The Plant Selector*. New York: Sterling, 1998.

Dirr, Michael A. *Dirr's Hardy Trees & Shrubs: An Illustrated Encyclopedia*. Portland, OR: Timber Press, 1997.

Dirr, Michael A. *Manual of Woody Landscape Plants*. Champaign, IL: Stripes Publishing Company, 1977.

DiSabato-Aust, Tracy. *The Well-Tended Perennial Garden: Planting and Pruning Techniques*. Portland, OR: Timber Press, 1998.

Ellefson, Connie, Tom Stephens, and Doug Welsh. *Xeriscape Gardening: Water Conservation for the American Landscape*. New York: Macmillan, 1992.

Ellis, Barbara and Bradley, Fern Marshall. *The Organic Gardener's Handbook of Natural Insects and Disease Control*. Emmanus, PA: Rodale Press, 1992.

Environmentally Friendly Gardening: Easy Composting. San Ramon, CA: Ortho Books, 1992.

The Family Handyman Landscape Projects: Planning, Planting & Building for a More Beautiful Yard and Garden. New York: Reader's Digest, 1998.

Fell, Derek. *Derek Fell's Handy Garden Guides*. New York: Friedman/Fairfax.

Fell, Derek. *The Encyclopedia of Flowers*. New York: Michael Friedman Publishing Group, Inc., 1994.

Ferguson, Nicola. *Right Plant, Right Place: The Indispensable Guide to the Successful Garden*. New York: Fireside Books, 1992.

Field, Ann and Gretchen Scoble. *The Meaning of Flowers*. San Francisco: Chronicle Books, 1998.

Fish, Margery. *We Made a Garden*. United Kingdom: W.H. & L. Collinridge Ltd., 1956.

Flowerdew, Bob. *Good Companions: A Guide to Gardening with Plants That Help Each Other*. New York: Summit Books, 1991.

Frieze, Charlotte M. *The Zone Garden Series*. New York: Fireside Books, 1997.

A Garden for All Seasons. London/New York: Reader's Digest, 1991.

Garden Design. New York: Meigher Communications.

Gardens Illustrated. London: John Brown Publishing.

Greenwood, Pippa. *Basic Gardening: 101 Essential Tips*. New York: DK Publishing, 1998.

Greenwood, Pippa. *The New Gardener: The Practical Guide to Gardening Basics*. New York: Dorling Kindersley, 1995.

Grey, Mara. *The Lazy Gardener*. New York: Macmillan, 1998.

Harmonious Technologies. *Backyard Composting: Your Complete Guide to Recycling Yard Clippings*. Ojai, CA: Harmonious Press, 1992.

Harper, Pamela J. *Designing with Perennials*. New York: Macmillan Publishing, 1991.

Heilenman, Diane. *Gardening in the Lower Midwest: A Practical Guide for the New Zones 5 and 6*. Indiana University Press, 1994.

Heriteau, Jacqueline. *American Horticultural Society Flower Finder*. New York: Simon & Schuster, 1992.

Hill, Lewis. *Pruning Made Easy: A Gardener's Guide to When and How to Prune Everything, from Flowers to Trees*. Pownal, VT: Storey Books, 1998.

Hillier, Malcolm. *Container Gardening Through the Year*. New York: DK Publishing, 1998.

Holmes, Roger and Rita Buchanan. *Home Landscaping: Mid-Atlantic Region*. Upper Saddle River, NJ: Creative Homeowner Press, 1998.

Holmes, Roger and Rita Buchanan. *Home Landscaping: Northeast Region*. Upper Saddle River, NJ: Creative Homeowner Press, 1998.

Holmes, Roger and Rita Buchanan. *Home Landscaping: Southeast Region*. Upper Saddle River, NJ: Creative Homeowner Press, 1998.

Hynes, Erin. *Rodale's Weekend Gardener: Create a Low-Maintenance Landscape to Enjoy Year-Round*. Emmanus, PA: Rodale Press, 1998.

Jackson, Richard and Carolyn Hutchinson. *How to Win at Gardening: A Practical A-To-Z Guide to a Better Garden*. New York: Reader's Digest, 1998.

Jaworski, Henry. *Summer Bulbs*. Shelburne, VT: Chapters, 1998.

Jay, Roni. *Gardens of the Spirit: Create Your Own Sacred Space*. New York: Sterling, 1998.

Joyce, David and John Elsey. *The Perfect Plant for Every Site, Habitat, and Garden Style*. New York: Stewart, Tabori & Chang, 1998.

King, Michael and Piet Oudolf. *Gardening with Grasses*. Portland, OR: Timber Press, 1998.

Kolls, Rebecca. *Rebecca's Garden: Four Seasons to Grow On*. New York: Avon Books, 1998.

Kourik, Robert and Deborah Jones. *The Lavender Garden: Beautiful Varieties to Grow and Gather*. San Francisco: Chronicle Books, 1998.

Lima, Patrick. *The Art of Perennial Gardening*. Somerville, MA: Firefly, 1998.

Loewer, Peter. *Step-By-Step Wildflowers & Native Plants*. Des Moines, IA: Meredith Corp., 1995.

Longley, Susanna. *The Weekend Gardener*. New York: Reader's Digest, 1998

Lovejoy, Ann. *Gardening from Scratch: How to Turn Your Empty Lot Into a Living Garden*. New York: Macmillan, 1998.

MacCaskey, Michael and National Gardening Association Editors. *Gardening for Dummies*. Foster City, CA: IDG Books, 1996.

Marken, Bill and National Gardening Association Editors. *Annuals for Dummies*. Foster City, CA: IDG Books, 1998.

Marken, Bill and National Gardening Association Editors. *Container Gardening for Dummies*. Foster City, CA: IDG Books, 1998.

Marshall, Fern, ed. *Rodale's All-New Encyclopedia of Organic Gardening*. Emmaus, PA: Rodale Press, 1992.

Martin, Deborah L., and Grace Gershuny, eds. *The Rodale Book of Composting: Easy Methods for Every Gardener*. Emmaus, PA: Rodale Press, 1992.

McGourty, Fred and Pam Harper. *Perennials: How to Select, Grow and Enjoy*. Los Angeles: Price Stern Sloan, 1985.

Mitchell, Henry. *Henry Mitchell on Gardening*. Boston: Houghton Mifflin, 1998.

Murray, Elizabeth. *Monet's Passion*. San Francisco, CA: Pomegranate Art Books, 1989.

Noordhuis, Klaas T. and David Tomlinson, ed. *The Garden Plants Encyclopedia*. Somerville, MA: Firefly, 1998.

O'Connor, Jane and Emma Sweeney. *The Complete Idiot's Guide to Gardening*. New York: Alpha Books, 1996.

Ogden, Shepherd. *Step By Step Organic Vegetable Gardening*. HarperCollins, 1992.

Organic Gardening. Emmaus, PA: Rodale Press.

Pick the Right Plant: A Sun & Shade Guide to Successful Plant Selection. Alexandria, VA: Time-Life Books, 1998.

Proctor, Rob. *Country Flowers: Wild Classics for the Contemporary Garden*. New York: Running Heads, Inc., 1991.

Raworth, Jenny and Val Bradley. *The Complete Guide to Indoor Gardening*. New York: Abbeville, 1998.

Reddell, Rayford Clayton. *All-America Roses*. San Francisco: Chronicle Books, 1998.

Richardson, Beth. *Gardening with Children*. Newtown, CT: Taunton, 1998.

Riley Smith, Mary. *The Front Garden: New Approaches to Landscape Design*. Houghton Mifflin, 1991.

Roach, Margaret. *A Way to Garden: A Hands-On Primer for Every Season*. New York: Clarkson Potter, 1998.

Rutledge, Cooper. *Backyard Battle Plan: The Ultimate Guide to Controlling Wildlife Damage in Your Garden*. New York: Penguin, 1998.

Schneck, Marcus. *Creating a Butterfly Garden*. New York: Fireside Books, 1994.

Schultz, Warren and Carol Spier. *Garden Details: Accents, Ornaments, and Finishing Touches for Your Garden*. New York: Friedman/Fairfax, 1998.

Seidenberg, Charlotte. *The Wildlife Garden: Planning Backyard Habitats*. Jackson, MS: University Press of Mississippi, 1995.

Seton, Susannah. *Simple Pleasures of the Garden: Stories, Recipes & Crafts from the Abundant Earth*. Emeryville, CA: Conari Press, 1998.

Smith, Charles W.G. *The Big Book of Gardening Secrets*. Pownal, VT: Storey Books, 1998.

Smittle, Delilah, ed. *Rodale's Complete Garden Problem Solver: Instant Answers to the Most Common Gardening Questions*. Emmanus, PA: Rodale Press, 1998.

Stell, Elizabeth P. *Secrets to Great Soil: A Grower's Guide to Composting, Mulching, and Creating Healthy, Fertile Soil for Your Garden and Lawn*. Pownal, VT: Storey Books, 1998.

289

Stuckey, Maggie. *Gardening from the Ground Up: Rock-Bottom Basics for Absolute Beginners*. New York: St. Martin's Press, 1998.

Tatroe, Marcia and National Gardening Association Editors. *Perennials for Dummies*. Foster City, CA: IDG Books, 1997.

Taylor, Patricia A. *Easy Care Perennials*. Fireside Books, 1989.

Taylor, Patricia A. *Easy Care Shade Flowers*. Fireside Books, 1993.

Taylor, Patrick. *Making Gardens: An Essential Guide to Planning and Planting*. Portland, OR: Timber Press, 1998.

Taylor's Master Guide to Gardening. Boston, New York: Houghton Mifflin, 1994.

Taylor's Pocket Guide to Herbs and Edible Flowers. Houghton Mifflin Co., 1990.

Thomas, Ian. *The Culpeper Guides: How to Grow Herbs*. Exeter, Devon, England: Webb & Bower, 1988.

Turner, Carole B. *Seed Sowing and Saving: Step-by-Step Techniques for Collecting and Growing More Than 100 Vegetables, Flowers, and Herbs*. Pownal, VT: Storey Books, 1998.

Uber, William C. *Water Gardening Basics*. Upland, CA: Dragonflyer Press, 1988.

Walheim, Lance and National Gardening Association Editors. *Roses for Dummies*. Foster City, CA: IDG Books, 1997.

White, Hazel. *Paths and Walkways: Simple Projects, Contemporary Designs*. San Francisco: Chronicle Books, 1998.

White, Hazel. *Water Gardens: Simple Projects, Contemporary Designs*. San Francisco: Chronicle Books, 1998.

Williams, Bunny and Nancy Drew. *On Garden Style*. New York: Simon & Schuster, 1998.

Williams, Carol. *Bringing a Garden to Life*. New York: Bantam, 1998.

Wyman, Donald. *Wyman's Gardening Encyclopedia*. Macmillan Publishing Co., 1971.

Yepsen, Roger. *1,001 Old-Time Garden Tips: Timeless Bits of Wisdom on How to Grow Everything Organically, from the Good Old Days When Everyone Did*. Emmanus, PA: Rodale Press, 1998.

Yepsen, Roger B., Jr. *The Encyclopedia of Natural Insect and Disease Control*. New York: Rodale Press, 1984.

Your Organic Garden with Jeff Cox. Emmaus, PA: Rodale Press, 1994.

Magazines

American Homestyle and Gardening
New York Times Co.
110 Fifth Ave.
New York, NY 10017 USA
Phone: (212)878-8700
Fax: (212)463-1269

Atlanta Homes and Lifestyles
Wiesner Inc.
1100 Johnson Ferry Rd. NE, Ste. 595
Atlanta, GA 30342 USA
Phone: (404)252-6670
Fax: (404)252-6673
E-mail: althomes@aol.com

Build and Green
Build and Green
2922 W. 6th Ave., Studio D
Vancouver, BC, Canada V6K 1X3
Phone: (604)730-1940
Fax: (604)730-7860

Canadian Gardening
Camar Publications Ltd.
130 Spy Ct.
Markham, ON, Canada L3R 5H6
Phone: (905)475-8440
Fax: (905)475-9246

Carolina Gardener
P.O. Box 4504
Greensboro, NC 27404 USA

Country Home
Meredith Corp
1716 Locust St.
Des Moines, IA 50309-3023 USA
Phone: (515)284-2015
Fax: (515)284-2552
E-mail: countryh@asm.mdp.com

Fine Gardening
The Taunton Press, Inc.
63 S. Main St.
P.O. Box 5506
Newtown, CT 06470 USA
Phone: (203)426-8171
Fax: (203)270-6751
Toll-free: 800-283-7252

Fleurs, Plantes et Jardins
Editions Versicolores Inc.
1320 Blvd. St. Joseph
St.-Joseph, PQ, Canada G2K 1G2
Phone: (418)628-8690
Fax: (418)628-0524

Flower & Garden
KC Publishing, Inc.
700 W. 47th St., Ste. 310
Kansas City, MO 64112 USA
Phone: (816)531-5730
Fax: (816)531-3873

Green World
Green World
12 Dudley St.
Randolph, VT 05060-1202 USA
E-mail: gx297@cleveland.freenet.edu

The Herb Quarterly
Long Mountain Press, Inc.
P.O. Box 689
San Anselmo, CA 94979-0689 USA
Phone: (415)455-9540
Fax: (415)455-9541
Toll-free: 800-371-4372

Horticulture
98 N. Washington St.
Boston, MA 02114 USA
Phone: (617)742-5600
Fax: (617)367-6364
E-mail: hortmag@aol.com

House Beautiful
Hearst Corporation
1700 Broadway
New York, NY 10019 USA
Toll-free: 800-289-8696

Journal of Therapeutic Horticulture
American Horticultural Therapy Association
362A Christopher Ave.
Gaithersburg, MD 20879-1280 USA
Phone: (301)948-3010
Fax: (301)869-2397

Kitchen Garden
The Taunton Press
63 S. Main St.
P.O. Box 5506
Newtown, CT 06470-5506 USA
Phone: (203)426-8171
Fax: (203)426-3434
Toll-free: 800-888-8286

Martha Stewart at Home
Time Inc.
Time-Life Bldg., Rockefeller Center
1271 Avenue of the Americas
New York, NY 10020-1300 USA
Phone: (212)522-1212
Fax: (212)765-2699

Minnesota Horticulturist
Minnesota State Horticultural Society
1755 Prior Ave. N.
Falcon Heights, MN 55113 USA
Phone: (612)643-3601
Fax: (612)643-3638
Toll-free: 800-676-6747

The National Gardener
102 S. Elm Ave.
St. Louis, MO 63119 USA
Phone: (314)968-1664

National Gardening
National Gardening Association
180 Flynn Ave.
Burlington, VT 05401 USA
Phone: (802)863-1308
Fax: (802)863-5969
URL: http://www.garden.org
Toll-free: 800-538-7476

Organic Gardening
Rodale Press, Inc.
33 E. Minor St.
Emmaus, PA 18098 USA

General GardeningWebsites

Adventures in Gardening: http://www.gardenguy.com

American Association of Botanical Gardens and Arboreta: http://www.mobot.org/AABGA

American Community Gardening Association: http://communitygarden.org

American Horticultural Society: http://www.ahs.org

Better Homes and Gardens: http://www.bhglive.com/gardening/index.html

Calendar of Gardening Events: http://www.gardencalendar.com

The Compost Resource Page: http://www.oldgrowth.org/compost

Digital Seed: http://www.digitalseed.com

293

The Garden Catalog List: http://www.cog.brown.edu/gardening/cat.html

Garden.com by Garden Escape: http://www.garden.com

The Garden Gate: http://www.prairienet.org/ag/garden/homepage.html

GardenNet: http://gardennet.com

Garden Pages: http://www.gardenpages.com

Garden Planet: http://www.worldleader.com/garden/index.htm

Garden Solutions: http://www.gardensolutions.com/cgi-bin/WebObjects/GardenSolutions

The Garden Spider's Web: http://www.gardenweb.com/spdrsweb

Garden Town: http://www.gardentown.com/index.html

Garden Web: http://www.gardenweb.com

Garden Web Ring: http://www.webring.com

Gardening.com: http://www.gardening.com

Herb Finder: http://www.woodny.com/garden/herbfinder.html

HGTV (Home & Garden Television): http://www.hgtv.com

HomeArts: Bloom!: http://homearts.com/depts/garden/00gardcl.htm

Horticulture Online: http://www.hortmag.com

Lawn Institute: http://www.lawninstitute.com

Master Composter: http://www.mastercomposter.com

Mr. Grow: http://www.mrgrow.com

Natural Gardening Online Catalog: http://www.naturalgardening.com

Nuseryman.com: http://www.nurseryman.com

Pacific Northwest Gardening: http://www.nwgardening.com

Plant Adviser: http://www.plantadviser.com

Plant World: http://www.plantworld.com

Southern Gardening: http://www.southerngardening.com

Sunset: http://www.sunsetmag.com

Traditional Gardening: http://traditionalgardening.com

The Trellis: http://wormsway.com/trellis.html

USDA Home Gardening: http://www.usda.gov/news/garden.htm

Virtual Gardener: http://www.pathfinder.com/vg

WebGarden: http://www.hcs.ohio-state.edu/hcs/WebGarden.html

Weekend Gardener: http://www.chestnut-sw.com/weekend.html

Botanical Garden Websites

Arnold Arboretum: http://www.arboretum.harvard.edu

Atlanta Botanical Garden: http://www.atlgarden.com

Australian National Botanic Garden: http://osprey.erin.gov.au/index.html

Birmingham Botanical Gardens: http://www.bbgardens.org

Boerner Botanical Gardens: http://uwm.edu/Dept/Biology/Boerner/index.html

Botanica: The Wichita Gardens: http://www.botanica.org

Brooklyn Botanic Garden: http://www.bbg.org

Chicago Botanic Garden: http://www.chicago-botanic.org

Desert Botanical Garden:
   http://cissus.mobot.org/AABGA/Members.page/desrt.bot.grdn.html

Descanso Gardens: http://www.descanso.com

Fioli Historical House & Gardens: http://www.fioli.org

Franklin Park Conservatory & Botanical Garden: http://www.fpconservatory.com

Huntington Botanical Garden: http://www.huntington.org/BotanicalDiv/HEH
   BotanicalHome.html

Huntsville-Madison County Botanical Garden: http://www.hsvbg.org

Idaho Botanical Garden: http://www.avocet.net/ibg

Jerusalem Botanical Garden: http://www6.huji.ac.il/~botanic

Kew Gardens: http://www.rbgkew.org.uk/index.html

The Lady Bird Johnson Wildflower Center: http://www.wildflower.org

Longwood Gardens: http://www.longwoodgardens.org

Missouri Botanical Garden: http://www.mobot.org

Mitchell Park Horticultural Conservatory: http://www.uwm.edu/Dept/Biology/domes

The Morton Arboretums: http://www.mortonarb.org

Mynelle Gardens: http://www.Instar.com/mynelle

Myriad Botanical Gardens: http://www.okccvb.org/myrgard/myrgard.html

Nani Mau Gardens: http://www.nanimau.com

The National Arboretum: http://www.ars-grin.gov/ars/Beltsville/na/index.html

National Garden (U.S. Botanical Garden): http://www.nationalgarden.org

New York Botanical Garden: http://www.nybg.org

The Niagra Parks Botanical Gardens: http://www.npbg.org

Olbrich Botanical Gardens: http://www.ci.madison.wi.us/olbrich/olbrich.html

Paronella Park: http://www.gspeak.com.au/paronella

QuadCity Botanical Gardens: http://www.qcbotanicalgardens.org

Quail Botanical Gardens: http://members.aol.com/quailbg/quail.html

Royal Botanical Gardens: http://www.rbg.ca

Royal Botanical Garden Edinburgh: http://www.rbge.org.uk

San Antonio Botanical Garden: http://www.sabot.org

Skylands: The New Jersey State Botanical Garden: http://www.njskylandsgarden.org

Sonnenberg Gardens: http://www.sonnenberg.org

The South Carolina Botanical Garden: http://agweb.clemson.edu/hort/scbg/intro.html

The State Botanical Garden of Georgia: http://uga.edu/~botgarden

Strybing Arboretum & Botanical Gardens: http://www.mobot.org/AABGA/member.pages/ strybing

Sydney Royal Botanic Garden: http://www.rbgsyd.gov.au

University of Delaware Botanic Gardens: http://bluehen.ags.udel.edu/udgarden.html

Associations

African Violet Society of America (AVSA)
2375 North
Beaumont, TX 77702 USA
(409) 839-4725, (409) 839-8484
Toll-Free: 800-770-AVSA
Fax: (409) 839-4329
E-mail: avsa@avsa.org
URL: http://www.avsa.org

The Alpine Garden Society
AGS Centre
Avon Bank
Pershore
Worcestershire WR10 3JP
United Kingdom
(UK) 01386 554790
Fax: (UK) 01386 554801
URL: http://www.alpinegardensoc.demon.co.uk/index.html#AGS

American Begonia Society (ABS)
157 Monument Rd.
Rio Dell, CA 95562-1617 USA
(707) 764-5407
Fax: (707) 764-5407

American Community Gardening Association (ACGA)
100 N. 20th St., 5th. Fl.
Philadelphia, PA 19103-1495 USA
(215) 988-8785
Fax: (215) 988-8810
E-mail: sallymcc@libertynet.org
URL: http://www.ag.arizona.edu/bradleyl/acga/main-frm.htm

American Daffodil Society (ADS)
1686 Grey Fox Trails
Milford, OH 45150 USA

(513) 248-9137
Fax: (513) 248-0898
E-mail: daffmlg@aol.com
URL: http://www.mc.edu/~adswww

American Dahlia Society (ADS)
c/o S. McQuithy Boyer
16816 CR 10
Bristol, IN 46507 USA
(219) 848-4888
E-mail: manorsam@aol.com
URL: http://www.dahlia.com/guide/index.html

American Fuchsia Society (AFS)
San Francisco County Fair Bldg.
9th Ave. & Lincoln Way
San Francisco, CA 94122 USA
(408) 257-0752
E-mail: sydnor@ix.netcom.com
URL: http://members.aol.com/amfuchsia/fuchs.as

American Gloxinia and Gesneriad Society (AGGS)
c/o Jessie Crisafulli
290 Federal St.
Belchertown, MA 01007 USA
(413) 323-6661
URL: http://aggs.org

American Hibiscus Society (AHS)
P.O. Drawer 321540
Cocoa Beach, FL 32932-1540 USA
(407) 783-2576
Fax: (407) 783-2576

American Horticultural Society (AHS)
7931 E. Boulevard Dr.
Alexandria, VA 22308 USA
(703) 768-5700
Toll-Free: 800-777-7931
Fax: (703) 768-8700
E-mail: gardenahs@aol.com
URL: http://www.ahs.org

American Hosta Society (AHS)
9448 Mayfield Rd.
Chesterland, OH 44026 USA

American Iris Society (AIS)
8426 Vinevalley Dr.

Sun Valley, CA 91352 USA
(818) 767-5512
Fax: (818) 767-8513

American Ivy Society (AIS)
P.O. Box 2123
Naples, FL 34106-2123 USA
(937) 862-4700, (941) 261-0388
Fax: (941) 261-8984
E-mail: 103630.3722@compuserve.com
URL: http://www.ivy.org

American Peony Society (APS)
250 Interlachen Rd.
Hopkins, MN 55343 USA
(612) 938-4706

American Primrose Society (APS)
41801 SW Burgarsky Rd.
Gaston, OR 97119-9407 USA
(503) 985-9596
URL: http://www.eskimo.com/~mcalpin/aps.html

American Rhododendron Society (ARS)
11 Pinecrest Dr.
Fortuna, CA 95540 USA
(707) 725-3043
URL: http://www.rhododendron.org/start.cfm

American Rose Society (ARS)
P.O. Box 30000
Shreveport, LA 71130-0030 USA
(318) 938-5402
Fax: (318) 938-5405
E-mail: ars@ars-hq.org
URL: http://www.ars.org

Azalea Society of America (ASA)
c/o Mrs. William Lorenz
P.O. Box 34536
West Bethesda, MD 20827-0536 USA
(703) 323-0114

Bonsai Clubs International (BCI)
P.O. Box 1176
Brookfield, WI 53008-1176 USA
(414) 860-8807
Fax: (414) 641-0757

E-mail: bonsairmt@aol.com
URL: http://www.bonsai-bci.com

Bromeliad Society (BSI)
c/o Carolyn Schoenau
P.O. Box 12981
Gainesville, FL 32604-0981 USA
(352) 372-6589
Fax: (352) 372-8823
E-mail: bsi@nervm.nerdc.ufl.edu

Cactus and Succulent Society of America (CSSA)
c/o Seymour Linden
1535 Reeves St.
Los Angeles, CA 90035 USA
(310) 556-1923
Fax: (310) 286-9629
E-mail: u4bia@aol.com
URL: http://www.cactus-mall.com/cssa

Cymbidium Society of America (CSA)
c/o Paula Butler
P.O. Box 2244
Orange, CA 92669 USA
(714) 532-4719
Fax: (714) 532-3611

Dynamics International Gardening Association (DIGA)
Drawer 1165
Asheboro, NC 27204-1165 USA

Epiphyllum Society of America (ESA)
P.O. Box 1395
Monrovia, CA 91017 USA
(310) 670-8148

Garden Club of America (GCA)
598 Madison Ave.
New York, NY 10022 USA
(212) 753-8287
Fax: (212) 753-0134

Garden Writers Association of America (GWAA)
c/o Robert C. LaGasse
10210 Leatherleaf Ct.
Manassas, VA 22111 USA
(703) 257-1032
Fax: (703) 257-0213
URL: http://www.hygexpo.com/gwaa

Gardeners of America (GOA)
5560 Merle Hay Rd.
P.O. Box 241
Johnston, IA 50131-0241 USA
(515) 278-0295
Fax: (515) 278-6245

Gardenia Society of America (GSA)
P.O. Box 879
Atwater, CA 95301 USA
(209) 358-2231

Heritage Rose Foundation
1512 Gorman St.
Raleigh, NC 27606-2919 USA
(919) 834-2591
E-mail: rosefoun@aol.com

Heritage Roses Group (HRG)
R.D. 1, Box 299
Clinton Corners, NY 12514 USA
(914) 266-3562

Hobby Greenhouse Association (HGA)
8 Glen Ter.
Bedford, MA 01730-2048 USA
(617) 275-0377
Fax: (617) 275-5693
E-mail: jhale@world.std.com
URL: http://www.hortsoft.com/hga.html

Indoor Gardening Society of America (IGSA)
944 S. Munroe Rd.
Tallmadge, OH 44278-3363 USA
(212) 666-5522

International Geranium Society (IGS)
P.O. Box 92734
Pasadena, CA 91109-2734 USA
(619) 727-0309
Fax: (818) 908-8867

International Lilac Society (ILS)
9500 Sperry Rd.
Kirtland, OH 44094 USA
(216) 946-4400
Fax: (216) 256-1655

International Oleander Society (IOS)
P.O. Box 3431

Galveston, TX 77552-0431 USA
(409) 762-9334

International Water Lily Society (IWLS)
1401 Johnson Ferry Rd.
Ste. 328 G, No. 12
Marietta, GA 30062 USA
(770) 977-3564

Los Angeles International Fern Society (LAIFS)
P.O. Box 90943
Pasadena, CA 91109 USA
(818) 441-3148, (310) 803-6887

Median Iris Society (MIS)
682 Huntley Heights Dr.
Ballwin, MO 63021 USA

National Council of State Garden Clubs (NCSGC)
4401 Magnolia Ave.
St. Louis, MO 63110-3492 USA
(314) 776-7574
Fax: (314) 776-5108

National Fuchsia Society (NFS)
c/o Rietkerk's
11507 E. 187th St.
Artesia, CA 90701 USA

National Gardening Association (NGA)
180 Flynn Ave.
Burlington, VT 05401 USA
(802) 863-1308
Fax: (802) 863-5962

North American Fruit Explorers (NAFEX)
1716 Apples Rd.
Chapin, IL 62628 USA
(217) 245-7589
URL: http://www.nafex.org

North American Gladiolus Council (NAGC)
c/o Eugene Demer
2624 Spurgin Rd.
Missoula, MT 59801 USA
(406) 728-7871

North American Heather Society (NAHS)
c/o Karla Lortz
E. 502 Haskel Hill Rd.

Shelton, WA 98584 USA
(360) 427-5318
Fax: (360) 427-5318
E-mail: heaths@gte.net
URL: http://www.humbold1.com/heathers

North American Lily Society (NALS)
P.O. Box 272
Owatonna, MN 55060 USA
(507) 451-2170
E-mail: nats@ll.net
URL: http://www.lilies.org

North American Rock Garden Society (NARGS)
c/o Jacques Mommens
P.O. Box 67
Millwood, NY 10546 USA
(914) 762-2948
E-mail: mommens@ibm.net
URL: http://www.nargs.org

Pacific Orchid Society of Hawaii (POS)
c/o Doug B. Schafer
1778 Hoolana St.
Pearl City, HI 96782 USA
(808) 455-7541

Plumeria Society of America (PSA)
P.O. Box 22791
Houston, TX 77227-2791 USA
(713) 780-8326

Reblooming Iris Society (RIS)
4 Marland Ave.
Towsonton, MD 21286 USA
(410) 337-9118

Rose Hybridizers Association (RHA)
21 S. Wheaton Rd.
Horseheads, NY 14845-1077 USA
(607) 562-8592
E-mail: lpeterso@stny.lrun.com

Seed Savers Exchange (SSE)
3076 N. Winn Rd.
Decorah, IA 52101 USA
(319) 382-5990
Fax: (319) 382-5872

Society for Japanese Irises (SJI)
9823 E. Michigan Ave.
Galesburg, MI 49053 USA
(616) 665-7500

Society for Louisiana Irises (SLI)
Box 40175
University of Southwestern Louisiana
Lafayette, LA 70504 USA
(318) 856-5859

Society for Pacific Coast Native Irises (SPCNI)
4333 Oak Hill Rd.
Oakland, CA 94605 USA
(510) 638-0658

Society for Siberian Irises (SSI)
c/o Ruth Wilder
802 Camellia Dr.
Anderson, SC 29625 USA
(803) 224-6966

Species Iris Group of North America (SIGNA)
c/o Richard Kiyomoto
486 Skiff St.
North Haven, CT 06473 USA
(203) 789-7238

Catalogs

Appalachian Gardens
Box 82
Waynesboro, PA 17268-0082
(717) 762-4312
Fax: (717) 762-7532

Autum Glade Botanicals
46857 W. Ann Arbor Trail
Plymouth, MI 48170
Fax: (313) 459-2604

Bently Seeds, Inc.
16 Railroad Avenue
Cambridge, NY 12816
(518) 677-2603
Fax: (518) 677-5676

Berlin Seeds / Raker's Greenhouse and Nursery
5371 County Road 77

Millersburg, OH 44654
(216) 893-2811

Bluestone Perennials
7211 Middle Ridge Rd.
Madison, OH 44057
(216) 428-7535
Fax: (216) 428-7198

Bovees Nursery
1737 S.W. Coronado
Portland, OR 97219
(503) 244-9341

Brittingham Plant Farms
P.O. Box 2538
Salisbury, MD 21802
(410) 749-5153
Fax: (800) 749-5148

The Bulb Crate
2560 Deerfield Rd.
Riverwoods, IL 60015
(708) 317-1414

W. Atlee Burpee & Co.
300 Park Ave.
Warminster, PA 18991-0001
(800) 888-1447

Carroll Gardens
P.O. Box 310
4444 E. Main St.
Westminster, MD 21158
(800) 638-6334

The Cook's Garden
P.O. Box 535
Londonderry, VT 05148
(802) 824-3400
Fax: (802) 824-3027

DeGiorgi Seed Company
6011 "N" St.
Omaha, NE 68117-1634
(402) 731-3901
Fax: (402) 731-8475

Earl May Seed Company
208 North Elm Street

Shanandoah, IA 51603-0099
(712) 246-1020

Farmer Seed & Nursery
P.O. Box 129
818 NW 4th St.
Fairbault, MN 55021
(507) 334-1623

Forest Farm
990 Tetherow Rd.
Williams, OR 97554-9599
(503) 846-6963

Gallina Canyon Ranch
P.O. Box 706
Abiquiu, NM 87510
(505) 685-4888
Fax: (505) 685-4888

Gardener's Eden
P.O. Box 7307
San Francisco, CA 94120-7307
(800) 822-9600

Gardener's Supply Company
128 Intervale Rd.
Burlington, VT 05401-2850
(802) 660-4600
Fax: (802) 660-4600

Gardens Alive!
5100 Schenley Pl.
Lawrenceburg, IN 47025
(812) 537-8650
Fax: (812) 537-8660

The Gourmet Gardener
8650 College Blvd., Suite 2051N
Overland Park, KS 66210-1806
(913) 345-0490

Greer Gardens
1280 Goodpasture Rd.
Eugene, OR 97401-1794
(503) 686-8266
Fax: (503) 686-8266

Gurney's Seed & Nursery Co.
110 Capital St.

Yankton, SD 57079
(605) 665-1671

Henry Field's Heritage Gardens
1 Meadow Ridge Rd.
Shenandoah, IA 51601-0700
(605) 665-5188

Iris City Gardens
502 Brighton Place
Nashville, TN 37205-2556
(615) 386-3778

Jackson & Perkins
1 Rose Lane
Medford, OR 97501-0701
(800) 292-GROW

Johnny's Select Seeds
Foss Hill Road
Albion, ME 04910-9731
(207) 437-4301
Fax: (207) 437-2165

Judy's Perennials
1206 Maple Ave.
Downers Grove, IL 60615
(708) 969-6514

J. W. Jung Seed Co.
335 S. High Street
Rondolf, WI 53956

Klehm Nursery
Route 5, Box 197 Penny Rd.
South Barrington, IL 60010-9555
(800) 553-3715

The Landis Valley Museum
2451 Kissel Hill Rd.
Lancaster, PA 17601
(717) 569-0401

Langenbach Fine Tool Co.
P.O. Box 453
Blairstown, NJ 07825
(800) 362-1991
Fax: (201) 383-0844

Laurie's Landscape

2959 Hobson Rd.

Downers Grove, IL 60517
(708) 969-1270

Le Jardin du Gourmet
P.O. Box 75
St. Johnsbury Center, VT 05863-0075
(800) 659-1446
Fax: (802) 748-9592

Lee Gardens
Box 5
Tremont, IL 61568
(309) 925-5262

A.M. Leonard
P.O. Box 816
6665 Spiker Rd.
Piqua, OH 45356-0816
(800) 543-8955, (513) 773-2696

Liberty Seed Company
P.O. Box 806
New Philadelphia, OH 44663
(800) 541-6022
Fax: (216) 364-6415

Mellinger's
2310 W. South Range Road
North Lima, OH 44452-9731
(216) 549-9861

Milaeger's Gardens
4838 Douglas Ave
Racine, WI 53402-2498
(414) 639-2371

The Natural Gardening Company
217 San Anselmo Ave.
San Anselmo, CA 94960
(415) 456-5060
Fax: (415) 721-0642

The Natural Garden
38 W443 Highway 64
St. Charles, IL 60174
(708) 584-0150

Nich Gardens
1111 Dawson Rd.

Chapel Hill, NC 27516
(919) 967-0078

Nichols Garden Nursery
1190 North Pacific Highway
Albany, OR 97321-4580
(503) 928-9280
Fax: (503) 967-8406

Nor'East Miniature Roses, Inc.
P.O. Box 307
Rowley, MA 019696
(508) 948-7964
Fax: (508) 948-5487

Park Seed Company
P.O. Box 46
Highway 254 North Cokesbury Road
Greennwood, SC 29647-0001
(803) 223-7333

Pinetree Garden Seeds
Box 300
New Glouchester, ME 04260
(207) 926-3400
Fax: (207) 926-3886

The Propagators Private Stock
8805 Kemman Rd.
Hebron, IL 60034

Riverhead Perennials
5 Riverhead Lane
East Lyme, CT 06333
(203) 437-7828

Roslyn Nursery
211 Burrs Lane
Dix Hills, NY 11746
(516) 643-9347

Seeds of Change
P.O. Box 15700
Santa Fe, NM 87506-5700
(505) 438-8080
Fax: (505) 438-7052

Seed Savers Exchange
3076 North Winn Rd.
Decorah, IA 52101

Sequoia Nursery
2519 E. Noble Ave.
Visalia, CA 93292
(209) 732-0190
Fax: (209) 732-0192

Sheffield's Seed Company, Inc.
273 Auburn Road, Route 34
Locke, NY 13092
(315) 497-1058

Shephard's Garden Seeds
30 Irene St.
Torrington, CT 06790-6627
(203) 482-3638
Fax: (203) 482-0532

R.H. Shumways
P.O. Box 1
Graniteville, SC 29829-0001
(803) 663-9771

Silver Creek Supply, Inc.
R.D. #1, Box 70
Port Trevorton, PA 17864
(717) 374-8010

Smith & Hawken
117 E. Strawberry Dr.
Mill Valley. CA 94941
(800) 776-3336

Southern Perennials and Herbs
98 Bridges Rd.
Tylertown, MS 39667
Fax: (601) 684-3729
E-Mail: sph@neosoft.com

Spring Hill Nurseries
6523 N. Galena Road, P.O. Box 1758
Peoria, IL 61651-9968

Springvale Farm Nursery, Inc.
Moxier Hollow Rd.
Hamburg, IL 62054
(618) 232-1108

Stark Bros. Nurseries and Orchards Co.
P.O. Box 10
Louisiana, MO 63353-0010

Sunrise Enterprises
P.O. Box 330058
West Hartford, CT 06133-0058
(203) 666-8071
Fax: (203) 665-8156

Surry Gardens
P.O. Box 145
Surry, ME 04684
(207) 667-4493

Thompson & Morgan
P.O. Box 1308
Jackson, NJ 08527
(800) 363-2225
Fax: (908) 363-9356

Totally Tomatoes
P.O. Box 1626
Augusta, GA 30903-1626
(803) 663-0016
Fax: (803) 663-9772

Trees on the Move
P.O. Box 462
Cranbury, NJ 08512
(609) 395-1366

Tripple Brook Farm
37 Middle Road
Southhampton, MA 01073
(413) 527-4626

TyTy Plantations
P.O. Box 159
TyTy, GA 31759
(912) 382-0400

Vermont Bean Seed Co.
Garden Ln.
Fair Haven, VT 05743
(802) 273-3400
Fax: (803) 663-9772

Wayside Gardens
1 Garden Lane
Hodges, SC 29695-0001
800) 845-1124

Weiss Brothers Nursery
11690 Colifax Highway
Grass Valley, CA 95945
(916) 272-7657

White Flower Farm
P.O. Box 50
Litchfield, CT 06759-0050
(800) 503-9624
Fax: (860) 496-1418

White Oak Nursery
6145 Oak Court
Peoria, IL 61614
(309) 693-1354

Wildseed Farms
1101 Campo Rosa Rd., P.O. Box 308
Eagle Lake, TX 77434
(800) 848-0078
Fax: (409) 234-7407

Willhite Seed Incorporated
P.O. Box 23
Poolville, TX 76487
(800) 828-1840
Fax: (817) 599-5843

Winterthur Museum And Gardens
Winterthur, DE 19735
(800) 767-0500

Wood Prairie Farm
RFD 1, Box 64
Bridgwater, ME 04735-9989
(800) 829-9765
Fax: (800) 829-6494

Worms Way Indoor/Outdoor Garden Supply
4620 South State Road
Bloomington, IN 47401
(812) 876-6446

Wrenwood of Berkeley Springs
Route 4, Box 361
Berkeley Springs, WV 25411
(304) 258-3071

Index

313

JANUARY

What's appearing or blooming indoors or out?

_____ _____
_____ _____
_____ _____
_____ _____

What insect or disease problems are appearing?

_____ _____
_____ _____
_____ _____

Record steps taken to remedy insect/disease problems:

_____ _____
_____ _____
_____ _____

Task list for this month: _____
_____
_____
_____
_____

Plants to buy: _____
_____
_____
_____

Other: _____
_____
_____
_____

Weather observations:

Date _____ Date _____ Date _____ Date _____
Rainfall _____ Rainfall _____ Rainfall _____ Rainfall _____
Avg Temp _____ Avg Temp _____ Avg Temp _____ Avg Temp _____

Date _____ Date _____ Date _____ Date _____
Rainfall _____ Rainfall _____ Rainfall _____ Rainfall _____
Avg Temp _____ Avg Temp _____ Avg Temp _____ Avg Temp _____

Date _____ Date _____ Date _____ Date _____
Rainfall _____ Rainfall _____ Rainfall _____ Rainfall _____
Avg Temp _____ Avg Temp _____ Avg Temp _____ Avg Temp _____

Date _____ Date _____ Date _____ Date _____
Rainfall _____ Rainfall _____ Rainfall _____ Rainfall _____
Avg Temp _____ Avg Temp _____ Avg Temp _____ Avg Temp _____

Date _____ Date _____ Date _____ Date _____
Rainfall _____ Rainfall _____ Rainfall _____ Rainfall _____
Avg Temp _____ Avg Temp _____ Avg Temp _____ Avg Temp _____

Date _____ Date _____ Date _____ Date _____
Rainfall _____ Rainfall _____ Rainfall _____ Rainfall _____
Avg Temp _____ Avg Temp _____ Avg Temp _____ Avg Temp _____

Date _____ Date _____ Date _____ Date _____
Rainfall _____ Rainfall _____ Rainfall _____ Rainfall _____
Avg Temp _____ Avg Temp _____ Avg Temp _____ Avg Temp _____

Date _____ Date _____ Date _____
Rainfall _____ Rainfall _____ Rainfall _____
Avg Temp _____ Avg Temp _____ Avg Temp _____

Planning (things to change next month or next year): _____
_____
_____
_____
_____
_____
_____
_____
_____

331

FEBRUARY

Date: _____

What's appearing or blooming indoors or out?

_____   _____
_____   _____
_____   _____
_____   _____

What insect or disease problems are appearing?

_____   _____
_____   _____
_____   _____

Record steps taken to remedy insect/disease problems:

_____   _____
_____   _____
_____   _____

Task list for this month:_____

_____
_____
_____
_____

Plants to buy: _____

_____
_____
_____

Other: _____

_____
_____
_____

Weather observations:

Date _____ Date _____ Date _____ Date _____
Rainfall _____ Rainfall _____ Rainfall _____ Rainfall _____
Avg Temp _____ Avg Temp _____ Avg Temp _____ Avg Temp _____

Date _____ Date _____ Date _____ Date _____
Rainfall _____ Rainfall _____ Rainfall _____ Rainfall _____
Avg Temp _____ Avg Temp _____ Avg Temp _____ Avg Temp _____

Date _____ Date _____ Date _____ Date _____
Rainfall _____ Rainfall _____ Rainfall _____ Rainfall _____
Avg Temp _____ Avg Temp _____ Avg Temp _____ Avg Temp _____

Date _____ Date _____ Date _____ Date _____
Rainfall _____ Rainfall _____ Rainfall _____ Rainfall _____
Avg Temp _____ Avg Temp _____ Avg Temp _____ Avg Temp _____

Date _____ Date _____ Date _____ Date _____
Rainfall _____ Rainfall _____ Rainfall _____ Rainfall _____
Avg Temp _____ Avg Temp _____ Avg Temp _____ Avg Temp _____

Date _____ Date _____ Date _____ Date _____
Rainfall _____ Rainfall _____ Rainfall _____ Rainfall _____
Avg Temp _____ Avg Temp _____ Avg Temp _____ Avg Temp _____

Date _____ Date _____ Date _____ Date _____
Rainfall _____ Rainfall _____ Rainfall _____ Rainfall _____
Avg Temp _____ Avg Temp _____ Avg Temp _____ Avg Temp _____

Date _____ Date _____ Date _____
Rainfall _____ Rainfall _____ Rainfall _____
Avg Temp _____ Avg Temp _____ Avg Temp _____

Planning (things to change next month or next year): _____

_____

_____

_____

_____

_____

_____

_____

MARCH

What's appearing or blooming indoors or out?

Date: _____

_____ _____
_____ _____
_____ _____
_____ _____

What insect or disease problems are appearing?

_____ _____
_____ _____
_____ _____

Record steps taken to remedy insect/disease problems:

_____ _____
_____ _____
_____ _____

Task list for this month:_____

_____
_____
_____
_____

Plants to buy: _____

_____
_____
_____

Other: _____

_____
_____
_____

Weather observations:

Date _____ Date _____ Date _____ Date _____
Rainfall _____ Rainfall _____ Rainfall _____ Rainfall _____
Avg Temp _____ Avg Temp _____ Avg Temp _____ Avg Temp _____

Date _____ Date _____ Date _____ Date _____
Rainfall _____ Rainfall _____ Rainfall _____ Rainfall _____
Avg Temp _____ Avg Temp _____ Avg Temp _____ Avg Temp _____

Date _____ Date _____ Date _____ Date _____
Rainfall _____ Rainfall _____ Rainfall _____ Rainfall _____
Avg Temp _____ Avg Temp _____ Avg Temp _____ Avg Temp _____

Date _____ Date _____ Date _____ Date _____
Rainfall _____ Rainfall _____ Rainfall _____ Rainfall _____
Avg Temp _____ Avg Temp _____ Avg Temp _____ Avg Temp _____

Date _____ Date _____ Date _____ Date _____
Rainfall _____ Rainfall _____ Rainfall _____ Rainfall _____
Avg Temp _____ Avg Temp _____ Avg Temp _____ Avg Temp _____

Date _____ Date _____ Date _____ Date _____
Rainfall _____ Rainfall _____ Rainfall _____ Rainfall _____
Avg Temp _____ Avg Temp _____ Avg Temp _____ Avg Temp _____

Date _____ Date _____ Date _____ Date _____
Rainfall _____ Rainfall _____ Rainfall _____ Rainfall _____
Avg Temp _____ Avg Temp _____ Avg Temp _____ Avg Temp _____

Date _____ Date _____ Date _____
Rainfall _____ Rainfall _____ Rainfall _____
Avg Temp _____ Avg Temp _____ Avg Temp _____

Planning (things to change next month or next year): _____
_____
_____
_____
_____
_____
_____
_____
_____
_____

APRIL

Date: _____

What's appearing or blooming indoors or out?

_____   _____
_____   _____
_____   _____
_____   _____

What insect or disease problems are appearing?

_____   _____
_____   _____
_____   _____

Record steps taken to remedy insect/disease problems:

_____   _____
_____   _____
_____   _____

Task list for this month:_____

_____
_____
_____
_____

Plants to buy: _____

_____
_____
_____

Other: _____

_____
_____
_____

Weather observations:

Date _____ Date _____ Date _____ Date _____
Rainfall _____ Rainfall _____ Rainfall _____ Rainfall _____
Avg Temp _____ Avg Temp _____ Avg Temp _____ Avg Temp _____

Date _____ Date _____ Date _____ Date _____
Rainfall _____ Rainfall _____ Rainfall _____ Rainfall _____
Avg Temp _____ Avg Temp _____ Avg Temp _____ Avg Temp _____

Date _____ Date _____ Date _____ Date _____
Rainfall _____ Rainfall _____ Rainfall _____ Rainfall _____
Avg Temp _____ Avg Temp _____ Avg Temp _____ Avg Temp _____

Date _____ Date _____ Date _____ Date _____
Rainfall _____ Rainfall _____ Rainfall _____ Rainfall _____
Avg Temp _____ Avg Temp _____ Avg Temp _____ Avg Temp _____

Date _____ Date _____ Date _____ Date _____
Rainfall _____ Rainfall _____ Rainfall _____ Rainfall _____
Avg Temp _____ Avg Temp _____ Avg Temp _____ Avg Temp _____

Date _____ Date _____ Date _____ Date _____
Rainfall _____ Rainfall _____ Rainfall _____ Rainfall _____
Avg Temp _____ Avg Temp _____ Avg Temp _____ Avg Temp _____

Date _____ Date _____ Date _____ Date _____
Rainfall _____ Rainfall _____ Rainfall _____ Rainfall _____
Avg Temp _____ Avg Temp _____ Avg Temp _____ Avg Temp _____

Date _____ Date _____ Date _____
Rainfall _____ Rainfall _____ Rainfall _____
Avg Temp _____ Avg Temp _____ Avg Temp _____

Planning (things to change next month or next year): _____
_____
_____
_____
_____
_____
_____
_____
_____

MAY

What's appearing or blooming indoors or out?

_____   _____
_____   _____
_____   _____
_____   _____

What insect or disease problems are appearing?

_____   _____
_____   _____
_____   _____

Record steps taken to remedy insect/disease problems:

_____   _____
_____   _____
_____   _____

Task list for this month:_____
_____
_____
_____
_____

Plants to buy: _____
_____
_____
_____

Other: _____
_____
_____
_____

338

Weather observations:

Date _____
Rainfall _____
Avg Temp _____

Date _____
Rainfall _____
Avg Temp _____

Date _____
Rainfall _____
Avg Temp _____

Date _____
Rainfall _____
Avg Temp _____

Date _____
Rainfall _____
Avg Temp _____

Date _____
Rainfall _____
Avg Temp _____

Date _____
Rainfall _____
Avg Temp _____

Date _____
Rainfall _____
Avg Temp _____

Date _____
Rainfall _____
Avg Temp _____

Date _____
Rainfall _____
Avg Temp _____

Date _____
Rainfall _____
Avg Temp _____

Date _____
Rainfall _____
Avg Temp _____

Date _____
Rainfall _____
Avg Temp _____

Date _____
Rainfall _____
Avg Temp _____

Date _____
Rainfall _____
Avg Temp _____

Date _____
Rainfall _____
Avg Temp _____

Date _____
Rainfall _____
Avg Temp _____

Date _____
Rainfall _____
Avg Temp _____

Date _____
Rainfall _____
Avg Temp _____

Date _____
Rainfall _____
Avg Temp _____

Date _____
Rainfall _____
Avg Temp _____

Date _____
Rainfall _____
Avg Temp _____

Date _____
Rainfall _____
Avg Temp _____

Date _____
Rainfall _____
Avg Temp _____

Date _____
Rainfall _____
Avg Temp _____

Date _____
Rainfall _____
Avg Temp _____

Date _____
Rainfall _____
Avg Temp _____

Date _____
Rainfall _____
Avg Temp _____

Date _____
Rainfall _____
Avg Temp _____

Date _____
Rainfall _____
Avg Temp _____

Date _____
Rainfall _____
Avg Temp _____

Planning (things to change next month or next year): _____

_____

_____

_____

_____

_____

_____

_____

_____

JUNE

What's appearing or blooming indoors or out?

_____ _____
_____ _____
_____ _____
_____ _____

What insect or disease problems are appearing?

_____ _____
_____ _____
_____ _____

Record steps taken to remedy insect/disease problems:

_____ _____
_____ _____
_____ _____

Task list for this month:_____

_____
_____
_____
_____

Plants to buy: _____

_____
_____
_____

Other: _____

_____
_____
_____

340

Weather observations:

Date _____	Date _____	Date _____	Date _____
Rainfall _____	Rainfall _____	Rainfall _____	Rainfall _____
Avg Temp _____	Avg Temp _____	Avg Temp _____	Avg Temp _____
Date _____	Date _____	Date _____	Date _____
Rainfall _____	Rainfall _____	Rainfall _____	Rainfall _____
Avg Temp _____	Avg Temp _____	Avg Temp _____	Avg Temp _____
Date _____	Date _____	Date _____	Date _____
Rainfall _____	Rainfall _____	Rainfall _____	Rainfall _____
Avg Temp _____	Avg Temp _____	Avg Temp _____	Avg Temp _____
Date _____	Date _____	Date _____	Date _____
Rainfall _____	Rainfall _____	Rainfall _____	Rainfall _____
Avg Temp _____	Avg Temp _____	Avg Temp _____	Avg Temp _____
Date _____	Date _____	Date _____	Date _____
Rainfall _____	Rainfall _____	Rainfall _____	Rainfall _____
Avg Temp _____	Avg Temp _____	Avg Temp _____	Avg Temp _____
Date _____	Date _____	Date _____	Date _____
Rainfall _____	Rainfall _____	Rainfall _____	Rainfall _____
Avg Temp _____	Avg Temp _____	Avg Temp _____	Avg Temp _____
Date _____	Date _____	Date _____	Date _____
Rainfall _____	Rainfall _____	Rainfall _____	Rainfall _____
Avg Temp _____	Avg Temp _____	Avg Temp _____	Avg Temp _____
Date _____	Date _____	Date _____	
Rainfall _____	Rainfall _____	Rainfall _____	
Avg Temp _____	Avg Temp _____	Avg Temp _____	

Planning (things to change next month or next year): _____
_____
_____
_____
_____
_____
_____
_____
_____

JULY

What's appearing or blooming indoors or out?

_____ _____
_____ _____
_____ _____
_____ _____

What insect or disease problems are appearing?

_____ _____
_____ _____
_____ _____

Record steps taken to remedy insect/disease problems:

_____ _____
_____ _____
_____ _____

Task list for this month:_____
_____
_____
_____
_____

Plants to buy: _____
_____
_____
_____

Other: _____
_____
_____
_____

342

Weather observations:

Date _____ Date _____ Date _____ Date _____
Rainfall _____ Rainfall _____ Rainfall _____ Rainfall _____
Avg Temp _____ Avg Temp _____ Avg Temp _____ Avg Temp _____

Date _____ Date _____ Date _____ Date _____
Rainfall _____ Rainfall _____ Rainfall _____ Rainfall _____
Avg Temp _____ Avg Temp _____ Avg Temp _____ Avg Temp _____

Date _____ Date _____ Date _____ Date _____
Rainfall _____ Rainfall _____ Rainfall _____ Rainfall _____
Avg Temp _____ Avg Temp _____ Avg Temp _____ Avg Temp _____

Date _____ Date _____ Date _____ Date _____
Rainfall _____ Rainfall _____ Rainfall _____ Rainfall _____
Avg Temp _____ Avg Temp _____ Avg Temp _____ Avg Temp _____

Date _____ Date _____ Date _____ Date _____
Rainfall _____ Rainfall _____ Rainfall _____ Rainfall _____
Avg Temp _____ Avg Temp _____ Avg Temp _____ Avg Temp _____

Date _____ Date _____ Date _____ Date _____
Rainfall _____ Rainfall _____ Rainfall _____ Rainfall _____
Avg Temp _____ Avg Temp _____ Avg Temp _____ Avg Temp _____

Date _____ Date _____ Date _____ Date _____
Rainfall _____ Rainfall _____ Rainfall _____ Rainfall _____
Avg Temp _____ Avg Temp _____ Avg Temp _____ Avg Temp _____

Date _____ Date _____ Date _____
Rainfall _____ Rainfall _____ Rainfall _____
Avg Temp _____ Avg Temp _____ Avg Temp _____

Planning (things to change next month or next year): _____
_____
_____
_____
_____
_____
_____
_____

AUGUST

Date: _____

What's appearing or blooming indoors or out?

_____ _____
_____ _____
_____ _____
_____ _____

What insect or disease problems are appearing?

_____ _____
_____ _____
_____ _____

Record steps taken to remedy insect/disease problems:

_____ _____
_____ _____
_____ _____

Task list for this month:_____
_____
_____
_____
_____

Plants to buy: _____
_____
_____
_____

Other: _____
_____
_____
_____

344

Weather observations:

Date _____   Date _____   Date _____   Date _____
Rainfall _____   Rainfall _____   Rainfall _____   Rainfall _____
Avg Temp _____   Avg Temp _____   Avg Temp _____   Avg Temp _____

Date _____   Date _____   Date _____   Date _____
Rainfall _____   Rainfall _____   Rainfall _____   Rainfall _____
Avg Temp _____   Avg Temp _____   Avg Temp _____   Avg Temp _____

Date _____   Date _____   Date _____   Date _____
Rainfall _____   Rainfall _____   Rainfall _____   Rainfall _____
Avg Temp _____   Avg Temp _____   Avg Temp _____   Avg Temp _____

Date _____   Date _____   Date _____   Date _____
Rainfall _____   Rainfall _____   Rainfall _____   Rainfall _____
Avg Temp _____   Avg Temp _____   Avg Temp _____   Avg Temp _____

Date _____   Date _____   Date _____   Date _____
Rainfall _____   Rainfall _____   Rainfall _____   Rainfall _____
Avg Temp _____   Avg Temp _____   Avg Temp _____   Avg Temp _____

Date _____   Date _____   Date _____   Date _____
Rainfall _____   Rainfall _____   Rainfall _____   Rainfall _____
Avg Temp _____   Avg Temp _____   Avg Temp _____   Avg Temp _____

Date _____   Date _____   Date _____   Date _____
Rainfall _____   Rainfall _____   Rainfall _____   Rainfall _____
Avg Temp _____   Avg Temp _____   Avg Temp _____   Avg Temp _____

Date _____   Date _____   Date _____
Rainfall _____   Rainfall _____   Rainfall _____
Avg Temp _____   Avg Temp _____   Avg Temp _____

Planning (things to change next month or next year): _____
_____
_____
_____
_____
_____
_____
_____

SEPTEMBER

What's appearing or blooming indoors or out?

_____ _____

_____ _____

_____ _____

_____ _____

What insect or disease problems are appearing?

_____ _____

_____ _____

_____ _____

Record steps taken to remedy insect/disease problems:

_____ _____

_____ _____

_____ _____

Task list for this month:_____

_____

_____

_____

_____

Plants to buy: _____

_____

_____

_____

Other: _____

_____

_____

_____

346

Weather observations:

Date _____   Date _____   Date _____   Date _____
Rainfall _____   Rainfall _____   Rainfall _____   Rainfall _____
Avg Temp _____   Avg Temp _____   Avg Temp _____   Avg Temp _____

Date _____   Date _____   Date _____   Date _____
Rainfall _____   Rainfall _____   Rainfall _____   Rainfall _____
Avg Temp _____   Avg Temp _____   Avg Temp _____   Avg Temp _____

Date _____   Date _____   Date _____   Date _____
Rainfall _____   Rainfall _____   Rainfall _____   Rainfall _____
Avg Temp _____   Avg Temp _____   Avg Temp _____   Avg Temp _____

Date _____   Date _____   Date _____   Date _____
Rainfall _____   Rainfall _____   Rainfall _____   Rainfall _____
Avg Temp _____   Avg Temp _____   Avg Temp _____   Avg Temp _____

Date _____   Date _____   Date _____   Date _____
Rainfall _____   Rainfall _____   Rainfall _____   Rainfall _____
Avg Temp _____   Avg Temp _____   Avg Temp _____   Avg Temp _____

Date _____   Date _____   Date _____   Date _____
Rainfall _____   Rainfall _____   Rainfall _____   Rainfall _____
Avg Temp _____   Avg Temp _____   Avg Temp _____   Avg Temp _____

Date _____   Date _____   Date _____   Date _____
Rainfall _____   Rainfall _____   Rainfall _____   Rainfall _____
Avg Temp _____   Avg Temp _____   Avg Temp _____   Avg Temp _____

Date _____   Date _____   Date _____
Rainfall _____   Rainfall _____   Rainfall _____
Avg Temp _____   Avg Temp _____   Avg Temp _____

Planning (things to change next month or next year): _____

_____
_____
_____
_____
_____
_____
_____
_____

347

OCTOBER

What's appearing or blooming indoors or out?

_____   ___

_____   ___

_____   ___

_____   ___

What insect or disease problems are appearing?

_____   ___

_____   ___

_____   ___

Record steps taken to remedy insect/disease problems:

_____   ___

_____   ___

_____   ___

Task list for this month:_____

_____

_____

_____

_____

Plants to buy: _____

_____

_____

_____

Other: _____

_____

_____

_____

348

Weather observations:

Date _____   Date _____   Date _____   Date _____
Rainfall _____   Rainfall _____   Rainfall _____   Rainfall _____
Avg Temp _____   Avg Temp _____   Avg Temp _____   Avg Temp _____

Date _____   Date _____   Date _____   Date _____
Rainfall _____   Rainfall _____   Rainfall _____   Rainfall _____
Avg Temp _____   Avg Temp _____   Avg Temp _____   Avg Temp _____

Date _____   Date _____   Date _____   Date _____
Rainfall _____   Rainfall _____   Rainfall _____   Rainfall _____
Avg Temp _____   Avg Temp _____   Avg Temp _____   Avg Temp _____

Date _____   Date _____   Date _____   Date _____
Rainfall _____   Rainfall _____   Rainfall _____   Rainfall _____
Avg Temp _____   Avg Temp _____   Avg Temp _____   Avg Temp _____

Date _____   Date _____   Date _____   Date _____
Rainfall _____   Rainfall _____   Rainfall _____   Rainfall _____
Avg Temp _____   Avg Temp _____   Avg Temp _____   Avg Temp _____

Date _____   Date _____   Date _____   Date _____
Rainfall _____   Rainfall _____   Rainfall _____   Rainfall _____
Avg Temp _____   Avg Temp _____   Avg Temp _____   Avg Temp _____

Date _____   Date _____   Date _____   Date _____
Rainfall _____   Rainfall _____   Rainfall _____   Rainfall _____
Avg Temp _____   Avg Temp _____   Avg Temp _____   Avg Temp _____

Date _____   Date _____   Date _____
Rainfall _____   Rainfall _____   Rainfall _____
Avg Temp _____   Avg Temp _____   Avg Temp _____

Planning (things to change next month or next year): _____

_____

_____

_____

_____

_____

_____

_____

_____

NOVEMBER

What's appearing or blooming indoors or out?

_____ _____
_____ _____
_____ _____
_____ _____

What insect or disease problems are appearing?

_____ _____
_____ _____
_____ _____

Record steps taken to remedy insect/disease problems:

_____ _____
_____ _____
_____ _____

Task list for this month: _____
_____
_____
_____
_____

Plants to buy: _____
_____
_____
_____

Other: _____
_____
_____
_____

Weather observations:

Date _____   Date _____   Date _____   Date _____
Rainfall _____   Rainfall _____   Rainfall _____   Rainfall _____
Avg Temp _____   Avg Temp _____   Avg Temp _____   Avg Temp _____

Date _____   Date _____   Date _____   Date _____
Rainfall _____   Rainfall _____   Rainfall _____   Rainfall _____
Avg Temp _____   Avg Temp _____   Avg Temp _____   Avg Temp _____

Date _____   Date _____   Date _____   Date _____
Rainfall _____   Rainfall _____   Rainfall _____   Rainfall _____
Avg Temp _____   Avg Temp _____   Avg Temp _____   Avg Temp _____

Date _____   Date _____   Date _____   Date _____
Rainfall _____   Rainfall _____   Rainfall _____   Rainfall _____
Avg Temp _____   Avg Temp _____   Avg Temp _____   Avg Temp _____

Date _____   Date _____   Date _____   Date _____
Rainfall _____   Rainfall _____   Rainfall _____   Rainfall _____
Avg Temp _____   Avg Temp _____   Avg Temp _____   Avg Temp _____

Date _____   Date _____   Date _____   Date _____
Rainfall _____   Rainfall _____   Rainfall _____   Rainfall _____
Avg Temp _____   Avg Temp _____   Avg Temp _____   Avg Temp _____

Date _____   Date _____   Date _____   Date _____
Rainfall _____   Rainfall _____   Rainfall _____   Rainfall _____
Avg Temp _____   Avg Temp _____   Avg Temp _____   Avg Temp _____

Date _____   Date _____   Date _____
Rainfall _____   Rainfall _____   Rainfall _____
Avg Temp _____   Avg Temp _____   Avg Temp _____

Planning (things to change next month or next year): _____

_____

_____

_____

_____

_____

_____

_____

_____

DECEMBER

What's appearing or blooming indoors or out?

_____ ____
_____ ____
_____ ____
_____ ____

What insect or disease problems are appearing?

_____ ____
_____ ____
_____ ____

Record steps taken to remedy insect/disease problems:

_____ ____
_____ ____
_____ ____

Task list for this month:_____

_____
_____
_____
_____

Plants to buy: _____

_____
_____
_____

Other: _____

_____
_____
_____

Weather observations:

Date _____
Rainfall _____
Avg Temp _____

Date _____
Rainfall _____
Avg Temp _____

Date _____
Rainfall _____
Avg Temp _____

Date _____
Rainfall _____
Avg Temp _____

Date _____
Rainfall _____
Avg Temp _____

Date _____
Rainfall _____
Avg Temp _____

Date _____
Rainfall _____
Avg Temp _____

Date _____
Rainfall _____
Avg Temp _____

Date _____
Rainfall _____
Avg Temp _____

Date _____
Rainfall _____
Avg Temp _____

Date _____
Rainfall _____
Avg Temp _____

Date _____
Rainfall _____
Avg Temp _____

Date _____
Rainfall _____
Avg Temp _____

Date _____
Rainfall _____
Avg Temp _____

Date _____
Rainfall _____
Avg Temp _____

Date _____
Rainfall _____
Avg Temp _____

Date _____
Rainfall _____
Avg Temp _____

Date _____
Rainfall _____
Avg Temp _____

Date _____
Rainfall _____
Avg Temp _____

Date _____
Rainfall _____
Avg Temp _____

Date _____
Rainfall _____
Avg Temp _____

Date _____
Rainfall _____
Avg Temp _____

Date _____
Rainfall _____
Avg Temp _____

Date _____
Rainfall _____
Avg Temp _____

Date _____
Rainfall _____
Avg Temp _____

Date _____
Rainfall _____
Avg Temp _____

Date _____
Rainfall _____
Avg Temp _____

Date _____
Rainfall _____
Avg Temp _____

Date _____
Rainfall _____
Avg Temp _____

Date _____
Rainfall _____
Avg Temp _____

Date _____
Rainfall _____
Avg Temp _____

Planning (things to change next month or next year): _____

_____

_____

_____

_____

_____

_____

_____

_____

JANUARY

Date: _____

What's appearing or blooming indoors or out?

_____ _____
_____ _____
_____ _____
_____ _____

What insect or disease problems are appearing?

_____ _____
_____ _____
_____ _____

Record steps taken to remedy insect/disease problems:

_____ _____
_____ _____
_____ _____

Task list for this month:_____
_____
_____
_____
_____

Plants to buy: _____
_____
_____
_____

Other: _____
_____
_____
_____

Weather observations:

Date _____   Date _____   Date _____   Date _____
Rainfall _____   Rainfall _____   Rainfall _____   Rainfall _____
Avg Temp _____   Avg Temp _____   Avg Temp _____   Avg Temp _____

Date _____   Date _____   Date _____   Date _____
Rainfall _____   Rainfall _____   Rainfall _____   Rainfall _____
Avg Temp _____   Avg Temp _____   Avg Temp _____   Avg Temp _____

Date _____   Date _____   Date _____   Date _____
Rainfall _____   Rainfall _____   Rainfall _____   Rainfall _____
Avg Temp _____   Avg Temp _____   Avg Temp _____   Avg Temp _____

Date _____   Date _____   Date _____   Date _____
Rainfall _____   Rainfall _____   Rainfall _____   Rainfall _____
Avg Temp _____   Avg Temp _____   Avg Temp _____   Avg Temp _____

Date _____   Date _____   Date _____   Date _____
Rainfall _____   Rainfall _____   Rainfall _____   Rainfall _____
Avg Temp _____   Avg Temp _____   Avg Temp _____   Avg Temp _____

Date _____   Date _____   Date _____   Date _____
Rainfall _____   Rainfall _____   Rainfall _____   Rainfall _____
Avg Temp _____   Avg Temp _____   Avg Temp _____   Avg Temp _____

Date _____   Date _____   Date _____   Date _____
Rainfall _____   Rainfall _____   Rainfall _____   Rainfall _____
Avg Temp _____   Avg Temp _____   Avg Temp _____   Avg Temp _____

Date _____   Date _____   Date _____
Rainfall _____   Rainfall _____   Rainfall _____
Avg Temp _____   Avg Temp _____   Avg Temp _____

Planning (things to change next month or next year): _____
_____
_____
_____
_____
_____
_____
_____
_____

FEBRUARY

Date: _____

What's appearing or blooming indoors or out?

_____ _____

_____ _____

_____ _____

_____ _____

What insect or disease problems are appearing?

_____ _____

_____ _____

_____ _____

Record steps taken to remedy insect/disease problems:

_____ _____

_____ _____

_____ _____

Task list for this month:_____

_____

_____

_____

_____

Plants to buy: _____

_____

_____

_____

Other: _____

_____

_____

_____

356

Weather observations:

Date _____
Rainfall _____
Avg Temp _____

Date _____
Rainfall _____
Avg Temp _____

Date _____
Rainfall _____
Avg Temp _____

Date _____
Rainfall _____
Avg Temp _____

Date _____
Rainfall _____
Avg Temp _____

Date _____
Rainfall _____
Avg Temp _____

Date _____
Rainfall _____
Avg Temp _____

Date _____
Rainfall _____
Avg Temp _____

Date _____
Rainfall _____
Avg Temp _____

Date _____
Rainfall _____
Avg Temp _____

Date _____
Rainfall _____
Avg Temp _____

Date _____
Rainfall _____
Avg Temp _____

Date _____
Rainfall _____
Avg Temp _____

Date _____
Rainfall _____
Avg Temp _____

Date _____
Rainfall _____
Avg Temp _____

Date _____
Rainfall _____
Avg Temp _____

Date _____
Rainfall _____
Avg Temp _____

Date _____
Rainfall _____
Avg Temp _____

Date _____
Rainfall _____
Avg Temp _____

Date _____
Rainfall _____
Avg Temp _____

Date _____
Rainfall _____
Avg Temp _____

Date _____
Rainfall _____
Avg Temp _____

Date _____
Rainfall _____
Avg Temp _____

Date _____
Rainfall _____
Avg Temp _____

Date _____
Rainfall _____
Avg Temp _____

Date _____
Rainfall _____
Avg Temp _____

Date _____
Rainfall _____
Avg Temp _____

Date _____
Rainfall _____
Avg Temp _____

Date _____
Rainfall _____
Avg Temp _____

Date _____
Rainfall _____
Avg Temp _____

Planning (things to change next month or next year): _____
_____
_____
_____
_____
_____
_____
_____
_____

MARCH

What's appearing or blooming indoors or out?

_____ _____

_____ _____

_____ _____

_____ _____

What insect or disease problems are appearing?

_____ _____

_____ _____

_____ _____

Record steps taken to remedy insect/disease problems:

_____ _____

_____ _____

_____ _____

Task list for this month:_____

_____

_____

_____

_____

Plants to buy: _____

_____

_____

_____

Other: _____

_____

_____

_____

Weather observations:

Date _____ Date _____ Date _____ Date _____
Rainfall _____ Rainfall _____ Rainfall _____ Rainfall _____
Avg Temp _____ Avg Temp _____ Avg Temp _____ Avg Temp _____

Date _____ Date _____ Date _____ Date _____
Rainfall _____ Rainfall _____ Rainfall _____ Rainfall _____
Avg Temp _____ Avg Temp _____ Avg Temp _____ Avg Temp _____

Date _____ Date _____ Date _____ Date _____
Rainfall _____ Rainfall _____ Rainfall _____ Rainfall _____
Avg Temp _____ Avg Temp _____ Avg Temp _____ Avg Temp _____

Date _____ Date _____ Date _____ Date _____
Rainfall _____ Rainfall _____ Rainfall _____ Rainfall _____
Avg Temp _____ Avg Temp _____ Avg Temp _____ Avg Temp _____

Date _____ Date _____ Date _____ Date _____
Rainfall _____ Rainfall _____ Rainfall _____ Rainfall _____
Avg Temp _____ Avg Temp _____ Avg Temp _____ Avg Temp _____

Date _____ Date _____ Date _____ Date _____
Rainfall _____ Rainfall _____ Rainfall _____ Rainfall _____
Avg Temp _____ Avg Temp _____ Avg Temp _____ Avg Temp _____

Date _____ Date _____ Date _____ Date _____
Rainfall _____ Rainfall _____ Rainfall _____ Rainfall _____
Avg Temp _____ Avg Temp _____ Avg Temp _____ Avg Temp _____

Date _____ Date _____ Date _____
Rainfall _____ Rainfall _____ Rainfall _____
Avg Temp _____ Avg Temp _____ Avg Temp _____

Planning (things to change next month or next year): _____
_____
_____
_____
_____
_____
_____
_____
_____

APRIL

What's appearing or blooming indoors or out?

_____ _____

_____ _____

_____ _____

_____ _____

What insect or disease problems are appearing?

_____ _____

_____ _____

_____ _____

Record steps taken to remedy insect/disease problems:

_____ _____

_____ _____

_____ _____

Task list for this month:_____

_____

_____

_____

_____

Plants to buy: _____

_____

_____

_____

Other: _____

_____

_____

_____

Weather observations:

Date _____
Rainfall _____
Avg Temp _____

Date _____
Rainfall _____
Avg Temp _____

Date _____
Rainfall _____
Avg Temp _____

Date _____
Rainfall _____
Avg Temp _____

Date _____
Rainfall _____
Avg Temp _____

Date _____
Rainfall _____
Avg Temp _____

Date _____
Rainfall _____
Avg Temp _____

Date _____
Rainfall _____
Avg Temp _____

Date _____
Rainfall _____
Avg Temp _____

Date _____
Rainfall _____
Avg Temp _____

Date _____
Rainfall _____
Avg Temp _____

Date _____
Rainfall _____
Avg Temp _____

Date _____
Rainfall _____
Avg Temp _____

Date _____
Rainfall _____
Avg Temp _____

Date _____
Rainfall _____
Avg Temp _____

Date _____
Rainfall _____
Avg Temp _____

Date _____
Rainfall _____
Avg Temp _____

Date _____
Rainfall _____
Avg Temp _____

Date _____
Rainfall _____
Avg Temp _____

Date _____
Rainfall _____
Avg Temp _____

Date _____
Rainfall _____
Avg Temp _____

Date _____
Rainfall _____
Avg Temp _____

Date _____
Rainfall _____
Avg Temp _____

Date _____
Rainfall _____
Avg Temp _____

Date _____
Rainfall _____
Avg Temp _____

Date _____
Rainfall _____
Avg Temp _____

Date _____
Rainfall _____
Avg Temp _____

Date _____
Rainfall _____
Avg Temp _____

Date _____
Rainfall _____
Avg Temp _____

Date _____
Rainfall _____
Avg Temp _____

Date _____
Rainfall _____
Avg Temp _____

Planning (things to change next month or next year): _____

_____

_____

_____

_____

_____

_____

_____

_____

MAY

What's appearing or blooming indoors or out?

_____ _____
_____ _____
_____ _____
_____ _____

What insect or disease problems are appearing?

_____ _____
_____ _____
_____ _____

Record steps taken to remedy insect/disease problems:

_____ _____
_____ _____
_____ _____

Task list for this month:_____

_____
_____
_____
_____

Plants to buy: _____

_____
_____
_____

Other: _____

_____
_____
_____

Weather observations:

Date _____   Date _____   Date _____   Date _____
Rainfall _____   Rainfall _____   Rainfall _____   Rainfall _____
Avg Temp _____   Avg Temp _____   Avg Temp _____   Avg Temp _____

Date _____   Date _____   Date _____   Date _____
Rainfall _____   Rainfall _____   Rainfall _____   Rainfall _____
Avg Temp _____   Avg Temp _____   Avg Temp _____   Avg Temp _____

Date _____   Date _____   Date _____   Date _____
Rainfall _____   Rainfall _____   Rainfall _____   Rainfall _____
Avg Temp _____   Avg Temp _____   Avg Temp _____   Avg Temp _____

Date _____   Date _____   Date _____   Date _____
Rainfall _____   Rainfall _____   Rainfall _____   Rainfall _____
Avg Temp _____   Avg Temp _____   Avg Temp _____   Avg Temp _____

Date _____   Date _____   Date _____   Date _____
Rainfall _____   Rainfall _____   Rainfall _____   Rainfall _____
Avg Temp _____   Avg Temp _____   Avg Temp _____   Avg Temp _____

Date _____   Date _____   Date _____   Date _____
Rainfall _____   Rainfall _____   Rainfall _____   Rainfall _____
Avg Temp _____   Avg Temp _____   Avg Temp _____   Avg Temp _____

Date _____   Date _____   Date _____   Date _____
Rainfall _____   Rainfall _____   Rainfall _____   Rainfall _____
Avg Temp _____   Avg Temp _____   Avg Temp _____   Avg Temp _____

Date _____   Date _____   Date _____
Rainfall _____   Rainfall _____   Rainfall _____
Avg Temp _____   Avg Temp _____   Avg Temp _____

Planning (things to change next month or next year): _____
_____
_____
_____
_____
_____
_____
_____
_____

363

JUNE

Date: _____

What's appearing or blooming indoors or out?

_____ ____
_____ ____
_____ ____
_____ ____

What insect or disease problems are appearing?

_____ ____
_____ ____
_____ ____

Record steps taken to remedy insect/disease problems:

_____ ____
_____ ____
_____ ____

Task list for this month:_____
_____
_____
_____
_____

Plants to buy: _____
_____
_____
_____

Other: _____
_____
_____
_____

364

Weather observations:

Date _____
Rainfall _____
Avg Temp _____

Date _____
Rainfall _____
Avg Temp _____

Date _____
Rainfall _____
Avg Temp _____

Date _____
Rainfall _____
Avg Temp _____

Date _____
Rainfall _____
Avg Temp _____

Date _____
Rainfall _____
Avg Temp _____

Date _____
Rainfall _____
Avg Temp _____

Date _____
Rainfall _____
Avg Temp _____

Date _____
Rainfall _____
Avg Temp _____

Date _____
Rainfall _____
Avg Temp _____

Date _____
Rainfall _____
Avg Temp _____

Date _____
Rainfall _____
Avg Temp _____

Date _____
Rainfall _____
Avg Temp _____

Date _____
Rainfall _____
Avg Temp _____

Date _____
Rainfall _____
Avg Temp _____

Date _____
Rainfall _____
Avg Temp _____

Date _____
Rainfall _____
Avg Temp _____

Date _____
Rainfall _____
Avg Temp _____

Date _____
Rainfall _____
Avg Temp _____

Date _____
Rainfall _____
Avg Temp _____

Date _____
Rainfall _____
Avg Temp _____

Date _____
Rainfall _____
Avg Temp _____

Date _____
Rainfall _____
Avg Temp _____

Date _____
Rainfall _____
Avg Temp _____

Date _____
Rainfall _____
Avg Temp _____

Date _____
Rainfall _____
Avg Temp _____

Date _____
Rainfall _____
Avg Temp _____

Date _____
Rainfall _____
Avg Temp _____

Date _____
Rainfall _____
Avg Temp _____

Date _____
Rainfall _____
Avg Temp _____

Date _____
Rainfall _____
Avg Temp _____

Planning (things to change next month or next year): _____
_____
_____
_____
_____
_____
_____
_____
_____

365

JULY

Date: _____

What's appearing or blooming indoors or out?

_____ _____
_____ _____
_____ _____
_____ _____

What insect or disease problems are appearing?

_____ _____
_____ _____
_____ _____

Record steps taken to remedy insect/disease problems:

_____ _____
_____ _____
_____ _____

Task list for this month:_____
_____
_____
_____
_____

Plants to buy: _____
_____
_____
_____

Other: _____
_____
_____
_____

Weather observations:

Date _____	Date _____	Date _____	Date _____
Rainfall _____	Rainfall _____	Rainfall _____	Rainfall _____
Avg Temp _____	Avg Temp _____	Avg Temp _____	Avg Temp _____

Date _____	Date _____	Date _____	Date _____
Rainfall _____	Rainfall _____	Rainfall _____	Rainfall _____
Avg Temp _____	Avg Temp _____	Avg Temp _____	Avg Temp _____

Date _____	Date _____	Date _____	Date _____
Rainfall _____	Rainfall _____	Rainfall _____	Rainfall _____
Avg Temp _____	Avg Temp _____	Avg Temp _____	Avg Temp _____

Date _____	Date _____	Date _____	Date _____
Rainfall _____	Rainfall _____	Rainfall _____	Rainfall _____
Avg Temp _____	Avg Temp _____	Avg Temp _____	Avg Temp _____

Date _____	Date _____	Date _____	Date _____
Rainfall _____	Rainfall _____	Rainfall _____	Rainfall _____
Avg Temp _____	Avg Temp _____	Avg Temp _____	Avg Temp _____

Date _____	Date _____	Date _____	Date _____
Rainfall _____	Rainfall _____	Rainfall _____	Rainfall _____
Avg Temp _____	Avg Temp _____	Avg Temp _____	Avg Temp _____

Date _____	Date _____	Date _____	Date _____
Rainfall _____	Rainfall _____	Rainfall _____	Rainfall _____
Avg Temp _____	Avg Temp _____	Avg Temp _____	Avg Temp _____

Date _____	Date _____	Date _____
Rainfall _____	Rainfall _____	Rainfall _____
Avg Temp _____	Avg Temp _____	Avg Temp _____

Planning (things to change next month or next year): _____
_____
_____
_____
_____
_____
_____
_____
_____

AUGUST

Date: _____

What's appearing or blooming indoors or out?

_____ _____
_____ _____
_____ _____
_____ _____

What insect or disease problems are appearing?

_____ _____
_____ _____
_____ _____

Record steps taken to remedy insect/disease problems:

_____ _____
_____ _____
_____ _____

Task list for this month:_____
_____
_____
_____
_____

Plants to buy: _____
_____
_____
_____

Other: _____
_____
_____
_____

Weather observations:

Date _____   Date _____   Date _____   Date _____
Rainfall _____   Rainfall _____   Rainfall _____   Rainfall _____
Avg Temp _____   Avg Temp _____   Avg Temp _____   Avg Temp _____

Date _____   Date _____   Date _____   Date _____
Rainfall _____   Rainfall _____   Rainfall _____   Rainfall _____
Avg Temp _____   Avg Temp _____   Avg Temp _____   Avg Temp _____

Date _____   Date _____   Date _____   Date _____
Rainfall _____   Rainfall _____   Rainfall _____   Rainfall _____
Avg Temp _____   Avg Temp _____   Avg Temp _____   Avg Temp _____

Date _____   Date _____   Date _____   Date _____
Rainfall _____   Rainfall _____   Rainfall _____   Rainfall _____
Avg Temp _____   Avg Temp _____   Avg Temp _____   Avg Temp _____

Date _____   Date _____   Date _____   Date _____
Rainfall _____   Rainfall _____   Rainfall _____   Rainfall _____
Avg Temp _____   Avg Temp _____   Avg Temp _____   Avg Temp _____

Date _____   Date _____   Date _____   Date _____
Rainfall _____   Rainfall _____   Rainfall _____   Rainfall _____
Avg Temp _____   Avg Temp _____   Avg Temp _____   Avg Temp _____

Date _____   Date _____   Date _____   Date _____
Rainfall _____   Rainfall _____   Rainfall _____   Rainfall _____
Avg Temp _____   Avg Temp _____   Avg Temp _____   Avg Temp _____

Date _____   Date _____   Date _____
Rainfall _____   Rainfall _____   Rainfall _____
Avg Temp _____   Avg Temp _____   Avg Temp _____

Planning (things to change next month or next year): _____
_____
_____
_____
_____
_____
_____
_____
_____

369

SEPTEMBER

What's appearing or blooming indoors or out?

_____ _____
_____ _____
_____ _____
_____ _____

What insect or disease problems are appearing?

_____ _____
_____ _____
_____ _____

Record steps taken to remedy insect/disease problems:

_____ _____
_____ _____
_____ _____

Task list for this month:_____
_____
_____
_____
_____

Plants to buy: _____
_____
_____
_____

Other: _____
_____
_____
_____

Weather observations:

Date _____
Rainfall _____
Avg Temp _____

Date _____
Rainfall _____
Avg Temp _____

Date _____
Rainfall _____
Avg Temp _____

Date _____
Rainfall _____
Avg Temp _____

Date _____
Rainfall _____
Avg Temp _____

Date _____
Rainfall _____
Avg Temp _____

Date _____
Rainfall _____
Avg Temp _____

Date _____
Rainfall _____
Avg Temp _____

Date _____
Rainfall _____
Avg Temp _____

Date _____
Rainfall _____
Avg Temp _____

Date _____
Rainfall _____
Avg Temp _____

Date _____
Rainfall _____
Avg Temp _____

Date _____
Rainfall _____
Avg Temp _____

Date _____
Rainfall _____
Avg Temp _____

Date _____
Rainfall _____
Avg Temp _____

Date _____
Rainfall _____
Avg Temp _____

Date _____
Rainfall _____
Avg Temp _____

Date _____
Rainfall _____
Avg Temp _____

Date _____
Rainfall _____
Avg Temp _____

Date _____
Rainfall _____
Avg Temp _____

Date _____
Rainfall _____
Avg Temp _____

Date _____
Rainfall _____
Avg Temp _____

Date _____
Rainfall _____
Avg Temp _____

Date _____
Rainfall _____
Avg Temp _____

Date _____
Rainfall _____
Avg Temp _____

Date _____
Rainfall _____
Avg Temp _____

Date _____
Rainfall _____
Avg Temp _____

Date _____
Rainfall _____
Avg Temp _____

Date _____
Rainfall _____
Avg Temp _____

Date _____
Rainfall _____
Avg Temp _____

Date _____
Rainfall _____
Avg Temp _____

Planning (things to change next month or next year): _____
_____
_____
_____
_____
_____
_____
_____
_____

OCTOBER

What's appearing or blooming indoors or out?

What insect or disease problems are appearing?

Record steps taken to remedy insect/disease problems:

Task list for this month:

Plants to buy:

Other:

372

Weather observations:

Date _____
Rainfall _____
Avg Temp _____

Date _____
Rainfall _____
Avg Temp _____

Date _____
Rainfall _____
Avg Temp _____

Date _____
Rainfall _____
Avg Temp _____

Date _____
Rainfall _____
Avg Temp _____

Date _____
Rainfall _____
Avg Temp _____

Date _____
Rainfall _____
Avg Temp _____

Date _____
Rainfall _____
Avg Temp _____

Date _____
Rainfall _____
Avg Temp _____

Date _____
Rainfall _____
Avg Temp _____

Date _____
Rainfall _____
Avg Temp _____

Date _____
Rainfall _____
Avg Temp _____

Date _____
Rainfall _____
Avg Temp _____

Date _____
Rainfall _____
Avg Temp _____

Date _____
Rainfall _____
Avg Temp _____

Date _____
Rainfall _____
Avg Temp _____

Date _____
Rainfall _____
Avg Temp _____

Date _____
Rainfall _____
Avg Temp _____

Date _____
Rainfall _____
Avg Temp _____

Date _____
Rainfall _____
Avg Temp _____

Date _____
Rainfall _____
Avg Temp _____

Date _____
Rainfall _____
Avg Temp _____

Date _____
Rainfall _____
Avg Temp _____

Date _____
Rainfall _____
Avg Temp _____

Date _____
Rainfall _____
Avg Temp _____

Date _____
Rainfall _____
Avg Temp _____

Date _____
Rainfall _____
Avg Temp _____

Date _____
Rainfall _____
Avg Temp _____

Date _____
Rainfall _____
Avg Temp _____

Date _____
Rainfall _____
Avg Temp _____

Planning (things to change next month or next year): _____
_____
_____
_____
_____
_____
_____
_____
_____

NOVEMBER

What's appearing or blooming indoors or out?

_____

_____

_____

_____

What insect or disease problems are appearing?

_____

_____

_____

Record steps taken to remedy insect/disease problems:

_____

_____

_____

Task list for this month:_____

_____

_____

_____

_____

Plants to buy: _____

_____

_____

_____

Other: _____

_____

_____

_____

374

Weather observations:

Date _____
Rainfall _____
Avg Temp _____

Date _____
Rainfall _____
Avg Temp _____

Date _____
Rainfall _____
Avg Temp _____

Date _____
Rainfall _____
Avg Temp _____

Date _____
Rainfall _____
Avg Temp _____

Date _____
Rainfall _____
Avg Temp _____

Date _____
Rainfall _____
Avg Temp _____

Date _____
Rainfall _____
Avg Temp _____

Date _____
Rainfall _____
Avg Temp _____

Date _____
Rainfall _____
Avg Temp _____

Date _____
Rainfall _____
Avg Temp _____

Date _____
Rainfall _____
Avg Temp _____

Date _____
Rainfall _____
Avg Temp _____

Date _____
Rainfall _____
Avg Temp _____

Date _____
Rainfall _____
Avg Temp _____

Date _____
Rainfall _____
Avg Temp _____

Date _____
Rainfall _____
Avg Temp _____

Date _____
Rainfall _____
Avg Temp _____

Date _____
Rainfall _____
Avg Temp _____

Date _____
Rainfall _____
Avg Temp _____

Date _____
Rainfall _____
Avg Temp _____

Date _____
Rainfall _____
Avg Temp _____

Date _____
Rainfall _____
Avg Temp _____

Date _____
Rainfall _____
Avg Temp _____

Date _____
Rainfall _____
Avg Temp _____

Date _____
Rainfall _____
Avg Temp _____

Date _____
Rainfall _____
Avg Temp _____

Date _____
Rainfall _____
Avg Temp _____

Date _____
Rainfall _____
Avg Temp _____

Date _____
Rainfall _____
Avg Temp _____

Planning (things to change next month or next year): _____
_____
_____
_____
_____
_____
_____
_____
_____
_____

DECEMBER

What's appearing or blooming indoors or out?

_____

_____

_____

_____

What insect or disease problems are appearing?

_____

_____

_____

Record steps taken to remedy insect/disease problems:

_____

_____

_____

Task list for this month:_____

_____

_____

_____

_____

Plants to buy: _____

_____

_____

_____

Other: _____

_____

_____

_____

Weather observations:

Date _____
Rainfall _____
Avg Temp _____

Date _____
Rainfall _____
Avg Temp _____

Date _____
Rainfall _____
Avg Temp _____

Date _____
Rainfall _____
Avg Temp _____

Date _____
Rainfall _____
Avg Temp _____

Date _____
Rainfall _____
Avg Temp _____

Date _____
Rainfall _____
Avg Temp _____

Date _____
Rainfall _____
Avg Temp _____

Date _____
Rainfall _____
Avg Temp _____

Date _____
Rainfall _____
Avg Temp _____

Date _____
Rainfall _____
Avg Temp _____

Date _____
Rainfall _____
Avg Temp _____

Date _____
Rainfall _____
Avg Temp _____

Date _____
Rainfall _____
Avg Temp _____

Date _____
Rainfall _____
Avg Temp _____

Date _____
Rainfall _____
Avg Temp _____

Date _____
Rainfall _____
Avg Temp _____

Date _____
Rainfall _____
Avg Temp _____

Date _____
Rainfall _____
Avg Temp _____

Date _____
Rainfall _____
Avg Temp _____

Date _____
Rainfall _____
Avg Temp _____

Date _____
Rainfall _____
Avg Temp _____

Date _____
Rainfall _____
Avg Temp _____

Date _____
Rainfall _____
Avg Temp _____

Date _____
Rainfall _____
Avg Temp _____

Date _____
Rainfall _____
Avg Temp _____

Date _____
Rainfall _____
Avg Temp _____

Date _____
Rainfall _____
Avg Temp _____

Date _____
Rainfall _____
Avg Temp _____

Planning (things to change next month or next year): _____

_____

_____

_____

_____

_____

_____

_____

_____